Working Papers on Canadian Politics

SECOND ENLARGED EDITION

WORKING PAPERS
ON
CANADIAN POLITICS

John Meisel

McGill–Queen's University Press
Montreal and London 1975

To
RHS

First published 1972
Enlarged edition 1973
Second enlarged edition 1975

© 1975 McGill-Queen's University Press

ISBN 0-7735-0245-9

Legal deposit second quarter 1975
Bibliothèque nationale du Québec

Printed in Canada by
The Hunter Rose Company, Toronto

Contents

Foreword

THE FIRST EDITION

AS ATTESTED TO BY THE UBIQUITY OF SIDEWALK SUPERINTEND-
ents, there is a great appeal in seeing how other people work
or perhaps just in seeing other people working. One of the purposes of this volume is to exploit this appeal by providing
students with the chance of becoming academic sidewalk super-
intendents and by affording a view, through a paperback peephole, of how one scholar went about, in part at least, constructing
some political analyses.

The four papers fall into two categories: the first three are
preliminary examinations of data derived from a national survey.
The last was prepared for *One Country or Two?*, a collection
of essays on Canada's constitutional problems. A word about
each type of paper is in order.

In keeping with the somewhat unconventional character of the
present book, let us turn to the final paper first. Less academic
in the sense that it is rather impressionistic and less research
oriented, it grew out of some discussions with various colleagues
at Queen's who were persuaded that it would be worth-while if
a few English-speaking Canadians quickly set down their reactions to various aspects of French-English relations in Canada
in the late sixties. My task was to say something about the attitudes of Quebeckers towards the rest of the country—something
I found hard to do without also talking about English-speaking
Canadians' views of Quebec. At any rate, the paper was written
without consulting any primary or secondary sources, as a quick
reaction towards one aspect of Canada's problems—a piece of
journalism or pamphleteering more than anything else. It is
presented here because it was not previously published in its
entirety and because I believe that its ideas ought to have a
different audience than the readers of the volume for which it
was intended. The text included here is complete and is longer

than that published in *One Country or Two?*; it shows how the need to reduce a paper in length may also alter its general tone. The full version is considerably more pessimistic about Canada's prospects.

Another extrinsic feature of "Cancel Out and Pass On" is related to its characteristic of generalizing about attitudes Canadians hold towards one another on the basis of reflections and not the winnowing of findings of a survey. Some of the observations could, in fact, have been (and now are being) tested with the aid of the 1968 post-election interviews used so extensively in the other papers of this book, but this was impossible for technical reasons at the time the paper was being drafted. The point to be noted specifically in the present context is that the 1968 survey, while designed *inter alia* to probe into the way in which francophones and anglophones regard one another, did not emphasize this area and was in any event primarily concerned with the *partisan* and *electoral* aspects of the question. As the result of the munificent effects of serendipity, we can nevertheless check some of our originally unsubstantiated observations in the last of the present papers with the aid of a survey, designed largely for other purposes.

Each of the other three papers consists of a ground-clearing operation in which a vast body of original data is subjected to a first, only gently focused, examination. The papers enabled me to conduct broad-gauged surveys of several aspects of Canadian politics, and particularly of the attitudes of the mass public at the time of the 1968 election. They are part of a larger research project which utilizes these data more comprehensively and also more subtly in a forthcoming monograph on that election.

But while, as was indicated above, one of the purposes of publishing these preparatory working papers is to share with students one phase of the scholarly adventure, at least insofar as the work habits of a particular researcher are concerned, this is not the only purpose. The other two are to make some of the important data derived from the 1968 election survey available at least in part before the full-fledged study is published and to make more data available than would otherwise find their way into print. It is for this reason that the present papers are over-supported by tables containing more material than was always necessary. Of all the terms currently fashionable among social scientists, "parsimony" is thus beyond doubt the most inappropriate in characterizing these essays. But the present is one of the very rare occasions when it is out of place and inimical to our purposes. Since there is nevertheless great virtue in parsimony, I shall apply it in the remainder of this Foreword by resorting to a number of short, discrete comments.

The first three papers are largely descriptive and exploit only marginally their theoretical assumptions or implications. The overall research project out of which they grew is primarily concerned with exploring the role of parties and elections in the process converting needs into wants, wants into demands, and demands into outputs. This focus guides the design of the overall election study. It was ignored in the drafting of the present papers since their main task was to become familiar with and scan some of our data generally and to look for unanticipated insights and leads. It is nevertheless interesting that the "Bases of Support" essay concludes with some speculations closely tied to the theoretical preoccupation of the whole research project, although in the original outline of the paper this part was to have consisted of no more than a few sentences posing some general questions about the interpretation of our data. The fact that in the end I allowed them to stimulate me into quite an extensive set of reflections about the effectiveness of the Canadian party system indicates not only how difficult it may be to divorce empirical findings from their normative implications but also that the theoretical underpinnings of a piece of research tend to assert themselves even when one tries to keep them submerged.

On several occasions, even in this brief introduction, I have had to stress the fact that our peephole affords a view of the habits of a given scholar. He may, of course, be quite atypical of the general breed and of the workways of his profession. Although the point is self-evident, it needs to be stressed because it is dangerous to assume, as is sometimes done (usually implicitly), that there is only one approved way of conducting research or analysing social phenomena. Making these papers available in the present form as illustrations of one phase of an investigation is intended simply to demonstrate one of several possible approaches. There may be some, in fact, who will be quite critical of what they will term the theoretical laxness and fishing-expedition nature of some of the present papers. However, although the intellectual path I followed here may be different from theirs, I suspect that we end up roughly at the same place; we must for once accept the dictum that the end justifies the means.

Academic work is in some ways among the most co-operative and companionable of human occupations. It generates and thrives on the mutually enriching process of discussion, argument and counter-argument, challenge and response, attack and defence, focusing not on the personalities involved but on ideas. Like most scholars I have benefited enormously from the advice of students, colleagues and other friends to whom I have given or sent drafts of my work for comment, either informally because I knew they were interested or more formally, through the institutional setting provided for this kind of consultation—the academic workshop or conference organized by a professional association. The second and third papers were originally presented in the latter way. One of the commentators at the session organized to discuss the party image paper was Jean Laponce who happens to be both a friend and a colleague sharing many of my research interests. His comments at the meeting and in correspondence afterward identified some interesting methodological problems posed by the paper. This led me to recalculate some of the data and to write a postscript to it discussing these problems and indicating how they can be avoided or minimized. The reader prone to skimming is, therefore, advised to be sure to read the postscript as well as the paper dealing with party images.

The four papers were written over a period of two years and therefore exhibit some slight inconsistencies. Most result from the fact that the 1968 survey data were being analysed for the first time and that some ways of handling the data were being developed as the work was progressing. Thus, for instance, "No Answer" or "Do Not Know" responses, or thermometer type questions, were treated differently at different times until a final method was settled upon, as the result of the experience I have had in working with the data. Furthermore, the papers are reproduced here in much their original form, and little attempt has been made to impose complete stylistic unity. They nevertheless had to receive fairly rigorous attention from my publishers, and I should like to thank particularly Joan Harcourt of McGill-Queen's University Press for editing a difficult and unyielding manuscript with imagination, charity, and tact.

Since the substance and tone of the present volume are to be associated more with a workshop than with a shrine, reflecting the provisional character of the contents, the reader, and particularly students for whom it is primarily intended, should not lose sight of its informality. They should view its contents as they would the opening part of a seminar, to be followed by the response of all the members.

One of the advantages of presenting an inchoate work to a wider public than one's friends is that one can benefit from the comments of a larger number of interested readers, before freezing the complete analysis into its final mold. I therefore invite anyone moved by the ensuing pages to ask himself questions to which the answers are not provided, or if he wishes to suggest alternate interpretations or uses of the data, to offer comments on my acts of commission or omission, or simply if he desires additional information, to get in touch with me. There is no reason why books should lead to only a one-way flow of communication. For both selfish and altruistic reasons, I look forward to hearing from readers who might wish to discuss any aspect of the papers.

A NOTE ON THE ENLARGED EDITION

It became apparent just before the 1972 election that a second printing of the *Working Papers* would soon be required. Since I have for some time thought that elections need to be studied as part of a continuing process, as well as an individual event in time, I was provoked by the 1972 campaign, and the need to reprint this volume, to do just that. In thinking about the developments leading up to October 30, I related the events of 1972 to my long-term interest in the effectiveness of party systems, and the period of Canadian history following the King–St. Laurent era.

Technical considerations made it necessary that the final typescript be in the publishers' hands two weeks after polling day. The new essay was thus drafted in seven days, and no doubt bears signs of this haste. Its preoccupations, however, grew out of my general interest in some of the more subtle aspects of party politics, and the observations upon which my conclusions are based were gathered during the fifteen years preceding the hectic hours of final creation. Despite, or perhaps because of, the tensions induced by an inhuman deadline, I enjoyed writing "Howe, *Hubris* and '72" more than I did any other paper in this collection.

THE SECOND ENLARGED EDITION

The need for a new printing of the *Working Papers* provides an opportunity to add to the sketches collected in the two previous editions. The underlying scheme has been a concern for the institutional response to divisions in Canadian society, and particularly that of political parties and politicians. Chapter 6 extends the argument into the area of "religious voting," complementing not only its companions here, but also my recent *Cleavages, Parties, and Values in Canada* (London and Beverly Hills: Sage Publications, 1974).

Although the new paper was originally addressed to an almost exclusively non-Canadian audience, it focuses on a perplexing Canadian phenomenon: the continuing relation between religious affiliation and voting in federal elections. The present version, in keeping with others in this book, is unrevised but has been shortened slightly by the omission of some historical material well-known to Canadian readers.

In addition to shedding new light on the nature of religious voting in Canada, the paper illustrates how the analysis of specific data can lead to a greater awareness of the operation of a political system. The particular circumstances surrounding "religious voting" in Canada point to an important aspect of the whole party system. They suggest an explanation of the dominant position of the Liberal party in terms of its reliance upon two "pillars"—a majority of Catholics and a minority of Protestants possessed of certain well-defined demographic characteristics and attitudes. The voting pattern is thus seen as influencing particular kinds of decision-making and providing a structural inducement towards one-party dominance of a self-perpetuating character.

1

SOME BASES
OF PARTY SUPPORT
IN THE 1968
ELECTION

THE PURPOSE OF THIS PAPER IS TO EXAMINE SOME BASES OF party support in the 1968 Canadian General Election. It describes what a post-election survey showed to have been the major differences between those voting for the five main parties.[1] The approach is exceedingly general—our picture is more like the old-fashioned school photograph taken with a swivel-camera, than a series of individual portraits. We get a gently blurred view of the well-scrubbed little mugs neatly arranged in rows, even perhaps of the fleet-foot who ran behind, the moment the camera left him, so as to appear again at the other extremity. The lens has obviously glided lightly over each face, concerned with the whole ensemble and never probing very deeply into the innermost soul of any one scholar. We have no searching portrait here by a Velasquez or a Karsh but a more or less mechanical presentation, quickly given, of a statistical aggregate. This being the first *overall* report on the characteristics of the various partisans in the 1968 election, the purpose is not to test any given theory about Canadian politics, nor to probe extensively

The research project, of which this paper is a part, is supported by a Killam Award of the Canada Council. I happily acknowledge my debt to it and to several colleagues and collaborators, particularly Bill Irvine and George Perlin for advice, Kate Reed, Grace Skogstad and Merilyn Dasil for more direct assistance.

into any particular aspect of electoral behaviour.[2] It is rather, to scan the results so as to gain an impression of the nature of partisan support with respect to the voters' personal attributes, perceptions of election issues, general political predispositions, and perceptions of parties, leaders, candidates and the 1968 campaign.[3] A concluding part contains some speculations about the Canadian party system, prompted by an examination of the data discussed in the more descriptive sections of the paper.

PERSONAL ATTRIBUTES

A convenient way of looking at the usual socio-economic characteristics of the voters is to pit our findings against the conventional wisdom and accumulated lore of Canadian political science, noting such departures from the "norm" as seem to challenge previous studies or to indicate that the 1968 election prompted a new pattern of voter response. Since Professor Schwartz has produced an admirable review of the relevant major literature, we shall, as a rule, compare our data with her summary.[4] Like her we shall pay considerable attention to regional variations in voter support, in addition to surveying the total Canadian scene.

The reason for the preoccupation with geographic variation lies in the fabulous heterogeneity of Canada and hence in the nature of the data: as is being increasingly noted, generalizations about Canadian voting patterns on a national scale can be dangerously misleading and require to be supplemented by regional comparisons.[5] The election results and our survey show, for instance, enormous variation in party support between Quebec on the one hand, and the Atlantic provinces or the Prairies on the other. Sixty-eight percent of our respondents in Quebec indicated that they voted Liberal but only 45 percent of Prairie residents did so; an even more startling regional disparity applies to the Conservative voters: Mr. Stanfield's party received 53 percent of the vote in the Atlantic region but only 18 percent in Quebec. In addition to these global variations, however, there are also regional differences in the personal characteristics of the voters which give the parties a somewhat different image (and character) in different parts of the country. Some of these textures in the Canadian party fabric are noted, even in this very general overview of the 1968 election.

2

Religion

Nothing in the 1968 data suggests that the well-known importance of religion to party support has diminished. Catholics still show a strong preference for the Liberal party. Only in Quebec, no doubt because of the exceptionally strong appeal of the Liberals to the English population and to those who do not belong to Canada's two charter groups, does the *proportion* of Catholics among those voting Conservative or NDP exceed the *proportion* of Catholics among Liberal voters. While the numbers involved and the margins are small, the pattern is in sharp contrast with the findings of the 1965 post-election survey as summarized by Schwartz.[6] She shows that in Quebec, where 86 percent of the sample was Catholic, the corresponding Conservative and NDP proportions were only 83 and 77 percent. In the 1968 sample, as is seen in Table I,* the proportion of Catholics among those who voted in Quebec was 90 percent, the Conservative and NDP percentages being 94 and 97 percent, that is, higher than the total Quebec figure.[7]

The long-standing marked religious difference between Liberals and Conservatives in Ontario continued in 1968 and is, to all intents and purposes, matched in its intensity in the Atlantic provinces, where the Catholics' support for the Liberals was 22 percentage points above the regional average and where the Conservative lag was correspondingly large.[8]

The Liberal edge among Catholics in the Prairies is not nearly so impressive; it is nevertheless still substantial, although less so than in British Columbia—but the numbers involved here are dangerously low for safe generalizations.[9]

As in previous surveys, the NDP was shown to draw somewhat greater support among non-Catholics everywhere except in Quebec (where there are only 29 relevant cases) but the margins are not great.

Status: Occupation

After religion, it is the cluster of characteristics associated with status which reveal the greatest disparities between the supporters of the various parties in the 1968 election. We shall

---

*Tables to this paper will be found in the Appendix.

here avoid the conceptual and methodological difficulties posed by the term "class" by focusing on three of the dimensions usually linked to it. Mildred Schwartz has provided us with an excellent summary of the main Canadian findings, and with a useful account of the ambiguities and problems arising from them (pp. 75-84). Her major conclusion is supported by our 1968 data, namely that "class-based voting exists; what is missing are consistent class-based parties," although some Canadian parties come much closer to being so than others.

The point is illustrated admirably with respect to the occupations of the voters. No new partisan alignments emerge showing a shifting occupational base for party support. The Liberals still appeal most "evenly" to members of all occupations, *except for farmers* but, as with virtually all generalizations about electoral behaviour in Canada, there are regional exceptions. In Ontario, for instance (and also, of course, in Quebec) the Liberals, while doing *proportionately* less well among farmers and pensioners than among other occupational groups, still outdraw the other partries by substantial margins, as Table II shows. The Ontario case is particularly interesting because, whereas in the other regions the Liberal appeal to farmers is substantially below that made to the electorate as a whole (the national deviation, as indicated in Table III, is 18.1 and that in the Prairies 22.9 percentage points), in Ontario the farmers' support for the Liberals was only 1.8 percentage points below that of the provincial average.

Table III tells us that in the country as a whole the appeal of the Liberal party is still greatest among members of high status occupations and tends to diminish as one moves towards the less exalted occupational categories of unskilled labour, farming and the somewhat ambiguously ranked "pensioners". In eastern Canada Mr. Trudeau's party appealed slightly more strongly to voters in sales and clerical occupations than to those holding managerial or professional posts, but this pattern was reversed in the Prairies and marginally in British Columbia.

As one might expect, the Conservatives display an opposite tendency: their greatest appeal is to the less highly ranked occupations. But in Ontario, the party presents a relatively more attractive political choice to the highest ranking occupational groups since almost a third of them voted Conservative, but only

4

26.8 percent of our total Ontario sample indicated that this is how they had cast their ballots. It is interesting and suggestive with respect to the unavoidable speculation about possible band-wagon effects that their appeal to the highest-ranking occupations was strongest in the three areas of greatest overall Conservative strength—the Atlantic provinces, the Prairies and Ontario. In Ontario and the Atlantic provinces they attracted an above average level of support from members of the professional and managerial category and although in the Prairies their appeal to this group was below the regional average by 5.1 percentage points, this was caused by their uncommonly strong support among farmers—53.6 percent of whom voted Conservative, as compared with 37.1 percent for all the Conservatives in this region.

Schwartz mentions that "Conservative voters were less likely than the remainder to be manual workers and more likely to be farmers or outside the labour force," (p. 75) a summary which is confirmed by our data. These indicate, however, that among the manual workers, the unskilled were more disposed, than the skilled, to vote Conservative in 1968.

As in previous elections, the NDP attracted considerably more than its average regional and national support from skilled labour. It received an unusually high proportion of votes (compared with its regional averages) from pensioners in the Prairies and British Columbia, but not in Ontario, proportionately its third most rewarding hunting ground. Although the numbers involved are very small indeed, it is worth noting that the NDP received well above average support from holders of high-ranking occupations in Quebec. This points to that party's strong appeal to intellectuals in French Canada, and to its weak appeal as a mass party among French Canadians.

Status: Subjective Class

Our data for occupations are reinforced by the responses we elicited about the class self-perception of those included in our sample. The Liberal party received above average support from those who placed themselves in the upper class and, to a lesser extent from those who think that they belong to the middle class; its proportion of the vote from lower-class identifiers, on the other hand, is everywhere below average. This general pattern is modified in the Atlantic provinces and Quebec where Mr. Trudeau's party appealed proportionately less strongly to the upper class (but note the low number of cases in this cell in the Atlantic provinces). A contrast between occupation and subjective class is evident in Ontario where the pattern of Liberal support was less clear-cut with respect to occupations than elsewhere but no such blurring occurs in terms of class: Tables II and III show that the usual regularly descending slope of the line is very much in evidence. This somewhat inconsistent pattern may reflect simply an ambiguity in our indicators of status but the breakdown by the educational characteristics of our sample reminds us that caution is in order: unlike elsewhere, in Ontario the support of the Liberals among those who have had from nine to thirteen years of schooling is below their provincial average, and lower than their appeal to those with the least number of years of schooling. This phenomenon may be related to the Liberals' unusually strong appeal to unskilled workers in Ontario.

The class-base for the Conservative vote, as measured by our self-identification question, reveals tendencies similar to those noted in relation to the occupation of the electorate. Except in its regions of greatest strength, the party once identified with fat cats seems to appeal more to people who think of themselves as members of the lower and middle classes than of the upper class. But again, the Conservatives attract above average support from the upper class in areas of their greatest strength, the Atlantic region and to some extent also Ontario. The picture in the Prairies is again rather different; here the appeal is greatest, relatively speaking, among the middle class voters. The West coast pattern of Conservative support is atypical, however. Not only have the lower class voters given the party below average support, but a greater proportion of upper class identifiers than one would have expected gave the Conservatives their vote: although only 12.9 percent of our British Columbia respondents voted Conservative, 18.8 percent of their upper class identifiers did so. Nevertheless, three quarters of the British Columbian upper crust, measured this way, voted Liberal, and none at all NDP! This apparent hostility to the Left may also explain the 5.9 percentage point above average margin of the West Coast upper class Conservatives.

Except for Quebec, all regions show the NDP to have received below average support from upper class identifiers and correspondingly disproportionately strong favour among those who place themselves in the lower class. This confirms previous findings about the unusually strong working class appeal of the NDP in all regions except Quebec. Here, as was the case with our occupational breakdown, we see unmistakable traces of the party's exceptionally strong appeal to professionals (also noted by Schwartz, p. 82) and its limited appeal to rank and file Quebeckers. In a sense, the class role performed by the NDP elsewhere in Canada is assumed in Quebec by the Ralliement des Créditistes. Like their ideological associates in the Prairies and British Columbia the Quebec Social Crediters received a proportionately high number of votes from low class identifiers and correspondingly less support from the upper class.

Mildred Schwartz has suggested that the Créditistes were unique among Canadian parties in approaching a one-class character: sixty-one percent of those who voted for them were manual workers, a quarter of the total unskilled (p. 75). While similar results obtain for the 1968 election (sixty-two percent of Créditiste voters were labourers, 44 skilled and 18 unskilled) one wonders whether Professor Schwartz' interpretation is acceptable. In 1968, the NDP supporters included 59 percent labourers all across Canada (the Liberal and Conservative figures are 47 and 43 respectively) thus giving Mr. Douglas' party an almost equally strong working class support and robbing the Créditistes of the uniqueness ascribed them. Furthermore, the self-identification class data indicate that a larger proportion of NDP voters than Créditistes identified with the working class. Forty-nine percent of the latter did so, as compared with 62 percent of those voting NDP in the 1968 election.

Status: Education

The educational background of the electorate is not a particularly useful guide to its voting intentions. Schwartz was struck by the fact that the best educated Canadians seem to "reflect so faithfully the ebb and flow of party fortunes" (p. 87). The 1968 survey supports this conclusion. The Liberals received less than their average support from those with the lowest number of years of schooling and above average support from the middle and highest educated groups in each region except in Ontario. In all other instances the proportion of the Liberal vote increases with the number of years of formal education.

The Conservatives, on the other hand, received above average support from the least educated everywhere except in British Columbia, and less than would have been the case of a random distribution among those with more than thirteen years of schooling, except in the Atlantic region and Ontario. They differ from the Liberals also in another way: whereas the relation between education and the vote is usually represented by a straight line for the Trudeau supporters, the corresponding Conservative line is curvilinear.

Given the unmistakable working class strength among NDP voters, one would have expected the line relating their vote to educational background to be straight and to have a slope opposite that of the Liberals. This is the case only in British Columbia, however. In Quebec, for reasons we have noted, the slope of the line is similar to that of the Liberals and elsewhere the pattern is curvilinear. Generally, the NDP receives above average support from the least well-educated and less than the average from those who have gone to school longest but the pattern varies regionally. In Ontario, the proportion of High School educated who voted NDP was higher than the percentage of those with only a Public School education: a factor probably related to the strong NDP appeal in Ontario to skilled labour. The performance of the Créditistes and Social Crediters, on the other hand, is quite as one would have predicted: both parties received less than the average support from the best educated, then came the middle group to be followed by the least well-educated, who accorded the Social Credit parties above average support.

Length of Residence in Canada

Although one's status as a citizen or the length of time one has been in Canada are not usually considered important elements in one's class status, they often do affect how one is esteemed by others and in many instances also the chances one has had of finding one's feet and niche. Since over 80 percent of our sample were born in Canada, the period of immigration cannot be a vitally important element in the composition of any party's support, unless immigrants clustered in very large numbers to a particular party. We found in 1968 that Canadian-born voters supported the Liberals at a rate slightly below that of the population as a whole; this pattern was consistent in all regions. Post-Second World War immigrants, on the other hand, showed a marked preference for the government party (15.8 percentage points over their national average). In Quebec, although there were only 33 cases, *all* voted Liberal! Mr. Trudeau's party did less well among naturalized citizens who came to Canada before 1946 but even so received almost half of this group's vote, as Table II shows. Our data reinforce the observation of Schwartz who has noted the smaller proportion of early arrivals among Liberals compared to other parties (pp. 64-65). The Conservatives, on the other hand, appealed quite strongly to the group of earlier settlers compared with more recent arrivals, and not only in the Prairies, as one might have expected, but also in Ontario and particularly in British Columbia. It was only in the last-named province that the pre-1946 immigrants accorded the NDP a lower proportion of votes than its national portion: elsewhere its members gave the NDP more votes than would have been the case had there been a purely random distribution. Similarly, the very slight "disadvantage" of the NDP in Ontario among the native-born Canadians offsets its above average support from them in all the other regions.

We can conclude that in 1968 the Liberals continued to make an exceptionally strong appeal to post Second World War immigrants and that the Conservatives' considerable strength among the older settlers was attained in part, at least, at the cost of the Liberals. Canadian-born voters showed some preference for the Conservatives, among the major parties (*all* of the Créditiste supporters were, not unexpectedly, born in Canada). Eighty-five percent of those voting Conservative were born in Canada; the corresponding proportion of "native" Liberals was 81 percent and of the NDP 80 percent.

Origin

No marked changes have affected the traditional party allegiance of the major ethnic groups. The Liberals continue to be the party greatly favoured by French Canadians, particularly in areas in which francophones constitute a minority. The seemingly startling fact of their receiving less than an average vote from people of French origin in Quebec is explained by the party's phenomenally strong appeal, noted earlier, to Quebeckers of British and "other" origins. The Conservatives continue to be exceptionally attractive to voters whose ancestors came from the British Isles. Mr. Stanfield's party received almost 60 percent of "British" votes in their stronghold—the Atlantic region—but, more surprisingly perhaps, outdrew the Liberals among members of this ethnic group even in the Prairies, receiving 8.1 percentage points more votes from them than from all Prairie votes combined. The NDP also continued to receive above average support from people of British origin in 1968 but, as in previous elections, was favoured even more strongly by Canadians whose origin is neither British nor French.

In a different context we have assumed that it is possible to gauge the degree to which Canadians identify with the values of the English-speaking or French-speaking societies making up their country by looking at their linguistic practices.[10] Our respondents were therefore grouped into five categories, reflecting the degree to which they spoke English and/or French. Tables II and III show that the mixed group, comprising 105 people with only the most tenuous connections to either French- or English-speaking Canada, gave the Liberals overwhelming support and that nationally the Liberals received about two-thirds of the votes of the pure francophones and also of the partial English- and partial French-speakers. Only the pure anglophones provided the government party with a substantially below average proportion of votes but even half of them voted Liberal. Although the numbers are of necessity small, it is interesting to note that the partial English-speakers in Quebec were considerably more favourable to the Liberals even than the strongly pro-Liberal pure English-speakers.

Community Size

While Mildred Schwartz notes the contrasting appeal observed in the nineteen-sixties of the Liberals and Conservatives with respect to the size of the voters' community, she cites CIPO and other data analyzed by Alford to indicate the great regional variations associated with this difference (pp. 94-96). The 1968 survey suggests that here, at least, a more even Canadian pattern may be developing and that in one sense, we may be witnessing the "nationalization" of Canadian politics in relation to the respective urban and rural appeals of Canadian parties. Our tables show that the clear-cut national strength of the Liberals in the large centres, and the relatively stronger showing of the Conservatives in rural areas are to be found everywhere except in the Atlantic provinces where the Liberals and Conservatives reversed their normal pattern, as they have done with respect to so many other of our variables.

National figures indicate an orderly descent of the proportion of NDP support from levels considerably above the Canadian total in metropolitan areas and their suburbs through communities of smaller size to rural areas where the NDP did least well. Regional breakdowns are quite inconsistent, however, displaying a variety of curvilinear relationships. Without going into detail (the numbers frequently forbid this) we should note that, leaving the Atlantic region aside, the NDP received above average support in the largest centres in all regions and in communities of between a thousand and 99,999 inhabitants everywhere except in Quebec. But it received below average support in our second largest category of urban centres of 100,000 to half a million inhabitants in all regions, as well, of course, as in rural communities throughout Canada. Both Social Credit parties revealed more orderly and expected support patterns: they proved to have been heavily rural in their appeal.

Age

During the nineteen-fifties and sixties the Conservative party received disproportionate support from older voters. Only at the height of his short-lived electoral appeal in 1958 did Mr. Diefenbaker draw substantial numbers of votes from younger Canadians, but by 1962 the party returned to its earlier pattern of appealing particularly to older people (Schwartz, p. 98, where Peter Regenstreif's analysis of the "Diefenbaker Interlude" is summarized). During the same period, Social Credit in Quebec made an exceptionally effective appeal to the young-

11

est voters and the Liberals and NDP did not have a consistently greater appeal to any age group, although the former party, as Schwartz indicates, did somewhat less well among older voters. This overall pattern continued into the 1968 election which, nevertheless, calls for a few comments.

We must note, in the first place, that the usual atypical reversal of national trends in the Atlantic region did not manifest itself with respect to age. The proportion of the vote received by the Conservatives in eastern Canada varied directly with the age of the electorate, whereas the Liberals established an inverse relationship. Secondly, the Liberal party appears to have made a below average appeal to the youngest age group in Quebec and to have been favoured especially by the oldest voters there. The continued strong support from the youngest voters, received by the Ralliement des Créditistes cannot alone be responsible for this: although Mr. Caouette received a disproportionately small number of votes from the oldest age group, there were not enough Social Credit voters in our sample to affect the showing of the Liberals. In fact, all parties, except the Liberals, received more than an average proportion of votes from 21 to 30 year olds. One might have expected the NDP, as a party of protest, to make a particularly strong showing among the youngest voters but this did not happen in 1968, as indeed it had not in previous elections. In 1968 we see the opposite occurring. In its areas of greatest strength, the NDP received an above average proportion of votes from the oldest cohort in two instances (the Prairies and British Columbia) and from the middle age group in one (Ontario).

Sex

Mildred Schwartz reports that there is nothing very distinctive or noteworthy about the differences in electoral behaviour between men and women in Canada. There are, nevertheless some minor features of interest in our tables showing how each voted in 1968. It appears that women had a slightly greater predisposition for the Conservative party (compared with the Liberals) everywhere except in the Atlantic region, and that the NDP is decidedly a men's party, and particularly in its regions of greatest strength. The Ralliement des Créditistes also received more support from women than from men.

12

Summary

We can now attempt a quick review of the insights we have gained through an examination of the personal characteristics of the voters supporting each of the parties in the 1968 election. The first and most important observation concerns the general pattern of support. As one might have expected, no radical alignment of voter support occurred from 1965 to 1968 in the sense that any particular social group traditionally favouring a particular party bolted its favourite by abstaining or by switching, in large numbers, to another party. The 1968 contest was decidedly not a "critical" election, in V. O. Key's sense. In Canada as a whole, the Liberals continued to receive above average support from Catholics, people with high-ranking occupations, a higher class self-image, and more years of formal schooling. They also drew a somewhat disproportionately large number of new Canadians, particularly those who arrived since the end of the Second World War, and they continued to be strongly favoured by French-speaking Canadians, by younger rather than older voters, by the most urbanized segments of the population and ever so slightly, by men. The Conservatives present the opposite picture: they did proportionately better among Protestants than Catholics, among farmers and people scoring low on the conventional class indicators, among Canadian-born voters and particularly among immigrants who arrived before 1946, among anglophones, rural dwellers, older voters and women.

The NDP continued its pattern of receiving a greater proportion of votes from non-Catholics than from Catholics and from anglophones than from francophones, and to be very strongly associated with the working class in the sense that almost 60 per cent of its vote was derived from labourers and those identifying with the working class. Canadians whose origins are neither British nor French also accorded it above average support; women were much less inclined to vote for it than men, and urban voters more so than rural ones.

I shall withhold comment on the data reported so far until after we have had a look at some other aspects of partisan support. It is nevertheless appropriate to stress here how widely the support for Canadian parties fluctuates regionally and that the variation is not always homogeneous among the supporters of the respective parties. We have found, for instance, that the national patterns for the Conservatives and Liberals are reversed, or strongly modified, in the Atlantic region with respect to occupation, self-defined class, education, community size and language practice but they remain unchanged even in this region insofar as religion, origin and age are concerned. It seems that the reversal of party fortunes in the Atlantic region has disturbed the "normal" national patterns of party support. We also noted that in other areas where the Conservative party was stronger than elsewhere, its appeal to certain subgroups—those with more highly-rated occupations or class perceptions, for example— was proportionately much greater than in other regions where the party was decidedly the underdog.

ISSUE PERCEPTION

While the personal attributes of the respective supporters of the various parties are important aspects of electoral behaviour, particularly when the latter is viewed from a long-term perspective, the perception of the immediate political problems faced by the government, and of the election issues, is especially relevant to the study of the political significance of any given election.

Members of the national sample interviewed at the time of the 1968 election were asked two kinds of relevant questions: (1) "What do you personally feel are the most important problems the government should try to take care of as soon as possible?"[11] and (2) a series of specific questions inquiring how important a number of stated issues or problems were to the respondents "in deciding what to do about voting in this election," or "in thinking about the election." Items such as economic problems (inflation, unemployment, housing, etc.), welfare issues, the desirability of having majority government, and the place of Quebec in Canada were mentioned.

The two sets of questions are closely related, despite the fact that in a sense they tap entirely different kinds of responses (i.e. "To what problem(s) should the government now address itself?" and "How important was . . . X, Y or Z . . . in your decision how to vote?"). It is, in fact, possible to consider the first question as an open-ended invitation to the respondent to indicate what public issues seemed to be most important to

14

him at the time of the election and the series of itemized issues as a focused probe into their importance to the voting decision. The great similarity in the responses to the questions thus assessing the importance of "prompted" and "unprompted" issues supports our conclusion that the two classes of questions are closely related.

We shall look at the "unprompted" issues first. A comparison of the inter-party and inter-regional variations, as presented in Table IV, reveals that the latter are, in some instances, considerably greater than the former. Differences with respect to the importance of governmental action in the fields of housing, unemployment or the position of Quebec in Canada are quite startlingly wide between some regions and exceed most of the gaps separating the parties. There is also a greater readiness in some regions for respondents to mention problems about which they would like the government to do something. British Columbians reacted particularly vigorously in this context and residents of the Atlantic provinces rather lethargically. There is, indeed, a tendency for the vigor of the reaction to increase as one moves westward from the Atlantic to the Pacific, with British Columbians displaying the aforementioned veritable crescendo of interest. Some regions reveal a marked and deviant lack of interest in one or most fields of possible governmental activity. Thus a solution to the question of what place Quebec should occupy in Canada was of strikingly less interest to respondents in the Atlantic provinces than to those elsewhere, Quebeckers showed a substantially less than average interest in housing problems (ranked *first* in Ontario and the Prairies!) and Ontario and the Prairies both were less concerned about unemployment. On the other hand, Quebec and British Columbia residents much more than any others cited education—an area clearly under provincial jurisdiction—as one in which Ottawa should take some action. Quebec respondents showed by far the greatest concern in the field of labour relations. These regional differences are highly suggestive about geographic and ethnic variations in Canada's political cultures and some—like the relative lack of interest in unemployment shown by highly industrial Ontario—are downright puzzling.

Our concern here is with differences between the supporters of the parties, however, and it is to these that we now turn.

15

The widest margins, as was to be expected, separated the old from the new parties, although interesting differences, particularly in some regions, are to be noted also between Liberal and Conservative voters. The Liberals were more concerned with Quebec nationally but particularly in that province itself, although it is noteworthy that in British Columbia and in the Prairies a larger proportion of Liberal voters wanted the government to do something about this than in Quebec, and on the West Coast the proportion of concerned Conservatives, in this context, was even greater than that of the Liberals—almost a third of them mentioning this problem. (But N = 25!)

Using the means in Table IV as our measure indicating the degrees of worry over the various problems, we find that nationally the Liberals were more concerned than Conservatives about taxes and the question of Quebec and that the latter attached more importance to inflation. When the frequency of regional differences is taken into account, we find Liberals considering medicare of greater importance than Conservatives in four instances, taxes in three, and Quebec and housing in two. The Conservatives, on the other hand, were keener to see action with respect to welfare in three regions and in the fields of inflation and Quebec in two. The limited nature of these divergences between Conservative and Liberal voters suggests that in this context at least, the electorate was not deeply divided and that the Quebec issue may have been less of a factor in the election than has sometimes been held. It is important to remember, however, that we are recording only differences in the *importance* attached to the problems, not in what should be done about them.

The most surprising response of NDP voters to the question about what action the government should take concerns the low priority they assigned to unemployment. The figures for the country as a whole indicate that they—supporters of the most working class party—attached less importance to full employment than the other parties. This is a good example, however, of the usefulness of going beyond aggregate Canadian data: the regional breakdown makes it clear that the very low interest in this question of Prairie NDP voters is largely responsible for the curious national pattern. Almost one quarter of our NDP respondents came from the Prairies but while this accounts for the national figures, it does not explain the assessment of Canadian problems made by this group: sixty-nine percent of them identified with the working class and 43 percent gave labour as their occupation. Supporters of the other parties in this region were more concerned about unemployment than those who voted NDP. Table VI indicates that the response was somewhat similar to the direct question about the importance of unemployment as a factor in the respondent's voting decision: while NDP voters were more influenced by it than Conservatives (who included a larger percentage of farmers), they showed much less concern here than Liberals who contained about the same percentage of labourers, and a much smaller proportion of farmers. The latter may have accounted in part for the response of the NDP voters but if this was so, why did a large percentage of Conservatives, who included an even higher proportion of farmers, consider unemployment a problem calling for early governmental action? We must leave these queries unanswered, at least for the present.

Their respective reactions to tax problems constitute another curious disparity between the supporters of the older parties and of the NDP. A larger proportion of the latter identified it as one requiring early government attention. And once again it is the somewhat localized reaction in one region—Ontario this time—which can be identified as the principal factor in the strong NDP reaction nationally. Almost half of the NDP voters we interviewed came from Ontario. At this stage in our analysis we can only surmise that this response reflects the presence of the (primarily skilled) working class NDP supporters who may have felt the tax pinch more acutely than others, endowed with a greater cushion protecting the purchasing power of their incomes. If this assumption is correct, one would expect the NDP voters, particularly in Ontario, to be also more concerned about inflation which in fact they were, slightly. Table VI shows, however, that in responding directly to the question of how important inflation was to their voting decision, NDP voters in Ontario were only marginally more influenced by the increase in the cost of living than Liberals and Conservatives. We are therefore again compelled to defer a satisfactory explanation of the phenomenon mentioned in this paragraph.

Medicare was largely a dead issue by the time of the 1968

election. It ranked very low in the responses to questions tapping both the "prompted" and "unprompted" issues, as described above. It is nevertheless interesting that NDP voters, traditionally greatly concerned with government-operated health schemes, should have responded more vigorously to this issue than the adherents of the older parties and that their reaction was exceptionally vigorous in the Prairies, where the memories of the CCF's battle for medicare are apparently still to be reckoned with. The issue had also flared up anew at the provincial level in Saskatchewan and this may have renewed and strengthened its salience for some NDP voters in that province.

The relevance to NDP voters of medicare is a shade greater even than to the Créditistes—the voters who more than those for any other party, display the most consistently "underdog" set of responses—a larger proportion of them wanted the government to act in the fields of welfare, unemployment and education, and only a slightly smaller percentage in the areas of medicare and taxes. They were considerably less interested in housing and inflation, but the relevance of the latter issue is attested to by the fact that even so almost a third of the Créditistes mentioned it as requiring governmental action.

There were only eleven Social Credit voters from the Prairies in our sample and 23 in British Columbia. There is not much to be gained from making any observations about Social Credit supporters' reactions generally to what the government should do partly because of the smallness of the sample but also because, as Table IV shows, the responses of Prairie and British Columbia Social Crediters were so inconsistent and, indeed, incompatible. It would be interesting to know whether a similar disparity would be revealed in a larger, more reliable sample of Social Crediters.

The most impressive observation by far to emerge from our examination of the respondents' estimate of how various specified issues affected their voting decision concerns the importance attached to a majority government being elected. Table V tells us that seven out of ten of our respondents who voted cited the desirability of seeing a government majority as extremely or very important to them. The reaction was fairly uniform throughout the country; the Prairies—Canada's most prolific birthplace of "third" parties—being the only region worrying less about this issue. But even here almost two-thirds of the voters showed concern. This high regional score is caused largely by the unsurprising but great Liberal (78 percent) fear of minority government. Only slightly more than half of the NDP voters attached much importance to this issue and the Conservatives were much closer to the NDP than to the Liberals. That more than half of the NDP voters, even in the Prairies, indicated that the question of majority government was important to them offers eloquent testimony of the degree to which the idea of minority governments is frowned upon in Canada. The ubiquity of this reaction is demonstrated by the fact that even Créditiste voters mentioned it as a meaningful issue in the same proportion as NDP voters in the Prairies—just over half of them indicated that it was extremely or very important to them.

Nationally, the proportion of Liberal voters responding in this way was really impressive: nearly four out of five did so, as compared to fewer than two-thirds of Conservative supporters, 54 percent NDP voters, and 51 percent of those who backed Créditiste or Social Credit candidates. The very strong showing of Liberals on this issue does not, of course, prove that it was the main, or even any reason, for their supporting Mr. Trudeau's party. It must be surmised, however, that among the factors contributing to the Liberal vote, or at least to its explanation after the event, the issue of majority government was more important, and by a good deal, than any of the other issues mentioned.

NDP voters, much more than anyone else, cited economic factors as being of importance to their voting decision. As Table V shows, of the five issues mentioned specifically, 71 percent of Tommy Douglas' supporters indicated that they found "issues concerning the economy, like unemployment, housing, cost of living, inequality between Canadian regions or the drop in wheat sales" extremely or very important. Liberals and Conservatives, of whom a considerably larger proportion were worried about majority government, as we have just seen, responded to this question in proportionately small numbers. Economic issues were nevertheless, even for them, considerably more important than the next one mentioned most frequently—the place of Quebec in Confederation.

Before considering the reaction to Quebec, however, it will

be well to take a closer look at the economic issues. The general economic question from which we quoted in the previous paragraph was used as a "gateway" identifying those of our respondents who had a reasonably serious interest in economic aspects of the election. These 61 percent were then presented with a battery of supplementary questions, probing into the reaction to each of the more specific items listed, inquiring into their assessment of the government's handling of them and also into the distance they saw between their own position on them and those of the various parties. Ninety percent of those asked, as Table VI shows, said that the cost of living affected their voting decision, the proportion of the Conservatives being slightly higher than that of the NDP and both being a little more concerned about inflation than the Liberals. The percentage is so great that over half of the total sample actually mentioned this as important, placing it immediately after majority government in order of importance, if we overlook the multiple economic question in this context. The increasing cost of living (the problem we examined as the "unprompted" issue of inflation) thus appears as the second most important election issue, ranking only after that of majority government for Liberals and Conservatives, and well ahead of it insofar as NDP voters are concerned.

Housing was the issue evoking the next highest response among the specified economic items suggested to our respondents, coming a shade before unemployment. The regional breakdown in Table VI shows that the keen interest displayed in this issue by Ontario respondents, and to a lesser extent by those in British Columbia, is chiefly responsible. Differences between parties are not striking except perhaps for its uncommonly strong influence on NDP voters in British Columbia. The Liberals and Conservatives are generally very close on housing except in the Prairies where the latter showed considerably less concern than the other parties, possibly because 30 percent of them were farmers.

We noted earlier how surprisingly uninterested NDP voters had appeared to be in unemployment when they were asked to identify areas in which the new government should take prompt action. When asked specifically about this issue, they responded more positively, a somewhat larger proportion of Douglas supporters indicating that this issue was important in their voting decision than those voting for Trudeau or Stanfield candidates. The very high response of British Columbia NDP voters offset the startlingly low interest in this issue displayed by Prairie NDP supporters. But again no party came anywhere near the Créditistes in the degree to which they admitted to having been influenced by unemployment.

Two of the economic issues mentioned were not expected to have relevance everywhere in Canada. Thus regional inequality was unimportant to a large proportion of British Columbians and, to a lesser extent, Ontario voters, but mattered to almost two out of every three in the Atlantic provinces and was important in Quebec. There was generally little difference between the parties within each of the regions except for one instance—the Prairies. Here, surprisingly, the proportion of our respondents who worried about regional inequality—a matter generally held to be a major source of political discontent—was virtually as small as that in Ontario, and considerably smaller than in the Atlantic region and Quebec. Only NDP voters were concerned in large proportions, the number of Conservatives indicating that the matter was important to their vote being quite startlingly small. Even the Liberals took it more seriously!

Our Prairie respondents did not, however, disappoint our expectations with respect to wheat sales. This issue evoked high resonance in the Prairies (and not much of it elsewhere, of course) but again the differences between the parties are suggestive. Eighty-two percent of NDP supporters admitted to this problem influencing their voting decision, whereas only seven out of ten Conservatives did and the Liberal proportion was only slightly larger. It seems that the NDP voters were a good deal more concerned with these two regionally relevant problems in the Prairies than supporters of other parties and that the NDP vote here was to a somewhat greater extent influenced by local, rather than national, issues.

The great interest of Atlantic respondents in regional inequality takes us back to the more general—non-economic—questions on the importance of various issues to the voting decision. For the eastern sensitivity to regional problems leads one to expect Atlantic respondents also being highly responsive to another problem closely affecting their place in Confederation—

the Quebec issue. They stood out, however, as attaching the least importance to it. Over half of British Columbians reacted positively to this question, as is indicated in Table V, but only about a third of those on the east coast did so. The differences between parties was small although the Liberals were more influenced by the Quebec issue in the country as a whole. This Liberal edge is accounted for by their greater concern in the Atlantic and in Quebec since the regions west of the Ottawa river, a larger proportion of Conservatives claimed to have been affected by it. NDP voters showed less interest everywhere except in Quebec where, as we have noted before, their number was very small.

Medicare and welfare were of importance to a smaller number of respondents than the other issues, but in both cases the proportion among NDP voters (and also Social Crediters) was larger than among those voting for the older parties.

Two kinds of themes emerge from the above minutae as absorbing the Canadians in the 1968 election: one was concerned with the functioning of the political system, the other with the economy. The former was the more important electorally, according to our data, in that a larger number of voters declared to have been influenced in their decision on how to cast their ballot by their reaction to the issue of majority government. The other largely political question, that of the status of Quebec, was considerably less important. Among the economic issues, inflation was the most telling, particularly among the newer parties. It was, in fact, the relative importance attached to economic questions which was the chief distinguishing feature between the parties, ranging the Liberals, Conservatives and Social Crediters on one side, the NDP and Créditistes on the other. Despite this common feature of the two older parties, it would be a mistake to conclude that there were no other differences between their respective supporters on how they reacted to what the government should do, and what influenced them in their voting decision. While these differences were not profound, they were great enough to show that the sometimes-heard charge that the two old parties are simply tweedledums and tweedledees was incorrect, at least insofar as the two parties' electors in the 1968 election was concerned.

The personal characteristics of the kind I discussed earlier, and the totality of one's experiences—by no means all of them political—combine to give each individual a set of general predispositions which strongly influence how he or she perceives and assesses more narrowly political phenomena, like political parties and issues coming up in the course of elections. Much has been written on this subject, referring to these predispositions in terms of political style, the political or civic culture, national character insofar as it is held to affect politics, psychocultural traits related to politics, and so on. A good deal of the pertinent literature has led to considerable ambiguity and confusion but it has at the same time contributed much to our understanding of politics, particularly in a comparative context. We shall not pause here to define the terms or their content but simply report on a series of answers to questions in our survey which have been grouped so as to enable us to compare the bases of party support in Canada in terms of many of the dimensions of interest to students of political culture—to employ what has probably come to be the most commonly-used term among those listed above. As the Notes to Table VII in the Appendix show, the dimensions were usually derived from grouping answers to a small number of questions, so as to construct an index of, say, religiosity or authoritarianism. In utilizing scores of "low", "middle" and "high", we have applied no substantive criteria but have arbitrarily established cutting points in the various scores in such a way that a roughly equal proportion of respondents in the country as a whole fell into each of the three categories. In this preliminary paper no attempt is made to show which of the items in the various indices yielded satisfactory results when subjected to Guttman scaling and which failed to do so. Some of the items do scale and others do not. We have therefore refrained from calling the measures "scales". At this stage in our investigation, we have thought it desirable to use a variety of measures recognizing that they are anything but refined and that they are merely rough indices of certain general predispositions of our respondents.

One is struck forcibly in looking not only at national scores but also at the regional breakdowns by the startling variation in responses, quite independent of the vote. Indeed, regional variation is, in many instances, greater than that between the supporters of different parties. Canada, as is witnessed in Table VII, appears unmistakeably as a country differing most profoundly and systematically in its citizens' politically relevant general predispositions with the eastern portion—the Atlantic region and Quebec—diverging on virtually every dimension from the rest of the country, and by a substantial margin. Attitudes in the Prairies usually come fairly close to the national average since they tend to fall between the extreme to be found in eastern Canada and that at the other pole entertained generally in Ontario and British Columbia.

At the risk of adding to the already rather murky scene portrayed here, I will make some generalizations about the variation in outrageously subjective terms, without even defining them: eastern Canada is, generally, less progressive, more intolerant, and less politically keen and has a lower sense of political efficacy than the Prairies, with Ontario and particularly British Columbia displaying tendencies opposite those of the Atlantic and Quebec regions. To be a little more precise, the scores on our indices in the Atlantic region *and* Quebec were virtually identical and lowest in Canada with respect to moral liberalism (attitudes to homosexuality, divorce and the death penalty), the toleration of ethnic and religious minorities, and interest in foreign affairs and the election; they were highest on our authoritarianism index (intolerance of communists and homosexuals, acceptance of the death penalty).[12] Quebec respondents scored highest on our measure of religiosity (frequency of church attendance, the proportion of friends of the same religion as oneself, attitudes to spending money on churches); they were least "centralist," least generally optimistic about the future, and interestingly, had the lowest score by far of any region on the index gauging attitudes towards the rigorous enforcement of law and order. Respondents in the Atlantic region were less opposed to the separation of Quebec from Canada (less even than Quebeckers), and they had the lowest score on our measure of political efficacy and the highest with respect to political cynicism. At the other extreme, British Columbia (with Ontario almost always close behind) "led" in its

24

general optimism about the future and in its citizens' economic optimism, in its interest in the election and in foreign policy questions, in its moral liberalism, sense of efficacy, tolerance of minorities. It was least authoritarian and scored lowest on the religiosity item. Even when it is recognized that some of our measures overlap, and that all we can claim to be doing is to identify broadly defined general predispositions, the conclusion is quite inescapable that Canada is a country displaying a complex of political cultures which are regionally based. No one is likely to be knocked off his pins by the novelty of this observation, but the extent of the diversity of Canada's political cultures and its scope, as documented here, are quite astonishing.

Liberal voters, despite the fact that a sizeable portion of them lives in Quebec, showed themselves to be the most progressive, liberal, secular and politically interested and to feel politically effective. Table VII tells us that the support for Mr. Trudeau's party varied directly with religiosity, moral liberalism, interest in foreign affairs, greater importance being attached to the central government, interest in the election, a sense of efficacy, general optimism about the future and economic expectations; it varied inversely with authoritarianism, respect for law and order (an admittedly doubtful index of being progressive) and cynicism. Although it increased with toleration for minorities, there was no difference in the degree of Liberal support among those scoring low and medium on this dimension. The pattern among Conservative voters is virtually the opposite: their proportion increased with increases in the authoritarianism, law and order and cynicism scores and decreased with the respondents' higher moral liberalism, greater toleration of minorities, increased interest in foreign affairs, "centralism" with respect to Canadian federalism, higher interest in the election, a greater sense of efficacy and heightened optimism about the future generally and about one's economic prospects in particular. No national pattern was evident in attempts to relate the Conservative vote to our religiosity index.

Using the somewhat doubtful criteria of "left" and "right", we find that the characteristics associated with the former are much more in evidence among Liberal voters, and with the latter among Conservatives. One expects NDP voters to adopt more "left" or "liberal" positions than even the Liberals. While

25

our Table VII does show Mr. Douglas' supporters to be generally more "liberal" or to the "left" of the Conservatives, and to take "progressive" postures on most of our relevant dimensions, the slope of the respective lines is less incisive than for the Liberals. This is the case, for instance, with respect to the toleration of minorities, authoritarianism, and attitudes to law and order, as well as in the case of the less ideologically focused indices of a sense of efficacy and of economic optimism. This slight modification of a clear-cut pattern notwithstanding, we find more NDP supporters on the whole among those with a higher rather than a lower moral liberalism score, among those with lower authoritarianism, lower regard for law and order, greater toleration, a slightly greater interest in foreign affairs, and with a modestly higher, rather than a lower, sense of efficacy. The NDP vote seems to be unrelated to interest in the election and also to our "centralism" measure. On the other hand, we find that NDP support was greater among those displaying greater cynicism towards the political system, and among those who have rather poor expectations of the future and of their own economic prospects.

When the scores of the various partisans are examined within each of the five regions, it is found that the national pattern is modified and sometimes reversed for both the Liberals and the Conservatives most frequently in the Atlantic provinces, particularly among Liberal voters. The latter showed no regional departures from the national pattern with respect to the "centralism" and cynicism indices, and varied rather wildly from region to region in their toleration of minorities. Apart from these exceptions, the Atlantic region modified or reversed the Liberal national pattern with respect to every one of our dimensions! Only Quebec Liberals came anywhere near those in the Atlantic provinces in deviating from the predispositions of Liberals throughout Canada, and even they were considerably more "typically Canadian" than their more easterly neighbours.

Although the "contrary" set of attitudes of Liberals in the Atlantic provinces is matched by a similar deviation on the part of east coast Conservatives, they are joined, in differing from the party's national scores, by Tory voters in a greater number from other regions. As was the case with Liberal voters, the national pattern for Conservatives with respect to the "central-

26

ism" index held in every region. There was no discernible relationship between religiosity and the Conservative vote and the regional variations with respect to interest in the election are so diverse as to deprive the national sequence of much significance in anything except purely aggregative terms.

A regional analysis of our NDP respondents is somewhat hazardous since, with the exception of Ontario, the numbers in each region are small, falling to only 29 in Quebec. The "anatomy", so to speak, of the NDP voters' attitudes, when a regional breakdown is attempted, is so suggestive, however, that it deserves to be reported upon, despite the necessarily somewhat speculative nature of our comments.

In some of our earlier examination of NDP voters in Quebec, we found that they displayed quite atypical characteristics when compared with social democratic voters elsewhere in the country, and this pattern is maintained with respect to the general predispositions. On the whole, Quebec NDP supporters were more liberal and experienced greater confidence about their political competence and about the future, than NDP supporters in the other regions. British Columbia is the second area in which they were more liberal. If we divide our indices very roughly into three groups—those which cannot be judged as progressive/liberal or reactionary/illiberal (religiosity, attitudes to Quebec separatism, "centralism"), those which concern liberalism (moral liberalism, authoritarianism, law and order and toleration) and those pertaining to one's sense of competence and optimism (interest in foreign affairs, interest in the election, efficacy, cynicism, optimism about the future and economic optimism)—we find that the scores of NDP voters on the West Coast are on the whole very much more liberal on the liberalism dimensions but not very different, in their general direction, from the others with respect to political competence and optimism. Ontario respondents who, irrespective of party, were the second most progressive and politically competent-feeling and optimistic on the other hand, did not prove to be particularly progressive insofar as the NDP voters are concerned, can hardly be distinguished in this respect from those living in the Prairies who produced a larger proportion of NDP voters with low liberalism scores than with high ones. There is not much to choose from between the various regions on the political competence indices and one must generally conclude that the rather more tolerant and progressive showing of the NDP nationally is not reinforced by strikingly similar scores in the regions. Despite the small number of Quebec NDP voters in our sample, constituting about 9 percent of the total, it is often they who can be seen as pushing the NDP into the progressive column, so to speak, although of course, to single them out as the deciding factor is a highly arbitrary and probably indefensible act. One can however say that were it not for the Quebec NDP supporters who, it will be recalled, inhabit the most "illiberal" region, the NDP national total would be much less progressive than is actually the case. Lest it is thought, because of the importance in the Quebec CCF and NDP of anglophone activists, that the Quebec members of our sample are predominantly English-speaking, it must be noted that twenty-one of the twenty-nine are "pure French-speaking" according to our language scale, six are partial French and only two are English-speaking.

PARTY PERCEPTIONS

In attempting to interpret what the voters had in mind when passing their verdict during an election, it is important to know not only how they viewed the particular issues of that election but also how they perceived the parties contesting it. Our respondents were accordingly asked how they *liked* various aspects of the parties and also how *important* these were *in the voting decision*. The measure used in both cases was the so-called "thermometer question" in which the respondent is asked to indicate how much he likes or how important he considers certain phenomena to be by assigning them a score or degree on a hypothetical thermometer. In our case the thermometer was calibrated from 0 to 100. The responses indicate the *ranking* of the items to which a reaction is sought and the *distances* which separate, in the respondent's mind, the various items and, in this case, also the parties themselves.

The 2767 Canadians interviewed in our survey were asked, among a number of other relevant items, which must be left out of the present discussion, how much they liked the leaders, the work of the members of the various parties in the Parliament which sat before the 1968 election, each party's candidate in their riding, the parties' respective campaigns and each of the parties taken as a whole.

On the five party dimensions Liberals liked their leader best, as can be gleaned from Table VIII, a good deal better than the Liberal party as a whole, which ranked second. The score Mr. Trudeau received is, in fact, the highest recorded for any aspect of any party with the one interesting exception, that of Mr. Caouette, who was liked as much by Ralliement voters as Mr. Trudeau was by Liberals. The work of Liberal MPs in Parliament was rated less favourably by Liberal voters than any other party feature probed and was generally lacking in appeal. The only exception was the reaction of the Créditistes who, again interestingly, ranked their MPs' performance second. The MPs' work shared the cellar, to borrow a term from the sports pages, with the party's election campaign which, though being rated second highest by the Liberals, was put last by everyone else.

The Conservative party's traditional uneasy relation with its leader, exacerbated in the middle and late sixties by the rejection of Mr. Diefenbaker, was reflected in the scores recorded by Conservative voters. They liked the party leader less well than the candidates and the party as a whole but, as we shall see shortly, there was, not unexpectedly, regional variation in this respect. Mr. Douglas fared well with his party, receiving a score just a shade higher than the NDP as a whole. This result is a powerful indicator of the affection and/or respect the former Saskatchewan Premier enjoyed, since NDP voters are characteristically more party-oriented (as is partly shown by Table IX) than they are swayed by anything resembling any cult of personality.

The Créditistes were the most enthusiastic of our respondents, in the present context, registering higher "temperature readings" even than the Liberals who, with the NDP following closely behind, produced much higher scores than the Conservatives and the Social Credit voters. The Créditistes also revealed less variation in the deviation of the score of each item from the average, than any of the other parties (Liberals displayed the highest variation, then Conservatives, Social Crediters and the NDP supporters). In any event, they rated the leader well above the other items, as noted above, and thought least highly of their party's election campaign. Their score on this item (73) was, however, still higher than the Social Credit voters' highest rating, which they accorded their party's candidates.

Looking at the scores in various parts of the country, we find that the Liberals displayed almost no regional variation in the rank order of the five party features examined, except that the order of the party and the candidates was occasionally reversed. But the Conservative voters varied considerably from region to region. The leader was rated extremely well in the Atlantic provinces, of course, but was also rated highest in British Columbia, which is rather surprising despite Mr. Stanfield's maintaining a second home here. NDP voters varied their scores relatively little nationally as between the five party aspects tapped, but their regional rankings, while close, reveal considerable variation, at least insofar as the leader and party are concerned, with the candidates not far behind. The leader was rated first in the Prairies and British Columbia and was only one "degree" below the top-rated party taken as a whole in Ontario—NDP voters therefore liked Mr. Douglas particularly in the areas of the party's greatest strength.

A useful view of the Canadian party system is obtained from an examination of how the voters regard the parties which they do *not* support. This is one way of identifying the distance between parties, as perceived by the electorate. Looking at Canada as a whole, we find that Liberal voters liked every one of the dimensions of the Conservative party better than that of any other except their own. As far as they were concerned, in other words, the Conservative party was closest to their own choice. There were only two deviations from this pattern in Ontario and three in British Columbia. The pronounced Liberal preference for the Conservative party is in no way reciprocated nationally, however, with respect to the leader and the work of the party's MPs, since Conservative voters preferred the NDP in the former case, and the Créditistes in the latter. On the other three dimensions considered, the Conservatives did rank the Liberal party highest, with the Social Credit party next and, in each case, the NDP last. NDP voters liked no party better than the Liberals on any of our items when the national figures are aggregated, but in the Prairies, as the regional breakdown shows, they preferred the Conservatives with respect to all items except the leader. Their rather negative assessment of Mr. Stanfield is

30

also attested to by their ranking Mr. Caouette a hair above the Conservative leader nationally.

One may like one or more features of a given party and yet decide not to vote for it—either because other aspects are more important or for some other reason—its poor chances of election, for instance. The responses to the questions about how important a number of suggested party attributes were to the respondents' voting decisions are nevertheless sufficiently similar to those tapping affect, to indicate that there was a close connection in the respondents' minds between the two sets of questions. The closeness may reflect a substantive relationship between the two kinds of phenomena examined or possibly a somewhat blurred interpretation of the questions by the respondent; we assume that the latter is not pronounced, however, since on some dimensions there was considerable discrimination made between the two sets of related questions.

Looking at Canada as a whole, in Table IX, we find that the leader was the most important factor, among those suggested, in the voting decision. He was followed by the party taken generally, the candidates and, a long distance behind, the work of the elected Members in the previous Parliament. This particular ranking is influenced mightily by the very high proportion of Liberals in our sample, as seen when we control for party: more than half of the Liberal respondents were primarily influenced by the party leader, about a third by the party generally and only 9 percent by their local candidates. In the case of the Conservatives, about one-third each stated that the leader and the party were the chief factors, and one-quarter recognized the primacy of the candidate in the voting decision. The NDP supporters, almost half of whom indicated the party taken as a whole as the most important feature in their decision, thus confirmed the generally-held view that Canada's social democratic party is more ideologically oriented than the others, assuming, of course, that the importance assigned the party can be equated with a strong commitment to its ideology. Only about one-quarter of the NDP voters attached top priority to the leader and one-fifth picked the candidate. We see that the Liberals alone rated the leader in first place—a development which must be ascribed to Mr. Trudeau's extraordinary appeal to an important segment of the 1968 Canadian electorate.

Liberal voters differ from those supporting the other parties much more in the degree to which they consider the leader to have been an important factor than they do in relation to the role of the party as a whole in their voting decision. The scores for the party generally are fairly uniform from party to party, with only one exception—that of the NDP. The substantial lead of Mr. Trudeau in the eyes of the Liberal voters was obtained at the expense of Liberal candidates who were frequently downgraded as influential factors in the voting decision of those casting Liberal ballots.

As in so many of our other categories, we find that the position of the Liberals and Conservatives was reversed in the Atlantic region: the former attached greater importance to the party than to the leader and the latter reversed this order but, interestingly, did not attach the characteristically low Liberal importance to their candidates. Another interesting regional phenomenon revealed by this analysis concerns the importance accorded by Quebec Liberals to their party: the "score" was half that received by the leader in Quebec and was lower than that for the party taken as a whole in any region from the voters of all the parties.

We have come to expect the Conservative leader to be well received in the Atlantic provinces, but it came as a surprise that he was found to have been so important a factor influencing the electoral decision in British Columbia (but $N = 25$!). As expected, Mr. Stanfield was considered less important in the Prairies than anywhere else and the Conservative party was mentioned as most important by the largest proportion—43 percent of Conservative voters. While the leader was cited in first place by only a similar small proportion of voters in Ontario, the party as such received much less recognition—only a third of Conservative voters accorded it first place among the factors helping them to make their electoral choice. Ontario Conservatives attached greater importance to their party's candidates than Tory voters in any other region, almst a third crediting the most importance to them.

NDP voters rated the party as a whole highest when identifying causes of the voting decision. Ontario was the most party-oriented region among this strongly party-oriented group of electors, with the candidates being cited by an uncharacteristically low 15 percent. Elsewhere in Canada, about a quarter indicated that the "local man" was the chief factor in the voting decision.

It will be recalled that Créditiste voters expressed enormous liking for Mr. Caouette. This was not translated into holding him primarily responsible for their vote. As befits adherents to something which is as much a social movement as a party, a larger proportion cited the party as important, and second, interestingly, came the work of the party's MPs—among whom Mr. Caouette of course played a leading role. Only the NDP voters in Quebec came near to so recognizing their representatives' efforts in Parliament.

Generally, when regional variations are considered independent of party, we find that no dimension varied as much as the importance attached to the MP's work. Candidates were assigned first place among the causal factors by only 15 or 16 percent of the voters, quite uniformly across the land. Leaders were most important in Quebec, Ontario and British Columbia and the party as a whole in the Atlantic region and the Prairies. It is interesting that the work of MP's in Parliament, referred to above, should vary so much and be considered twice as important in Quebec than in the two regions immediately to the east and west of it. The explanation may lie in the already noted rather deviant cases of the Créditistes and the Quebec NDP voters, or possibly more likely, since this item was selected by more voters of the other parties as well in Quebec, than in other regions, in the greater survival, in Quebec, of a more personal political style and of greater importance still being attached to the way in which a deputy carries out his duties—in Parliament and elsewhere.

CONCLUDING COMMENTARY

Having presented a great many raw data, we now offer some commentaries on what we saw. In keeping with the preliminary and exploratory nature of the present piece, we shall simply tease out of the survey findings some observations of interest either to the professional student of politics and/or to the citizen trying to assess some of the "meaning" and consequences of the 1968 election. Since our principal focus here is the bases of

33

support for the parties, we shall approach our problem by looking at each of the groups of partisans more or less separately,
and then consider the implications of some of our data for an
understanding of the Canadian political system generally, of
Canada's party system and of the future, both in terms of governmental outputs and the way in which the game of politics is
likely to develop. Since some of the interpretative sallies concern
more than one party, however, we shall save a number of comments touching on the Liberals until we have also made some
remarks about the Conservative voters, and on the party system
generally, until after we have looked also at the NDP and the
Social Credit parties. Lest the reader's expectations have been
aroused too much by this auspicious-looking introduction, let me
hasten to present two disclaimers: our observations are merely
briefly sketched first impressions and the data are derived
entirely from our survey. While we speculate about, we bring no
empirical evidence to bear on other, critically important aspects
of parties: the behaviour and attitudes of leaders, policies imposed by uncontrollable circumstances or other external influences largely unrelated to the immediate attitudes of the voters.
We are, in other words, concentrating here on the voters,
sometimes perhaps falling into the trap of forgetting that its
voters, in a given election, are by no means the whole party.
Some of the ideas flowing out of the data are in the process
of being examined by proposing and testing causal models;
others must await the linking of the present data to other,
relevant information, or the creation and execution of new
research designs. Some bold (a respectable euphemism for
"wild"?) speculations or flights of fancy, suggested by the data,
but going well beyond them, are nevertheless presented.

Liberal Support

Two seemingly contradictory views of the Liberal party have
been popular elements in Canada's political folklore. The party
is seen, on the one hand, as the captive of French Canadians
and Catholics who are its principal supporters and thus allegedly
impose a sinister domination on Canada or, at least, who cast a
gloomy pall on the country's politics. The other portrait presents
the Liberals as the only truly national party appealing without

bias to all the groups and levels of society, and thus representing all interests with uncannily perfect precision. Neither optic is entirely accurate yet both have a basis of fact to sustain them. Both are also misleading.

Our survey (and all manner of other evidence) indicates that French Canadians and Catholics support Liberals in larger proportions than they do the other parties (except the Ralliement des Créditistes) or, to put it in the way we have normally used above, the proportion of the Liberal vote from francophones and Catholics is higher than the party's average vote. But, on the other hand, even allowing for this, no party is as broadly representative of the ethnic, religious, occupational or any other kind of Canadian grouping, as the Liberal. By comparison, the disproportion of Conservative support, for instance, is much greater: fifty-eight percent were of British origin, over 70 percent Protestant as against 33 percent French, and 53 percent Catholic for the Liberals. If any party can be accused of drawing, in a potentially dangerous manner, on only a partial electorate for support, it must be the Conservatives or the NDP, as Table I shows.

The nature of the Liberal party's support from francophones does, nevertheless, require closer scrutiny because it is by no means as one-sided as is often assumed. In the first place, we have noted that in Quebec itself, the party is, in a sense, less French and Protestant than the others. This does not mean, of course, that it receives less absolute support from francophones than the Conservatives and the NDP but that its *proportion* of voters who are not French Canadian is very much greater. In Quebec, the Liberal party is the party *par excellence*, of the English-speaking and ethnically non-French and non-British population. If any Canadian party had any electoral interest in espousing policies designed to satisfy English-speaking Quebeckers, it would be the Liberals. Furthermore, we have seen that the Quebec Liberals deviate markedly from Trudeau supporters elsewhere in the low rating they give the Liberal *party* generally, compared with other party features, and that they also produced a quite atypical age pattern: only in Quebec did Liberals do better among older than among younger voters. One is consequently tempted to conclude first that the Liberals are not quite as homogeneously French as some would have it and that in the stronghold of French Canada—Quebec—the party may be in danger of losing some ground in the future. Results in provincial elections, while only partially relevant, nevertheless support the interpretation suggested here: in the 1970 Quebec contest, the Liberal party appealed phenomenally strongly to anglophones and fared rather badly among younger voters.[13]

Who is likely to benefit in the long run from its losses, or to replace it even, in the event that the Liberal party were to lose its French Canadian support, particularly in the era following that dominated by Mr. Trudeau? The Liberal party has always benefitted from the electoral lack of appeal of alternatives to it and this fact, well outside our present capacity to examine, may repeat itself.[14] Another important aspect of the Liberal appeal to French Canadians concerns the party's reception by francophone non-Quebeckers which, as we have noted, is quite at variance with that of those residing in Quebec. Franco-Ontarians and Acadians gave overwhelming support to the Liberals and there is no indication of its being in any danger of disappearing. This feature of the Liberals' attraction may be related to the party's general tendency to be favoured by minorities to which we shall turn shortly, after taking another look at its alleged "perfect representativeness" insofar as Canadian society is concerned.

While more broadly representative than the other parties of the spectrum of socio-economic groupings usually considered relevant to an explanation of political behaviour, the Liberal party's supporters as a group nevertheless display certain biases (other than the ones mentioned above) which may ultimately have some consequences for the decisions made by the party leadership. The party, more than any other in Canada, appealed in 1968, as in previous elections, to the better-off segments of the public. On virtually every one of our relevant indicators we saw that Liberals obtained a larger proportion of the vote from those who had been favoured in life, whether in terms of the prestige of their occupation, their educational background, the degree of satisfaction displayed about how life has treated them or of any other of our dimensions. With the only exception of its appeal in the Atlantic provinces, to which we shall return later, the Liberal party appeared as the prestige party, drawing to itself the votes of the more privileged segments of the population.

Apart from the regional exception just mentioned, there were however some other departures from this pattern indicating not only the versatility of Canadian political behaviour but also the party's remarkable openness to support from diverse segments of society. The one group, for instance, to which nationally the Trudeau party seemed to hold singularly little attraction was the farmers yet, as we have seen, in Quebec and Ontario they gave the Liberals substantial margins of votes over the other parties, and in the latter province their proportion of the vote was only slightly below that received by the party from all the Ontario voters. In central Canada, therefore, the Liberal party was favoured by farmers and it is really among the western farmers that the Trudeau party had little appeal.

The overall image of the party in the West in fact differed somewhat from that in the East, if the nature of its support is taken as an indicator, for it was here particularly that the Liberals drew the support of the better-off segments of the population. This may in part be related to the lower percentage of French Canadians and Catholics in that part of Canada, two groups which, in aggregate terms, have been favoured somewhat less than others in the status they enjoy in Canada, but other factors are at play to several of which we shall return when we discuss some of the effects of minor parties on the Canadian party system.

We have already commented on the Liberals making a particularly strong appeal to the English-speaking minority in Quebec and to the French-speaking minorities in Ontario and the Atlantic provinces. They also received well above average support from recent immigrants to Canada particularly, as our Language Scale indicates, from those who still make extensive use of their mother tongue. There is, in fact, a strong suggestion in our data that the Liberals have done exceptionally well among Canadians only partially linked to or integrated into the dominant English-speaking culture. Support for this view is found in the overwhelming proportion of Liberal voters among the "mixed" category in our Language Scale, in the better Liberal showing among the "partial" rather than the "pure" French and English, and in the considerably greater favour found by the Liberals among "new Canadians" (those who arrived after 1945) than among "old settlers" (immigrants who came before

1945). The Liberals also received slightly less than their national proportion of votes from Canadian-born electors. The Liberal party thus appears as a party highly tolerant of minorities and its supporters also generally display a more tolerant attitude towards minorities, than the other parties, as we have seen.

These features are no doubt part and parcel of the generally "progressive" and "modern" nature of the Liberal clientele:[15] the party's appeal was greater to young voters than to old ones, to urban dwellers rather than to rural settlers, to Canadians with a high as distinct from a low sense of political efficacy, to people displaying relatively little cynicism about politics. In short, Liberal voters, more than those of the other parties, included what might be termed the most industrialized, urbanized, technocratic and managerial Canadians. In terms of its supporters, therefore, the Liberal party can be thought of as being most progressive or "modern", in the sense of appealing most to those elements in society which feel at home in the so-called "advanced," urbanized and highly technological world usually associated with urban North America. This is not to say, of course, that the supporters of the other parties were all, or even predominantly, antique rustics dwelling in some sort of retarded psychological middle age but rather that the Liberals, on the whole, contained a larger proportion of modern electors, as described here, than the others.

Although the Liberal voters were, in this sense, more progressive than the Conservatives and, in some way, more also than NDP voters, they were not markedly innovative, zealously bent on transforming the world. This is reflected in their general satisfaction with life so far, in their optimism, as well as in a number of other predispositions and particularly perhaps, in the manner in which, in their party perceptions, after their own, they preferred all aspects of the Conservative party. They showed impressive "old party" solidarity—much more so than we observed among the Conservatives, for instance.

In view of their rather urban, optimistic, tolerant and somewhat conservative physiognomy, it is not surprising that Liberal voters found Mr. Trudeau a highly attractive party leader. They were not alone in this, of course, since virtually the whole world saw in him an exceptionally impressive person, combining a number of features highly prized in democratic leaders, or lead-

ers of any sort, for that matter. Nevertheless, the rational, tolerant, sensible, responsible and rather conservative approach of
Mr. Trudeau, in conjunction with his indisputable charisma,
made him an ideal leader of the Liberal party. He would, no
doubt, have fared well at the head of another party but the
match between him and the Liberals was ideal. It is probably
this quite exceptional attraction of the leader which accounts
for the surprising downgrading by Liberal respondents of the
importance of the local candidate in their voting decision. The
Liberals, it will be recalled, differed only slightly from the other
parties (except the NDP) in the weight they gave the party
generally as a causal force in their voting decision; the extraordinary influence of the leader was attained at the expense of
the individual contestant in the ridings. We may be witnessing
here a convergence of two strands which, if they should reinforce and thus perhaps help to consolidate one another, may
have long-lasting effects on Liberal party support and, because
of the large proportion of the Canadian population involved, on
Canada's politics in the future. The modern and thus rather
cosmopolitan character of the Liberal electorate, already predisposed by its political style to approach contemporary problems from a large-scale, universalistic perspective, may have its
focus of attention directed away from local issues and personalities even more than would otherwise have been the case, by a
compellingly attractive national leader next to whom local candidates are likely to pale in colour and appeal. A centralizing
predisposition may thus be reinforced and rooted more deeply
than had the attractiveness of the national and local party personnel been roughly equal. The consequence of this experience
may outlast the presence of a fiercely attractive national leader
and may influence the manner of arriving at future partisan
decisions, even when conditions are vastly different. It is however useful, in this speculation, to recall that the party generally
was still considered of very great importance in their voting
decision, even by Liberal voters, and that so long as Quebeckers
choose the Liberal party in large numbers, there is little danger
of excessive centralization submerging local interests.

Conservative Support

It is generally safe to assume that for practically every statement made above about the Liberal party, the reverse holds for the Conservative voters. The major qualification concerns the profile of Conservatives in the Atlantic region who, as we have seen, with only few exceptions (age and religion, for instance) "look" the way the Liberals do elsewhere in Canada: on the East Coast the Conservative party received greater support from those with higher status, and it had the highest proportion of "progressive", tolerant, satisfied, etcetera, voters. The Liberals, on the other hand, appeared here as the party of the less favoured and the less enlightened. A related phenomenon may be observed in Ontario: although here the two old parties did not reverse their positions on most of our dimensions, the gap between them was often much smaller than elsewhere and in Ontario the Conservative supporters contained a greater proportion of people with a higher status and with more progressive ideas (always, of course, using the adjective in the highly arbitrary sense outlined above).

What are the reasons for this rather atypical aspect of Conservative support in the Atlantic regions and in Ontario? Numerous and complex, they are related to items such as the party's history in the region, its personnel and its position at the provincial level. *One* implication to be drawn from our data in this context concerns the likelihood that in politics, particularly in communities in which the party battle is essentially non-ideological, the appeal of a party to the better placed (in the socio-economic sense) electors depends on its credibility—on the probability of its achieving success. Those following the fortunes of the CCF and the NDP in Canada have noted that one of the obstacles in these parties' path to power has been the reluctance of many electors to "throw away" their vote by supporting what seemed to them the hopeless case of a candidate or party obviously incapable of attaining office. We may be witnessing the opposite but related phenomenon of voters being so impressed by the local aspects of a party—its local position, strongly-favoured, credible leader, well-known candidates, etcetera—to support it despite the overall low appeal elsewhere. And this kind of appeal will persuade high-status electors to support a party which, elsewhere, would likely deter them. In politics, as in other endeavours, nothing appears to succeed like success! The pattern is suggestive to the student of political change, and to one concerned with the relations between provincial and federal politics.

It is well-known that a federal party which also holds power provincially can benefit substantially in terms of obtaining party workers and otherwise adding to its sinews of electoral war. It is less widely perceived but likely equally important that a federal party enjoying a respectable presence at the provincial level derives important psychological benefits from its provincial credibility. The locally immensely popular Mr. Stanfield, already highly regarded as a fine provincial premier, no doubt gained further stature and support from his party having provided a successful government in Nova Scotia but also, within recent memory, in two other Atlantic provinces.

More important perhaps, a new leader with an exceptionally strong appeal in one or more regions may play an important role in starting the process ultimately leading to a realigning or deviating election by detaching support from its traditional moorings and shifting it into new channels. Changes in federal elections have often in the past been preceded by gradual shifts in provincial political configurations and governments, and it is likely that over and above the more obvious relationship between parallel party changes at the provincial and federal levels, the greater credibility of a successful provincial party and its leaders is an important element in influencing patterns of party support even federally.

One of the questions which arises concerns the durability of such changes. There is little doubt that Mr. Stanfield was greatly responsible for the exceptionally strong showing of the Conservatives in the Atlantic region (as Mr. Diefenbaker was before him). Will his support hold, now that he has changed the role of provincial premier for that of an electorally unsuccessful federal leader? And what would happen to the Conservative supporters in the Atlantic provinces if Mr. Stanfield were not to lead the party in the next election? The period preceding that of the 1968 election offers some instructive comparative material. Mr. Diefenbaker's drawing-power in the late 'fifties as the new federal leader was as great in the Prairies as Mr. Stanfield's in the Atlantic region a decade later and, it seems that he has exercised a "realigning influence" on that region and probably also, to a lesser extent, elsewhere in Canada. It is of course

41

the case that, despite his no longer being the party's national leader, he is still a prominent and active Conservative politician and that the Conservative party receiving a larger proportion of votes than the Liberals in Saskatchewan and Alberta in 1968 may be no more than a personal expression of loyalty. There is some confirmation for this interpretation in the extremely high rating the Conservative *party as such* received from its Prairie voters as influencing their voting decision—no doubt many who were still "following John" were compelled to express this by identifying the party rather than the leader, the work of the Conservative MPs or the candidates, as being most important to their voting decision. But whatever the reason for the 1968 loyalty to the Conservative party, it is likely that the prolonged practice of viewing the world through Conservative spectacles, so to speak, has predisposed a substantial number of Prairie voters in favour of the party and that this predisposition will not dissipate itself immediately.

To be sustained, however, this kind of predisposition and support have to establish their worth. Mr. Diefenbaker bound large numbers of Prairie voters to himself and to his party by his "native son" appeal, his political style and by party and government outputs which made of him a credible champion of the region. In 1958 he and his party also detached an important proportion of traditionally Liberal Quebec voters and encouraged them to vote Conservative. This was what we might term only a "deviating" influence, by contrast, in that it induced the voters to stray only temporarily from the traditional path to which they returned when they became convinced that the "newly-found" party and its leader would not, or could not, "deliver"—espouse and implement acceptable policies.

The possibility, hinted at here, that the influence and credibility of Mr. Stanfield and his party in the Atlantic region may have exercised a "realigning" effect on eastern Canada, insofar as party support goes, is of course still highly remote, and there are, in fact, some indicators pointing in the opposite direction. I raised an equally hypothetical possibility when noting the Liberals' relatively lower appeal in Quebec among the younger age groups and also the party's generally lower rating compared with its candidates, leader, etcetera. A similar troublesome phenomenon (from the party's viewpoint) was observed among Conservative supporters in the Atlantic region: the youngest cohort was considerably less enthusiastic about the party than older voters and, in part at least, the strong showing of Mr. Stanfield's candidates in eastern Canada may have to be ascribed not only to the leader's appeal and the party's prestige in the region but also to the relatively small proportion of young voters in the Atlantic region and to the absence of large metropolitan centres. The Liberals *did* attract more of the younger voters than the Conservatives and may hold their support and the process of urbanization will inevitably transform the culture of eastern Canada, thus perhaps depriving the Conservative party of some of the conditions predisposing voters in its favour.

In addition to attracting more "high status" support in its regions of particular strength—the Atlantic provinces and to a certain extent also in Ontario—the Conservatives display an interesting "status profile" also in the two western regions. Nationally the party, as we have seen, received a relatively higher proportion of votes from the least favoured, somewhat less from the middle groups, and least from those ranking highest. In the Prairies the graphs representing these relationships are often curvilinear, with the middle groups giving greater support to the Conservatives than those placed in the low categories. This may indicate a difference in the status of farmers but it also reflects the presence of parties with an even more pronounced "proletarian" appeal—the NDP and Social Credit. As we shall note below at greater length, the presence of a somewhat class-based party has important consequences for the physiognomy of the other parties and for the manner in which they perform their tasks in the political system.

Another consequence of a party's general proximity to power or of its image as a successful organization capable of making effective policy decisions may be detected in the difference in the respective appeals of Liberals and Conservatives to immigrants. The difference is striking in that the latter party did considerably better among the "older settlers", as we have seen, than among the "new" Canadians. There are a number of explanations, of course, as there seem to be for all the phenomena affecting voting behaviour. It is likely, for instance, that the tendency of a larger proportion of earlier settlers having been engaged in agriculture and having taken up residence in the

West is a factor explaining their greater predilection for the Conservative party. But the pattern holds in regions other than the West. The ethnic origin of different waves of immigrants is no doubt also relevant but the explanation which strikes me as being particularly plausible and germane to the present discussion concerns the timing of the immigrants' arrival in relation to who was in power at the time.

An overwhelming proportion of post-Second World War immigrants arrived in Canada under Liberal regimes and were in fact attracted by Liberal governments engaged, during periods of full employment, in aggressively seeking additions to Canada's manpower. Many came from strongly deferential societies in which respect for governmental and bureaucratic authority was pronounced, and gratitude high for favours and goodwill from those in authority. No wonder then that they were kindly predisposed towards what they thought to be their powerful benefactors—Liberal governments and the Liberal party. The latter, by the way, was aware of the process and astutely nursed this important element in its potential constituency. In any event, the image of power and authority—of being to the government mansion born, as well as the policies of successive Liberal governments, bound the new arrivals' loyalties firmly to the Liberal party. Their impression of the Conservatives, on the other hand, was that of a loser, never quite able to scale the heights of federal power.

Earlier waves of immigrants, on the other hand, came to be politically socialized into Canada at periods in which the Liberals were much less *the* government party (although many also came under Liberal regimes) and in which the Conservatives provided a viable, sometimes Ottawa-entrenched alternative. The Liberal party, as we saw, still attracted a greater proportion of these immigrants in 1968 than the Conservatives, but the disparity between the parties was much smaller and certainly nothing like that dividing them in relation to the support they drew from the recent arrivals. While the pattern just described applies particularly to immigrants belonging to neither of Canada's charter groups, it fits with only minor modifications also those of British ancestry.

The above comparison of Liberal and Conservative appeals to immigrants and ethnic minorities invites another short digression into a related difference between the parties. We noted earlier that Liberals were greatly favoured by francophones, particularly outside Quebec. Despite the qualifications we introduced on this point earlier, we concluded that the Liberal party was, more than the others, Canada's French party. It surprised us therefore that a larger proportion of Conservative than Liberal supporters favoured the separation of Quebec. The numbers are exceedingly small (54 Conservatives, 73 Liberals) since there was everywhere an overwhelming rejection of the separatist solution to the "Quebec problem", but the pattern is so consistent across the country (with the exception of the Atlantic region) that it calls for comment.

Questions in our survey probing related attitudes showed, not surprisingly, that Quebec respondents who favoured the separation of their province from Canada liked French Canadians a great deal and their support of separatism must therefore be considered an expression of French Canadian nationalism. This was so particularly for Liberals among whom those who favoured Quebec independence liked French Canadians even better than those opposed (no doubt because the latter included the many anglophone Quebec Liberals). Outside Quebec there was virtually no difference between Liberals and Conservatives supporting separation: voters for both parties in this category rated French Canadians quite low compared to the liking they expressed for other ethnic groups and compared to the degree to which French Canadians were liked by the very large number of respondents opposed to separation. Among the latter group, the difference between Liberals and Conservatives was quite pronounced[16] and we must therefore conclude that the Conservative party not only attracted substantially fewer French Canadians than the Liberals but also that its voters, particularly outside Quebec, liked francophone Canadians a lot less than did the corresponding group of Liberals. The greater Conservative support for the separation of Quebec must therefore be taken as reflecting hostility to French Canada rather than as a sign of sympathy for its nationalist aspirations.

Our final comment arising from a comparison of the bases of support for the Liberal and Conservative parties in the 1968 election concerns the considerably greater homogeneity of the Liberals. Although the argument is difficult to document, it is virtually certain that this difference affects the parties' respective capacities to adopt consistent postures towards policy questions. Liberal support, as we have seen, was much more evenly distributed across the country and displayed less regional variation in the way in which the voters looked at their party, particularly the leader. While both old parties normally try to evolve bundles of policies appealing to all Canadians, insofar as this is possible, the policy-forming process is, in each case, at least partly responsive to the membership of the party in the sense that the most active supporters, usually coming in the largest numbers from the regions of special strength, are likely to exercise a particularly great influence on the decisions reached. In the case of the Conservatives, for instance, the task of reconciling the demands of the most active members from the Atlantic and Prairie regions, and from Ontario, (or, to put it slightly differently, those of the vestigial Drew men, the Stanfield admirers and the Diefenbakerites) imposes extremely awkward tensions on the leadership which, as a consequence, makes it difficult for the national party to appear forceful and consistent both inside and outside the House of Commons. The greater heterogeneity of the Conservatives compared with the Liberals, as observed in 1968, existed in earlier periods and suggests that one of the neglected aspects in the assessments of Mr. Diefenbaker as national leader concerns precisely the lack of homogeneity of his party and the consequent strains on the Diefenbaker cabinets. The Liberals are, of course, not free of divisions, but they are less affected by the kind of structural predisposition to them which have plagued and continue to trouble the Conservatives.

Support for the NDP

The NDP is usually regarded as Canada's only national mass, left-wing party and, when its record is considered, this description is reasonably accurate, although it is not easy to define the meaning of left-wing in the North American, mass party context. We can obtain at least one impression of what the term may signify, when operationalized into day-to-day politics, by looking at a so-called left-wing party. The NDP is not, in terms of its 1968 support at least, an out-and-out party of the underdog. The personal attributes of its voters show it to have a strong appeal to what we might term the "better-off worse-off"

Canadians. It attracts a larger proportion of skilled than un-skilled workers, its vote does not vary directly with the age or the education of its supporters; it does better in urban than in rural areas but here again there are some irregularities and the graph showing the relationship is curvilinear. Usually thought of as a strongly British party, the NDP does indeed find that almost half of its voters were of British origin (a considerably smaller proportion, nevertheless, than among Conservatives) but of all Canadian parties its supporters contain the largest proportion of those whose ethnic origin is neither British nor French. It received little more than token support from French Canadians, and in Quebec drew a much less working-class and a more intellectual group of voters than elsewhere. The one out-standing aspect of the party, despite its *non-Lumpenproletariat* character, is its class base. About 60 percent of its vote came from labour and from individuals who thought of themselves as belonging to the working or lower class.

As a left-wing party, the NDP is reputed to have an ideology or at least a consistent batch of well-defined theoretical positions of a "progressive", welfare-statist kind, guiding its policies and actions. Insofar as its voters go, the party appears to be some-what less ideologically consistent than this reputation would lead one to believe, but it would be misleading to ignore the presence of some sort of ideological broth within which its supporters' positions seem to have developed. Our comments when we were describing the characteristics of NDP voters indi-cated how very heterogeneous the party appeared when viewed in this way. There were many, sometimes contradictory, regional variations not only with respect to the personal attributes of the voters but also in relation to the perceptions of issues and the party and in their general predispositions. But certain dominant strains stood out and were strongly in evidence among NDP voters in all the regions with only the occasional exception of the highly deviant Quebec group.

The two most outstanding common attributes, also strikingly differentiating NDP supporters from those of the older parties, concern which of the election issues were considered of the greatest importance and which of the party characteristics were most important to the voting decision. We have seen that eco-nomic problems were of far greater importance to NDP supporters than to those of all the other parties. One might assume that this was not so much a reflection of a certain general approach to public issues as of the class composition of the NDP voters but the much lower ranking of these issues by the roughly comparable class-based Créditistes and Social Crediters suggests that this is not a matter exclusively of occupational or class background. The degree to which NDP voters liked their party as such (as distinct from its leaders, candidates and parliamentary performance) and to which they assigned it importance in their voting decision indicates that personalities seem to play less of a role in their political choice-making than is the case with supporters of the other parties. Some of our questions, not reported upon here, also indicate that the strength of party attachment is greater among the NDP voters. All this leads us to conclude that the universal heed paid the party as a whole indicates that the NDP voters stand in a different relationship to it than that which prevails between other parties and their voters. The distinction refers to more than just a different perception of a political institution and relates to some general ideas or broad assumptions about government which, however loosely, can as accurately be considered ideological as anything else.

At the risk of abusing an already greatly over-extended word (but no more extended than "ideology"), I shall refer to this quasi-ideological dimension of the NDP supporters as a political style. In doing so, I realize that the NDP voters as described here are merely a statistical category and that to assert that they share a political style is nonsense. Nevertheless the term covers a wider spectrum of traits than ideology and is applied here in hopes that the reader (and the author, as he is swept along by his enthusiasm) does not forget that it is being used in a very special manner, by way of a short-hand term of convenience. The political style consists of only a moderately "progressive" or "liberal" outlook, as our general predispositions showed, more secular than that of other partisans, and one most concerned with economic issues.

Data not included in the tables cited above also show that although the NDP voters' sense of efficacy was similar to that of the Liberals, they had a markedly greater confidence in the capability of political institutions to affect human life. In response to three separate questions exploring this area, a larger percentage of NDP voters than of any other party indicated that they thought that it made a good deal of difference what the government in Ottawa does, and which party is in power federally and provincially.[17] NDP supporters thus appeared to believe more than other partisans that parties and governments can effectively influence affairs and, presumably, bring about changes sought by those controlling them. They accepted the view, in other words, that political decision-makers are capable of altering social and economic conditions.

NDP voters revealed a seemingly inconsistent attitude to at least one question: I expected their mildly socialist predisposition to imbue them with a belief in planning and, as a consequence, give them a pronounced centralist outlook, favouring the federal government having considerable powers relative to those of the provinces. We have seen that this is not the pattern established by the NDP voters who, while more centralist than the Conservatives and the two fiercely provincialist Social Credit groups, were nevertheless substantially less so than the Liberals and reflected very closely the pattern set by the electors of all the parties combined. One could view this greater provincial, rather than federal orientation as the result of a thoroughly modern concern for grass roots and popular, "participatory" democracy, not necessarily at variance with a good deal of planning, even perhaps part of it. But the age-profile of the NDP voters, some of their general predispositions and their response to regional issues suggest that they were simply more concerned with problems of a more local, regional nature and that their political vantage point was often provincial or regional rather than national.

It will be recalled that NDP voters stood out in the Prairies as being most concerned about wheat sales (the Social Credit voters can be ignored because of their small numbers), about regional inequality and about medicare which we had earlier taken to be partly a local issue in this instance. Welfare issues generally were more important to them than to supporters of other parties. NDP voters are revealed by these various responses to share a common basic concern for welfare, for economic problems and also for a somewhat less personalized politics than is preferred by supporters of the other parties and for a tendency to respond to regional issues and problems strongly, within the broad context of these shared predispositions. They emerge, as a consequence, not so much as one *national,* highly homogeneous group sharing certain philosophical predispositions which powerfully influence their electoral choice, but as loose regional groupings responding to their local problems within a roughly shared political outlook mildly resembling the political approach of west European social democratic parties. Although the Canadian leadership of the NDP has always been more homogeneous than this, and has presented us with a coherent party led by consistent and clearly oriented politicians, the NDP supporters appear more like a group of European voters supporting the various components of a somewhat loose alliance of the so-called left. The fact that they do obviously share a common political style and are frequently conscious of having certain political "habits" in common offers a fruitful and suggestive invitation to speculate about the consequences of the general political system in Canada on its party system and on the day-to-day political process, but this is hardly the place for such speculation. We have already moved to a dangerously distant point from our empirical anchor.

Créditistes and Social Crediters

Because of the small numbers involved in each case, it is dangerous to draw many conclusions from the data we have presented respectively about the Créditiste and Social Credit voters. This is particularly so since there are marked differences between the patterns displayed by the Prairie and British Columbia Social Crediters. The Quebec group does, in a way, resemble the NDP in appearing to have a distinct political style but, except for their concern with economic issues, the Créditistes seem to possess the very opposite characteristics of the NDP, particularly in their general predispositions. Although the Caouette followers have played a lively part in federal politics for some ten years, there is still doubt about their staying power as a political organization at the federal level. Their fortunes seem tied strongly to the personality of the leader and when he departs from the national scene, the party may lapse into oblivion, at least insofar as Ottawa is concerned.

50

All three Social Credit groupings do, however, share one characteristic with one another, and also with the NDP voters, which has important consequences for the other parties and for the Canadian party system: their appeal is much greater to the less privileged than to the more favoured, and they can therefore be considered parties attracting the voters of the poorer segments of the population who find the older parties unacceptable.

Consequences for the Political and Party Systems

One of the consequences is that the older parties are deprived of the support of these groups. To some extent, therefore, the demands of the less privileged are articulated in a different manner from that of other socio-economic groupings. The decision-makers of the older parties taken together are less exposed to the pressures of the underprivileged and, although they may be highly sensitive to this fact, the awareness cannot compensate for the constant structurally reinforced clamor to which they would be exposed if they were more dependent on its originators electorally. We have seen that the Liberal party, although receiving slightly less than average support from unskilled labourers, does count among its electors exactly the same proportion of skilled workers as there were among all the voters. It can therefore be argued that it, at least, does reflect, even structurally, the class composition of the country (leaving the farmers aside) and that within it, at least, the malrepresentation of the underdog cannot be detected. But it must, precisely because it is very much an omnibus party drawing on very wide support, adopt policies pleasing to a wide variety of interests and groups. It is also a party which has a disproportionately large number of "high class" voters. The better-off, the more formally educated, those feeling that they can be politically effective are much more likely to formulate and express their ideas, to bring them to the ears of the ultimate decision-makers and so persuade the latter to pay heed to their demands. This is so particularly in a pluralistic society accustomed to governments consulting organized groups, specially in the world of industry and business.

Under these conditions, the interests of the economic underdog are championed at the political level most vigorously, and somewhat more single-mindedly than is the case with broadly-based omnibus type parties, by those political organizations whose primary support is derived from the less-favoured sectors of society. In Canada, this is particularly the NDP and the Social Credit parties, and among the latter notably the Créditistes. But these parties, it is sometimes said are, because of their "minority" status, less effective than the old "government" parties. The student concerned with the capacity of the party system to respond to the needs and demands of various segments of society is confronted through this train of thought by the question of whether the interests of the least favoured economic and social groups in society *are* effectively championed within the Canadian party system.

A prior, more fundamental question is, of course, whether the neglect of certain interests is to be ascribed to flaws in the political system or whether it is simply impossible to achieve perfection. Have we done just about as well as can be expected and must we conclude that high levels of personal freedom, economic growth and the maintenance of a liberal civilized society cannot be reconciled with social justice? Or, to reformulate and extend the question into a more contemporary mode: can a pluralist, liberal democratic system achieve our highest social aims or is it necessary to resort to drastic reorganization, perhaps even violence, to bring about such cataclysmic social change as according full membership in our society even to the poorest and currently most neglected of its members? This question cannot even be contemplated here, although what we have said so far certainly leads us to it, but before it can be answered some less grandiose problems need to be settled, and our data are of some relevance to them.

They centre on the question of whether the Canadian party system, as it has operated and as it presents itself in our survey data, is particularly well-suited for the most effective translation of human needs into governmental outputs, particularly in the terms presented in this essay. Specifically, of course, this raises the question of whether the system of *one* major omnibus party, usually forming the government, opposed by a group of less widely based, more specialized parties, is in part responsible for our failure to fulfill our ideals. Would, for instance, a straight

52

two-party system have performed better, or alternatively, an even more fragmented system, less dominated by the particular characteristics and style of the Liberal party and by the "majoritarian bias" in our Parliamentary system? To answer even these more modest formulations of our major problem requires answers to questions about the role of governments in society, and of what is expected of *the* opposition and of opposition parties individually.

If it is assumed that the main task of the opposition parties, aside from the basic one of providing an alternative to the existing government, is to act as a watchdog, keeping the government on its toes not only in terms of the efficiency of its performance but also in responding to all the sectors of the community requiring services, then one may ask whether this is done best by one large powerful omnibus party, like that forming the government, also omnibus in nature, or whether better results follow from the splintering of the opposition into a number of more specialized, differently-based parties.

It is possible to argue that the existing process is virtually ideal: the party system reacts doubly or even triply to discontent, criticism and the requirements of the lowest economic groupings. The major party, drawing not inconsiderable support from this part of the community, does its best to serve it. If, however, its omnibus nature and the special pleading of more strategically placed voters or other organized supplicants should prevent a healthy internal sensitivity of the Liberal party to the needs of the poor and downtrodden, then the opposition parties, and particularly those most heavily indebted to them electorally, will take up cudgels on their behalf. In Canada the Conservatives—the major of the minor parties—will do so in part, for are they not essentially the party of the less-favoured? And even more certainly and single-mindedly the NDP—Canada's most strikingly class-based and ideologically appropriate party—has made it its hallmark to champion the interests of underprivileged Canadians, sometimes assisted by the Créditistes. The system thus assures that *all* parties—some within a general practice of maximizing support from all layers of society, others as the result of their special clientele—express the interests of those often considered overlooked by public and private decision-makers in bourgeois societies. The Parliamentary system, par-

53

ticularly as it operates in Canada, with its modified two-party system, is at least triply effective in assuring social justice.

Those doubting the usefulness of the most frequently invoked alternative—a fully-fledged multi-party system composed of more "programmatic" parties—claim that the possibly more effective single-mindedness and stridency expected to result would be more than offset by the likely strengthening of the major party as the result of the public's distaste for minority governments. Our data certainly offer overwhelming evidence that Canadians do not like minority governments. This strong feeling on the part of so many Canadians can be interpreted as a powerful factor in the frequent election to office of the Liberals who, because of their broad electoral base and widespread appeal, are often given the best chance of winning a Parliamentary majority. A fragmented opposition is thus held to strengthen the government, quite aside from splintering the opposition itself. There is no doubt some truth in this observation, but it is impossible to say whether this effect is greater or less than the salutary consequences of having several parties, boasting different leaders and drawing on widely diverging support, attacking and pressing the government, undaunted by the inhibition of expecting one day themselves to be the solitary formers of a government.

The formal framework of our Parliamentary system is, nevertheless, geared to a dialectic two-party interaction between the government and opposition party, assumed to take place in a highly routinized, gentlemanly manner dominated by the myth that all concerned are loyal advisers to the sovereign. The system has adjusted to the realities of its modern pluralist setting to some extent by allowing for the role played by a complex bureaucracy and for the interaction between the final decision-makers and organized groups of citizens likely to be affected by their decisions. Despite the partial adjustment, however, the system is basically still built on the premise of a dichotomy permeating politics and arising from the simple confrontation between *the* government party (having a majority of seats) and *the* opposition party (temporarily in a minority in *the* House). The fact that the dominant interactions and conflicts in the polity are economic, regional, politically structural (i.e. federal-provincial, provincial-municipal, federal-provincial-municipal, etcetera) is only imperfectly integrated into the formal theory and rhetoric of the system, and also into the actual rules of procedure guiding the working of Parliament, the central government and interaction between the various levels of government, which themselves now transcend the simple local-provincial-federal division of yesteryear.

The system has, as is stressed in much of the literature on liberal democracy and the two-party system, facilitated compromise and broad consensus among the effective decision-makers which was accepted as legitimate by the vast bulk of the population affected by them.

There is another way of reading our reality however which, though extending somewhat the argument presented at the opening of this section, merits being examined in greater detail. It begins by recognizing that the interests of the underprivileged are exceedingly difficult to meet, even to *try* to meet: they are immensely hard to define even, if one is really serious about it, and they are hard to express. Whatever the definition and formulation, however, the result is generally clear: the standards of living and the opportunities for personal development of an important proportion of Canadians are substantially below the levels expected according to the criteria accepted by most Canadians as being just and adequate and in keeping with the rhetoric of Canadian politics and the way in which social values are defined within it. This applies to Indians, Eskimoes, negroes and other ethnic minorities as well as to clusters of the poor both in highly urban and in rural slums. It would be difficult to find a well-informed person on the subject who is not appalled by the social and economic conditions of substantial numbers of Canadians. It would be equally hard to find one who would not readily agree that in part at least, these conditions prevail for reasons totally unrelated to the personality or personal characteristics of the individuals concerned.

The solutions of the problems posed by these economic and social disparities are economic, social and even, no doubt, partly psychological, but it would be robbing the "political" of any meaning if it were not recognized that in part they must also be political. Students of politics therefore ask themselves what is responsible for the political side of the problem-solving process having performed less-well than one would have wished.

55

The answers, like the problems, are to some extent universal and cannot be sought entirely by looking at the Canadian political system but there are, on the other hand, purely Canadian aspects which may be illuminated by some implications following from the foregoing portrait of Canadian electorates and parties.

Both Liberal and Conservative governments have, since the Second World War, introduced extensive welfare legislation benefitting virtually all levels of Canadian society and certainly the poor and least-favoured. The gap between the very rich and the very poor has not been noticeably narrowed, however, and on the whole the legislative output has provided relatively greater advantages to those who have already achieved some sort of take-off position in their standards of living than to those at the very bottom of the socio-economic and "opportunity" pyramid. This period was dominated by a series of efficient Liberal governments who did much to facilitate the extraction of Canadian natural resources and to some extent their processing (more often than not by American concerns), and who worked well with large commercial and industrial interests. There is little doubt that the creation of jobs and the general well-being of Canadians were very much in the minds of both the politicians and the powerful Ottawa mandarinate, as they formulated and implemented Canada's social and economic policy. Their frame of reference was one, however, which while favouring welfare, accepted a good deal of poverty and lack of material, social and psychic amenities as an inevitable, albeit deplorable, aspect of the *condition humaine,* at least for the time being. Liberal politicians and their competent, technocratic advisers in the bureaucracy thought of politics very much as the art of the possible, in which the possible was to be obtained by competent, safe, mildly reformist procedures, invariably stopping before one began reaching for the stars. They were, in short, prepared to tolerate conditions which, in the seventies, are increasingly being considered as intolerable.

The NDP, less encumbered with the need to act as broker for a large number of cross-cutting interests and avowedly representing the country's so-called working people, was a vigorous and determined spokesman for the less favoured and often pointed to conditions in which it thought to see the advantages

56

of some vested interests encroach on the well-being of the general public or some defenceless segment of it. Although it has often been remarkably effective in compensating for biases emanating from the structural and attitudinal characteristics of the government parties, the NDP has of course also been subject to the biases resulting from *its* specialized clientele and political style. Among the most important were the partnership with organized labour, substantially greater support from skilled rather than unskilled labour, the vestiges of important support from certain kinds of farmers in the West, and an ideological patina formed as the result of the acclimatization to Canada of certain ideas and procedures of west European social democratic movements. The need to reconcile these occasionally conflicting tendencies, to create an image which would prove attractive to a growing segment of a North American electorate and the inevitable socializing influences of the oldest of the Daughters of Parliament resulted in the NDP's protests and claims on behalf of the underdog being somewhat less strident and insistent than was probably necessary for a truly effective representation of the *most* neglected Canadians. The Ralliement des Créditistes, largely because of its novelty, size, ideas and its geographically and ethnically specialized constituency was even less effective than the NDP, despite its somewhat more proletarian (but rural) electorate.

It is by no means conclusive but certainly plausible to argue that a different kind of party system composed of parties displaying a variety of more or less narrow vested interests and political styles, from conservative, conciliatory ones to more strident and radical types—challenging the legitimacy of a system neglecting some group or problem—might produce a more just, egalitarian bundle of outputs than is the case at present. It might (and the conjecture can only be intensely hesitant) make the system more interesting to the very large proportion (25 percent in 1968, the year of an unusually lively and interesting election) of Canadians who do not bother voting and many of whom, in terms employed practically throughout this paper, must be considered as being outside the political and party system. They do not form any kind of clientele for the parties and, although lured by, and often needing them, do not seem to bite. It is among this group that the proportion of underprivileged and otherwise neglected citizens is exceptionally high.

In contemplating the implications of the above speculation, it is necessary to bear in mind that the suggestion implicit in it, namely that the party system and the Parliamentary system blunt the expression of demands from the most needy sections of the population, by failing to reach, fragmenting, neutralizing and partially syphoning off radical constituents from the decision-making process, imposes responsibilities on the party system that might well be placed elsewhere—namely on the shoulders of the electors. It is not necessarily the party system—the structure of parties and the relations prevailing among them—but the consciousness, attitudes and wishes of the electorate, perhaps even the most "neglected" sections of it themselves, which may be responsible. If this is the case, then one might conclude that the insensitivity of the system to certain human needs must be ascribed not to structural features of the party system—certainly not to them alone—but also to the wishes of the majority. The system may not be just but it is at least democratic in the conventional sense. If this is the situation, however, then one might raise the question whether a system thus constraining individuals so that they are unresponsive to some of the needs of their fellow-men, and possibly of their own self-development, is inadequate and requiring considerable reform. We cannot tackle problems of this kind of complexity here and must content ourselves with a more mundane one: assuming that a systematic neglect of the important requirements of certain groups actually occurs in Canada, is it likely that ultimately the neglected groups will adopt illegitimate means to seek redress or that gradually the legitimacy of the whole regime may be undermined, as the behaviour and output of parties fail to keep pace with changing attitudes of important segments of the public?

The various questions in our survey probing into the degree of confidence and trust Canadians have in the governmental process suggest that there is a considerable and widely-based (although by no means giddily enthusiastic) level of support for the regime. There is also an extremely strong preference for majority governments and any particular government is thus provided with a cushion of goodwill or credit, which allows it to tax the public's patience by some errors and incompetence, since there is the widely-held belief that unless another party obtains a majority of seats, government is not likely to be effective. This safety-valve notwithstanding, we have seen that a significant number of Canadians does not vote at all and another large group is prepared to vote for parties which are unlikely, to say the least, to have majorities in the near future. One of these —the Conservatives—still enjoys the image of being a potential majority party, although with only exceptional flurries (as the brief governments of Bennett and Diefenbaker have shown) the party has not been able to win majorities in Parliament since the First World War. Furthermore, we have seen that the bases of party support do not augur well for its future as a major party enjoying the kind of widespread and "modern" foundation bolstering the Liberals. The party's image nevertheless makes it a formidable alternative to the Liberals and, as the voting history of the NDP and more recently the Social Credit parties, and our survey data show, large numbers of Canadians are willing to risk a minority government when they feel like rejecting the Liberals. There is, in the Canadian system, therefore, a stabilizing and conservative factor composed, among other elements, of the attitudes of the public towards minority governments and of the broad and seemingly well-rooted support of the Liberals. On the other hand, there is also a flexibility and porousness provided by the willingness of the electorate to withhold support from the one majority party and distribute it among other claimants to power. It is of course not being suggested here that the voters make conscious decisions of this sort (as is sometimes foolishly assumed by those who insist that individual Canadians try to create a balance of power by supporting different parties at the provincial and federal levels) but rather that their behaviour and attitudes have made for the development of a system possessing the characteristics described above. This flexibility and porousness compels the government party to be forever on the alert (a ubiquitous condition in democratic regimes, accentuated in Canada by the circumstances just described) for new crosscurrents of opinion, and it also gives the so-called minor parties the opportunity to influence policies since they not only provide an alternative to reigning governments but also occasionally Parliamentary ma-

jorities to the party in power. The system which has not therefore, perhaps because of the absence of radical parties and of a
lively and widely shared philosophy of protest, moved dramatically towards meeting the needs of the underdog, is nevertheless
capable of responding to demands even of minorities, once they
are formulated. The trouble with Canada, from the viewpoint
of the reformer, is thus not so much the character of its party
system as the attitudes and priorities of the citizens, who have
not demanded of their party system that it help them move
visibly towards the establishment of a Just Society. The bases
of party support, as revealed in the study of the 1968 election,
indicates that there was, at that time at least, no "critical mass"
base for radical politics in Canada.

NOTES

1. Interviews were conducted across Canada with 2767 respondents chosen according to established sampling methods from the
preliminary Voters Lists. Details of the sample design may be obtained from the author.
2. This will be done in a forthcoming book on the 1968 election
for which this essay is a preliminary working paper.
3. The tables accompanying this discussion contain many interesting data not commented upon in the text. One of the reasons
for publishing this working paper before the major research report,
for which it is a kind of *étude*, is to make some of the data available
to interested scholars earlier than would otherwise be the case.

4. Mildred A. Schwartz, "Canadian Voting Behaviour," prepared for Richard Rose [ed.], *Comparative Electoral Behavior.* (New York: Free Press forthcoming). All references to her work in this paper will henceforth, unless specifically stated, refer to the mimeographed version of Prof. Schwartz's paper. Page references will be placed in brackets in the text, so as to avoid unnecessary footnotes.

5. The attention of readers interested in Canadian regionalism is directed to the papers arising out of the CPSA/SCSP 1970 Colloque by Lijphart, Noel, Bergeron, Irvine and Cameron in *The Canadian Journal of Political Science*, IV, 1 (March 1971), pp. 1-25; Donald E. Blake, "The Measure and Impact of Regionalism in Canadian Voting Behaviour," presented to the CPSA, June 1971 meetings and this author's Yale dissertation proposal, "Regionalism in Canadian Voting Behaviour—1908-1968;" Richard Simeon's "Allegiants, Deferentials, Rebels and the Alienated: Some Regional Dimensions of a Political Culture" (forthcoming) and Mildred Schwartz' forthcoming *The Divisions of Canada.* An earlier approach to the problem is in my "Conclusion: An Analysis of the National(?) Results," in my *Papers on the 1962 Elections.*

6. The survey, conducted by Converse, Meisel, Pinard, Regenstreif and Schwartz, comprised interviews with over 2100 respondents.

7. In this paper we usually adopt a different way of presenting our data, however, stressing the proportion of *votes* received by the *parties* from each studied group or subgroup. Thus to show the appeal of the Quebec Conservatives, for instance, to Catholics and "Others", we indicate in Table II that 19.0 percent of the former and 12.5 percent of the latter voted Conservative. Table III tells us that the party received 18.4 percent of the total Quebec vote; the above-mentioned 19.0 percent was 0.6 percentage points *above* the total, and the "Others' " 12.5 percent was 5.9 percent *below* it. We normally therefore examine the appeal of parties by looking at the deviation of the support given by each group examined from the total population of which it is part. The data on personal attributes mentioned in the present text are usually contained in Tables II and III although an occasional glance at Table I will also prove useful.

8. A closely related point to note here is that 13 percent of our Atlantic respondents were of French origin and that 73 percent of these voted Liberal.

9. When drafting the ensuing pages, we were occasionally tempted to refer to instances either supporting or challenging some of our generalizations, in which the number of cases was so small as to preclude the evidence being accepted unquestioningly. We normally resisted the temptation and the meticulous reader should therefore bear in mind, when now and then finding an inconsistency

between the text and the tables, that cases involving very small numbers have usually been ignored in our discussion.

10. "Language Continua and Political Alignments: The Case of French- and English-users in Canada," paper presented to the 7th World Congress of Sociology, 1970. Included in the present volume as "Values, Language and Politics in Canada."

11. The preamble to the question made it clear that the newly elected *federal* government was being referred to.

12. It will be noted that the same questions have occasionally been used in more than one index. This practice, while quite appropriate at this exploratory stage, has nevertheless dangers in that it leads to certain indices representing, in part at least, the same phenomena. Their cumulative effect, therefore, is not nearly as powerful as would otherwise be the case. Our moral liberalism and authoritarianism indices are a good example.

13. Cf Vincent Lemieux, Marcel Gilbert and André Blais, *Une élection de réalignement*, (Montreal, 1970), *passim*.

14. Although generally our data do not support the often-heard view that Canadians usually vote *against*, rather than *for* a party or a government.

15. I am again using these adjectives in a highly subjective way, knowing that I am conveying my *rough* meaning well enough but also cognizant of the looseness of my form of expression. The reader is asked to forgive this shorthand.

16. The scores were 67° for the Liberals and 58° among Conservatives.

17. The percentages were as follows:

It makes	Govt. in Ottawa				Party in Ottawa				Party in Province			
	L	PC	NDP	SC	L	PC	NDP	SC	L	PC	NDP	SC
A good deal of difference	57	60	65	36	37	26	38	16	38	35	41	20
Some difference	25	22	23	28	38	40	41	34	39	39	39	44
No difference	18	18	12	36	26	34	21	50	23	26	20	36

2

PARTY IMAGES
IN CANADA:
A REPORT ON
WORK IN PROGRESS

INTRODUCTION

IN INTERPRETING THE MEANING OF THE PARTY STRUGGLE AND
of elections at any given place and time it is imperative to have
a clear idea of how the voters perceive the parties competing for
their support. Among the large number of possible approaches
to the question of what are the images of the parties, a particularly promising technique is the so-called semantic differential
type of question which, as it is used here, invites the respondents
to place each party on a scale indicating where they think it fits
most appropriately with respect to various dimensions which are
presented in the form of simple word pairs. These pairs, which
may comprise such notions as Good-Bad, United-Split, Powerful-Weak and so on, are predetermined by the investigators involved; they consequently deprive this particular instrument of
the spontaneity of open-ended questions. The method, on the
other hand, has some great advantages both in terms of the

A paper presented to the Forty-Second Annual Meeting of the
Canadian Political Science Association, Winnipeg, June 1970. The two
national surveys on which this paper is based were made possible by
grants from the Canada Council, the Laidlaw Foundation (1965) and
the Izaak Killam Memorial Fund of the Canada Council (1968). I
should like to acknowledge the generosity of these granting bodies and
also the help I received specifically in the preparation of this paper from
the following: Paul Duncan, Gayle Grossman and Ann Spiller.

TABLE I : PARTY IMAGES EXPLORED IN EITHER 1965 OR 1968

	IDEAL			LIBERAL						CONSERVATIVE						NDP					
	1965	1968	Change 1965-1968	1965	1968	Change 1965-1968	Deviation from Ideal '65	Deviation from Ideal '68	Change in Deviation 65-68	1965	1968	Change 1965-1968	Deviation from Ideal '65	Deviation from Ideal '68	Change in Deviation 65-68	1965	1968	Change 1965-1968	Deviation from Ideal '65	Deviation from Ideal '68	Change in Deviation 65-68
ONLY 1965																					
Foolish-Wise	6.5		4.7			-1.8			4.3			-2.2			4.6			-1.9			
Strong Minded – Weak Minded	1.7		3.6			1.9			3.5			1.8			3.0			1.3			
Slow-Fast	5.2		3.6			-1.6			3.6			-1.6			4.5			-.7			
ONLY 1968																					
Concerned for Welfare – Unconcerned	1.4		2.9	3.0			1.5			2.5			1.6						1.1		
Good-Bad for Canadian Unity	1.3		2.6	3.3			1.3			3.4			2.0						2.1		
Religious – Non-Religious	3.1		3.6	3.5			.5			3.8			.4						.7		

analysis which it permits after the data have been gathered and in providing a highly useful tool for making comparisons over time and in cross-cultural studies.[1]

This paper is not an exhaustive or final application of the semantic differential approach to the study of parties. The reader who takes the trouble to look up some of the sources cited in the footnote will observe that the semantic differential can be used, in conjunction with various statistical techniques, in a number of subtle ways. While by no means all of these would be appropriate in the study of party images, some could have been applied here. The progress of our work did not, however, permit the utilization of some of the available refined tests and this paper is a rather early report on work in progress. The data, it will be seen, are fascinating and they are presented in a very simple way which permits a first, rough examination of their thrust and meaning. They tell us a good deal about the images Canadians had of their parties in 1965 and 1968 and they suggest a number of paths along which the answers to more conventional questions in election surveys should be analyzed.

METHOD AND THEORETICAL CONCERNS

While the theoretical relevance of the semantic differential type of question in our research should logically be presented first, its discussion will be more meaningful after we have sketched how we have used the type of question pioneered in an infinitely more sophisticated way by Charles E. Osgood and his associates.

Our data are derived from two national opinion surveys conducted after the 1965 and 1968 elections.[2] Comparisons between party images in the two elections are therefore made on the basis of interviews with two quite distinct samples, and not by talking twice to the same panel of electors.

Thirteen word pairs were used in each election,[3] but three from the earlier survey (Foolish—Wise, Strong-minded—Weak-minded, Slow—Fast) were dropped, and three new ones used in 1968 (Concerned for People's Welfare—Unconcerned for People's Welfare, Good for Canadian Unity—Bad for Canadian Unity, Religious—non-Religious). The mean scores are presented in Table I. Ten word pairs used in both elections are grouped to guide us to perceptions of three broad aspects of the parties:

Party Aspect	Word pair
(A) General Quality	Good—Bad
	Honest—Dishonest
	Exciting—Dull
(B) General Orientation	Modern—Out of Date
	Young—Old
	For the Working Class—For the Middle Class
	Left Wing—Right Wing
(C) Performance	Powerful—Weak
	Competent—Incompetent
	United—Split

The respondents were asked to score each Canadian party and also an Ideal party.[4] In this paper I shall concern myself only with the images of the Ideal party, of the Liberals, Conservatives and NDP. The Social Credit and Creditiste parties are left out of our discussion.

In filling out the questionnaire, each respondent was asked to "score" the Ideal and actual parties for each word pair on a seven-point scale. The seven positions on the scale were subsequently assigned a value from 1 to 7 and the mean score computed for each group or sub-group, for each party and for each word pair. The results were tabulated and, to facilitate analysis, were also summarized graphically, in the manner shown in Chart I.

Generally, the material presented here is derived from scanning the mean scores assigned by our respondents to the Ideal and actual parties on the ten dimensions, grouped into the three aspects shown above.

We have relied primarily on three measures:

(1) The *mean scores* as such, assigned the parties by one or the other of our two sets of respondents (1965 or 1968) taken as a whole or by some sub-group of them (e.g. Anglicans, people aged sixty years or more). This measure permits us to see how the respondents rated each party in "absolute" terms.

(2) *Deviations* between the mean scores assigned the Ideal party and each of the actual parties at one point in time, by the various groups whose perceptions are being examined. The deviation enables us to see how each group or sub-group rated

the actual parties in relation to its own criterion set by scoring the Ideal party.

(3) The *change in deviations from 1965 to 1968* between the Ideal and actual parties. This measure tells us whether the gap between the Ideal and actual parties has widened or narrowed in 1968, as compared with 1965.[5]

The relevance of the semantic differential type of question to the theoretical framework of my studies of Canadian parties and elections is very great but neither time nor space permit its discussion here. I shall simply indicate some of my theoretical concerns which greatly commend the technique to me. Because it is a convenient place to do so, I shall also catalogue a few of its general advantages in the study of elections and parties.

I am concerned with the responsiveness of parties to the needs, wants and demands of the total population and of sub-populations. In this context the opportunities provided to ask respondents to identify the position of an Ideal, as well as of actual parties, is of inestimable value. It permits us to conceive of the gap between the Ideal and actual parties as a measure of achievement or frustration. We have in this technique, therefore, a tool with which we can look at the perceptions people have of parties from the viewpoint of both the demand and support aspects of the political system.

The concept Party Identification, as used by scholars associated with the Michigan Survey Research Center has proven exceptionally rewarding, both theoretically and empirically, in efforts to describe and explain electoral behaviour.[6] Our two surveys suggest, however, that it may be almost inapplicable in Canada. On the basis of admittedly limited evidence (surveys of only two elections) we have found that party identification seems to be as volatile in Canada as the vote itself. If this is confirmed as being the case, we shall need a more stable measure of the long-term component of the vote, in Converse's sense.[7] Party images, as revealed, measured and organized with the aid of the semantic differential techniques may give us just such a measure. It could, where necessary, assume some of the explanatory role now performed by Party Identification and could also be used to extend the analysis of voting behaviour by being used in conjunction with it.

By providing a number of the dimensions in which party

images are scored, the technique is an exceptionally effective means of conducting comparisons of parties over time and cross-culturally. There are obvious dangers in providing and also in substituting these dimensions but the rewards of the technique are nevertheless great.

The data elicited through the type of question we have used in drafting this paper provide a highly subtle and nuanced way of examining party perceptions which admirably augments the yields provided by the more conventionally used questions. We have, of course, put a large number of the usual kind of question on our 1965 and 1968 questionnaires and do not propose to neglect them.

It is my purpose in this paper to share with interested colleagues some of the discoveries made with the assistance of the semantic differential type of question. My concern is to point to some of the highlights of the findings and to consider how they need to be analyzed further, *alone and in conjunction with the other data* in our surveys, to obtain the insights required if our theoretical preoccupations and our wish to describe and explain Canadian political realities in the sixties are to be satisfied.

The next section examines the perceptions of parties by the total Canadian population, and in the one which follows we summarize and make some highly selective (i.e. incomplete) comments on the party images of various subpopulations grouped by sex, age, education, religion, ethnic origin, period of immigration to Canada, region, and class. Limitations of space prevent us from reporting here also on the breakdowns by political variables: voting history, partisanship, a sense of efficacy and so on.

GLOBAL IMAGES

The Non-Respondents

Table II shows that those who did not answer the semantic differential questions, either by refusing to do so or by saying that they did not know how to score one or more of the word pairs (the two categories of responses are combined in the table), reacted quite differently to the various parties and also, to some extent, to the various word pairs.[8]

In both sets of interviews, the lowest refusal rate occurred in

WORD PAIRS	IDEAL		LIBERAL		CONSERVATIVE		NDP	
	1965	1968	1965	1968	1965	1968	1965	1968
Modern - Out of Date	4.1	3.2	5.4	3.0	7.0	4.2	16.1	10.3
Competent - Incompetent	4.2	2.4	5.5	3.6	7.1	4.5	16.0	10.8
Powerful - Weak	4.3	2.2	5.2	3.6	6.9	4.4	16.0	10.4
Foolish - Wise	4.3	-	5.7	-	7.1	-	16.4	-
For Working - For Middle Class	4.7	2.4	6.4	3.6	7.4	4.6	16.4	10.5
United - Split	4.2	2.5	5.6	3.8	7.0	4.9	16.6	10.9
Good - Bad	4.3	2.4	5.7	3.4	6.9	4.8	16.1	10.8
Left Wing - Right Wing	7.3	10.5	9.4	12.1	10.7	12.0	19.0	16.7
Strong - Weak Minded	4.4	-	5.8	-	7.0	-	16.3	-
Honest - Dishonest	3.8	2.2	5.7	3.2	6.9	4.6	16.2	10.6
Exciting - Dull	4.7	2.6	6.1	3.7	7.1	4.8	16.2	10.6
Young - Old	4.3	2.3	5.7	3.4	7.0	4.2	16.2	10.7
Slow - Fast	4.1	-	5.4	-	6.8	-	16.3	-
Concerned - Unconcerned	-	2.2	-	3.3	-	4.3	-	10.5
Good - Bad for Unity	-	2.3	-	3.7	-	4.5	-	11.0
Religious - Non-Religious	-	2.7	-	4.4	-	5.6	-	11.7

scoring the Ideal party, to be followed by the Liberals, the Conservatives and finally the NDP, which met with a significant non-response in both our surveys. The differences with respect to the actual parties was probably related to their "visibilities" but this, like so many of our observations, needs to be tested. One cannot overlook the possibility that the response rate also is related to the order in which the parties were mentioned. Social Credit and the NDP came last.

The semantic differential type of question seems to be quite congenial to Canadian respondents, as can be seen from the low refusal rate associated with the Ideal party, particularly in the 1968 survey. Our respondents were, furthermore, not at all reluctant to commit themselves about parties they knew something about, like the Liberals, and they responded fairly freely even when scoring less known parties like the NDP.

The refusal rate was, however, quite atypically high with respect to the Left Wing—Right wing continuum. This was probably so because our respondents did not understand its meaning or because they thought that the dimension was not compatible with the politics they know.[9] The reluctance of our samples to use the Left—Right scale is instructive not only

69

TABLE III: PARTY IMAGES, 1965 AND 1968 (MEAN SCORES)

	IDEAL			LIBERAL						CONSERVATIVE						NDP					
	1965	1968	Change 1965-1968	1965	1968	Change 1965-1968	Deviation from Ideal '65	Deviation from Ideal '68	Change in Deviation 65-68	1965	1968	Change 1965-1968	Deviation from Ideal '65	Deviation from Ideal '68	Change in Deviation 65-68	1965	1968	Change 1965-1968	Deviation from Ideal '65	Deviation from Ideal '68	Change in Deviation 65-68
(A) GENERAL QUALITIES																					
Good-Bad	1.4	1.4	.0	3.3	2.9	-.4	1.9	1.5	-.4	3.6	3.4	-.2	2.2	2.0	-.2	3.3	3.6	.3	1.9	2.2	.3
Honest-Dishonest	1.3	1.3	.0	3.3	2.6	-.7	2.0	1.3	-.7	2.9	2.8	-.1	1.6	1.5	-.1	2.6	2.8	.2	1.3	1.5	.2
Exciting-Dull	2.4	2.4	.0	4.1	3.2	-.9	1.7	.8	-.9	4.2	4.5	.3	1.8	2.1	.3	3.4	4.0	.6	1.0	1.6	.6
(B) GENERAL ORIENTATION																					
Modern-Out of date	2.0	2.0	.0	3.7	2.9	-.8	1.7	.9	-.8	4.3	4.3	.0	2.3	2.3	.0	2.7	3.5	.8	.7	1.5	.8
Young-Old	3.1	2.9	-.2	4.7	3.1	-1.6	1.6	.2	-1.4	4.9	4.6	-.3	1.8	1.7	-.1	2.9	3.5	.6	-.2	.6	.8
For Working Class- For Middle Class	3.4	3.5	.1	4.4	4.4	.0	1.0	.9	-.1	4.4	4.2	-.2	1.0	.7	-.3	2.7	2.7	.0	-.7	-.8	-.1
Left Wing-Right Wing	4.6	4.6	.0	4.3	4.4	.1	-.3	-.2	.1	4.6	4.4	-.2	.0	-.2	-.2	3.6	3.5	-.1	-1.0	-1.1	-.1
(C) PERFORMANCE																					
Powerful-Weak	2.0	2.0	.0	4.0	2.8	-1.2	2.0	.8	-1.2	4.3	4.4	.1	2.3	2.4	.1	4.6	4.9	.3	2.6	2.9	.3
Competent-Incompetent	1.4	1.5	.1	3.5	3.1	-.4	2.1	1.6	-.5	3.8	3.5	-.3	2.4	2.0	-.4	3.5	3.8	.3	2.1	2.3	.2
United-Split	1.7	1.6	-.1	3.6	2.7	-.9	1.9	1.1	-.8	4.0	3.6	-.4	2.3	2.0	-.3	3.0	3.5	.5	1.3	1.9	.6

CHART I. PERCEPTIONS OF PARTIES ON TEN DIMENSIONS
CANADA, 1965 and 1968
(mean scores)

A. General Qualities

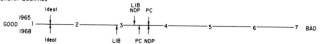

GOOD — 1965 / 1968 — BAD

HONEST — 1965 / 1968 — DISHONEST

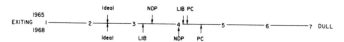

EXITING — 1965 / 1968 — DULL

B. General Orientation

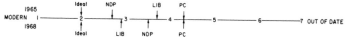

MODERN — 1965 / 1968 — OUT OF DATE

YOUNG — 1965 / 1968 — OLD

WORKING CLASS — 1965 / 1968 — MIDDLE CLASS

LEFT WING — 1965 / 1968 — RIGHT WING

C. Performance

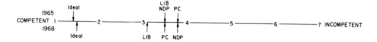

POWERFUL — 1965 / 1968 — WEAK

COMPETENT — 1965 / 1968 — INCOMPETENT

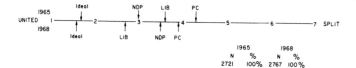

UNITED — 1965 / 1968 — SPLIT

	1965		1968	
	N	%	N	%
	2721	100%	2767	100%

because of what it tells us about how Canadians react to this particular political dimension but also because it underlines the acceptability of the other scales we have used.

The Ideal Party

Table III and Chart I (which presents the same material graphically) reveal that there is considerable variation between the parties and between the two elections with respect to a great many of the dimensions explored by us. The data also show, however, that in its perception of the Ideal party the Canadian electorate was anything but volatile in the period under discussion. If the ten dimensions for which we have data for both elections are tabulated according to magnitude of the change in the perception of the Ideal party, we obtain the following distribution:

TABLE IV: CHANGES IN PERCEPTIONS OF IDEAL PARTY 1965–1968[*]

NO CHANGE	CHANGE OF 0.1	CHANGE OF 0.2
Good–Bad (A)	Working–Middle Class (B)	Young–Old (B)
Honest–Dishonest (A)	Competent–Incompetent (C)	
Exciting–Dull (A)	United–Split (C)	
Modern–Out of Date (B)		
Left–Right (B)		
Powerful–Weak (C)		

[*]Letters (A) (B) (C) refer to party aspects as identified in the text and in Table II.

Of the six dimensions for which no change is registered in the mean score, three concern the General Qualities (A) of the parties (the letter after each word pair identifies the aspect, as presented on p. 66 above), two of the instances in which a change of 0.1 occurred fall into the "Performance" aspect (C), and the case in which the greatest change occurred reflects the greater preference, in the 1968 sample, for a younger Ideal party.

Since we are dealing with two separate samples, and the differences in the "expectations" from the Ideal party are small, we should be cautious about placing undue weight on interpretations of the above tabulation. It is nevertheless interesting that no change was generally registered with respect to dimensions which have moral connotations (e.g. Good—Bad, Honest—Dishonest) but that under the "Performance" heading (e.g. Competent—Incompetent, United—Split) some movement is noticeable in the expectations the total population had of the parties.

The 1968 election brought to an end a fairly long era of minority governments and of many seemingly fruitless procedural Parliamentary wrangles; the changes in the perceptions of what the Ideal party ought to be like may reflect the desire on the part of the public to see a tidier, more effective set of parties providing efficient government. This view fails to explain the absence of change with respect to the Powerful—Weak dimension, and the change in the class aspect of the Ideal party, but it is nevertheless plausible. It requires closer study.

To what can we ascribe the shifts in the perceptions of the Ideal party? It has often been argued that the presence of two new leaders, particularly of Mr. Trudeau, explains much of the outcome of the 1968 election. It is in this context that we must approach the greatest change of all recorded in the scores of the Ideal party: the move towards a younger Ideal party. It is possible that Mr. Trudeau, and the youth-oriented nature of his campaign, found some reflection in the way in which voters viewed the Ideal party. It is, however, also possible that the preference for youth reflects the generally changing attitude in the world towards younger people, and also the changing shape of the Canadian demographic tree. These points have implications for the interpretation of this whole paper; we shall return to it later.

On which dimensions are Canadians most decisive when contemplating an Ideal party? Table III and Chart I show that there are no dimensions on which the weighted mean approaches the 7 pole of the continuum but in several instances the Ideal party is placed near the 1. Thus the mean for Honesty—Dishonesty is 1.3 in both surveys, followed by Good—Bad (1.4) and Competent—Incompetent (1.4, 1.5), United—Split (1.7, 1.6), Powerful—Weak (2.0) and Modern—Out of Date (2.0). The two *moral* dimensions of our (A) category elicit the most clear-cut and decisive response, to be followed by all three dimensions in the Performance category (C). Only the Modern—Out of Date pair, of the four in the General Orientation group, appears unequivocally near one or the other of the two extremes. It is under this, the (B) aspect of the parties, that the most centrally placed score appears. On the Left Wing—Right Wing dimension, the mean fell a little distance from the centre towards the Right Wing pole (4.6), and on the For the Working Class—For the Middle Class dimension, the Ideal party placed between 3 and 4 (3.4, 3.5).

All this suggests that Canadians, taken as a whole, adopt a clear-cut, highly moral position when it comes to the general probity of their parties (although it must be noted that the Good—Bad dimension is somewhat equivocal as a measure of probity—it may tap effectiveness just as much), they prize the Performance of their parties next highly, and that they are somewhat less unanimous about the general Orientation of the parties, particularly with respect to social policy.

This last observation, while supported by the data mentioned so far, is strongly contradicted by the response of our 1968 sample to the invitation that they place the Ideal party on a scale created by the poles "Concerned for People's Welfare—Unconcerned for People's Welfare." The mean on this dimension, as Table I shows, was 1.4. While the wording used, and the fact that we are dealing with only two dimensions, prevents us from formulating general propositions on the basis of our welfare oriented dimensions, our findings are nevertheless suggestive. They lead one to speculate that a significant proportion of Canadians may almost unwittingly and automatically turn away from consciously thinking in terms of a class and from any formulation of social problems in class terms[10] but that they do not mind making judgements about the same kind of problems when they are discussed in terms of people's welfare. This is an area where some very useful work can be done on other data now in our possession and in the future, by a more extended application of the semantic differential technique.

Existing Parties

There are several ways in which the scores received by the parties can be compared and analyzed. The first consists of observing the "absolute" position of each party in 1965 and in 1968 and then noting what change, if any, had occurred. Taking the Good—Bad dimension for the Liberal party, for example, we see in Table III and Chart I that in 1965 the mean score was

3.3. By 1968 this had changed to 2.9, a drop of .4. By looking at each party it is possible to compare how each rated in 1965 and 1968 and how it fared in the period between. The scores of the parties can be compared.

A second approach stresses the relative position of the parties with respect to the various dimensions. Chart I is particularly helpful in indicating whether the distance between the parties is great or small, and how it changed in the course of time. Using the Good—Bad pair as our example again, we see that the Liberals scored 3.3 in 1965, the Conservatives 3.6, and the NDP 3.3. By 1968 the scores were 2.9, 3.4 and 3.6 respectively, indicating an "improvement" for the Liberals of .4, for the Conservatives of .2 and a "deterioration" for the NDP of .3.

Thirdly, it is useful to examine the distance between each party and the Ideal party. This enables one to escape the kind of value judgement I just made in suggesting that the Liberals' and Conservatives' image had improved and that of the NDP deteriorated, with respect to the Good—Bad dimension. In this particular case it was probably not irresponsibly daring to conclude that the Good pole is the favourable one, but the decision is not always quite as easy. By comparing the score of each party with that of the Ideal party it is possible to ascertain whether the actual parties have come closer, or moved farther away, from the image the public likes, and one can also of course measure the distance of each party from the Ideal.

TABLE V: TOTAL DEVIATION FROM IDEAL PARTY 1965-1968[*]

PARTY	1965	1968	DEVIATION
LIBERAL	16.2	9.3	−6.9
CONSERVATIVE	18.0	17.2	−0.8
NDP	12.4	16.4	+4.0

[*]Plus and minus signs are ignored in the case of the Left—Right and Working Class—Middle Class dichotomies. The minus sign indicating that the NDP was considered to be slightly younger than the Ideal Party was retained.

75

Finally, the comparison between the deviation of each party from the Ideal in 1965 and 1968 provides a measure of the *change* in its image, a measure which takes into account, when necessary, whether the public's "yardstick" had itself altered.

In analyzing our data we have used whichever of the above measures seemed most appropriate.

Changes from 1965 to 1968   Among the major and most persistent impressions given by the analysis of the scores received by the various parties is that of a great Liberal surge, of there being almost no change in the image of the Conservative party and of the deterioration in the public's conception of the NDP. The data are summarized in Table V which is derived from adding up the deviations from the Ideal party, for each of the ten dimensions.

The Liberals' image moved closer to that of the Ideal party by 6.9 points, the Conservatives improved slightly by 0.8 but the NDP slipped by 4.0. Chart I provides a graphic and rather dramatic illustration of the pattern for each of the ten dimensions. A careful examination of it (or of Table III) reveals that in 1965 the NDP was closer than the Liberals to the Ideal party no less than six times, that it and the Liberals were twice equidistant from it and that the Liberals surpassed the NDP in this respect only twice. In 1968 the Liberals were closer to the Ideal party nine times, and the NDP only once!

A similar comparison of the Liberals and the Conservatives confirms the generally unchanged perception of the Conservatives when they are ranked with the other parties along our ten dimensions.

Comparing the Conservatives and the NDP, we see that in 1965 they were closer to the Ideal party only twice, as compared to the eight instances in which the NDP was in greater proximity to it. By 1968 the two parties occupied the same position vis-à-vis the Ideal party once, the NDP was ahead three times, and the Conservatives five times. In the terms now under discussion, Mr. Stanfield's party was perceived a good deal better in 1968 than Mr. Diefenbaker's had been in 1965.

In the light of the virtual reversal of the positions of the NDP and of the Liberals in the period 1965 to 1968 it is instructive to see on which of the dimensions the position of the parties changed, and in what order. An interesting diagram emerges when our ten dimensions are ranked side by side for the Liberals and the NDP in descending order of gain (for the Liberals) or in ascending order of "loss" (in the case of the NDP) with respect to the Ideal party, over the period from 1965 to 1968:

DIAGRAM I: <u>Ranked Changes in Deviations from Ideal Party 1965 1968,</u>

<u>Liberal Party and NDP</u>

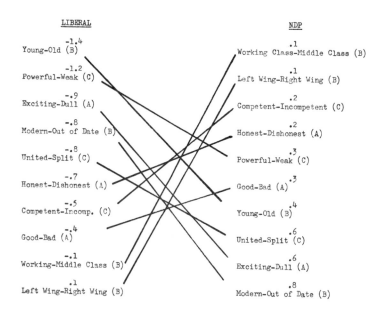

It appears from the diagram that, with only one or two exceptions, the dimensions in which the Liberals registered their greatest improvement from 1965 to 1968 were those in which the NDP suffered the most, and vice versa. The first, third, fourth and fifth dimensions in which the Liberals' image improved most were precisely the four in which the NDPs suffered the greatest decline. It is interesting that the diagonals with the least steep slope both depict the moral dimensions (Honesty—Dishonesty and Good—Bad), in which the *relative* ranking of the NDP appeared better than that of the Liberals. A similar pattern, at least with respect to the Honesty—Dishonesty dimension, emerges when the change in deviations of the Liberals

77

from 1965 to 1968 is compared with that of the Conservatives, as can be seen in Diagram II. It also, of course, shows that the general switch in the rankings observed between the NDP and the Liberals holds when the latter are being compared with the Conservatives: the four dimensions in which the Liberal image gained most, when compared with the Ideal party, are those in

DIAGRAM II: Ranked Changed in Deviations from Ideal Party, 1965-1968, Liberal and Conservative Parties

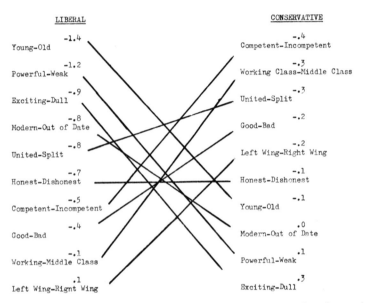

LIBERAL

-1.4	Young-Old
-1.2	Powerful-Weak
-.9	Exciting-Dull
-.8	Modern-Out of Date
-.8	United-Split
-.7	Honest-Dishonest
-.5	Competent-Incompetent
-.4	Good-Bad
-.1	Working-Middle Class
.1	Left Wing-Right Wing

CONSERVATIVE

-.4	Competent-Incompetent
-.3	Working Class-Middle Class
-.3	United-Split
-.2	Good-Bad
-.2	Left Wing-Right Wing
-.1	Honest-Dishonest
-.1	Young-Old
.0	Modern-Out of Date
.1	Powerful-Weak
.3	Exciting-Dull

which the perceptions of the Conservative party deteriorated most.

The ranking of the NDP and Conservative parties, with respect to the change in deviations from the Ideal party, produces a diagram which looks quite differently from its predecessors. The slope of the diagonals in Diagram III is on the whole considerably less steep, indicating that such favourable a change in the deviation from the Ideal party as the Conservatives were able to muster was not achieved, so to speak, at the cost of the NDP.

It is impossible to explain the changes in the rankings in terms of our three party aspects. No discernible pattern emerges

78

in terms of the General Qualities of the parties, their Orientation, or their Performance. But while the four top Liberal dimensions on which the other parties fared rather badly do not fit our categories, they are extremely suggestive.

DIAGRAM III: Ranked Changes in Deviation from Ideal Party, Conservative Party and NDP

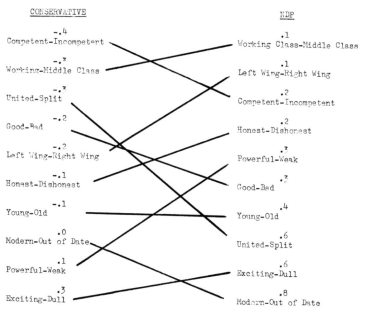

The Liberals gained most when appearing to be young, powerful, exciting and modern. These are the qualities emphasized by the campaign organized around Mr. Trudeau; these are the qualities which one would expect to appeal to an electorate grown restive under a number of minority governments.[11] The five dimensions on which the Liberals improved their showing most are all ones which are associated with an effective, forward-looking and active government; their five least improved dimensions are, with one important exception (Competent—Incompetent) related to more general aspects of the parties: Honesty, Goodness, being less Left Wing, and a shade closer to the middle class. On these dimensions the public image of the Liberals changed least. They have less to do than most of the

DIAGRAM IV: Ranked Deviations from the Ideal Party, 1968

(Smallest Deviation From 1968 Ideal)

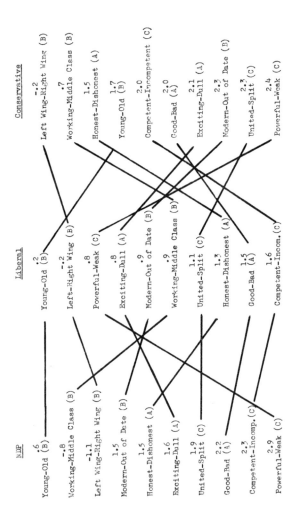

(Greatest Deviation From 1968 Ideal)

other dimensions with the capacity of a party to govern effectively.

In the light of the above, how can we explain the relatively modest improvement of the Liberals on the Competence scale and the relatively good showing on it of the Conservatives? The latter party improved its image only to a very modest extent, its greatest "advance", for example, being by only .4, whereas the Liberals' highest gain was a substantial 1.4. It is nevertheless still somewhat surprising that the Conservatives gained most with respect to their competence since the voters rejected them decisively at the polls. We confront the critical question, to which we at present still lack an answer: which particular dimension or combination of dimensions is most related to the voting decision?

It should also not be forgotten that the Liberals moved a slightly greater distance towards the Competence pole than the Conservatives but the improvement in their image was so much greater on other dimensions that the modest change here was relatively unimportant. For the Conservatives, on the other hand, even a modest improvement placed the changed dimension high on our list.

Another curious feature of the Conservative ranking is the improvement experienced by the party with respect to the Working Class—Middle Class dimension. In 1965, the Conservatives and Liberals were equidistant from the Ideal party. By 1968, the Liberal position had remained unchanged, but the Ideal party shifted one tenth of a point towards the Middle Class. The Conservatives, on the other hand, were viewed as being two tenths of a step in the scale closer to the working class side. The greater proximity of the Conservatives to the Ideal is therefore accounted for by a slight shift in the Ideal, and a small shift in the perception of the party. I am at a loss to explain the shift, but it should be noted that it really is very small and ranks high only because of the general stand-pat perception the voters accorded the Conservative party. But here, too, further work is required.

Party Images in 1968   We have so far talked almost exclusively in terms of the *changes* which have occurred in the images Canadians had of the major parties between 1965 and 1968. In Diagram IV the perceptions of the parties are presented again by

DIAGRAM V: Ranked and Spaced Deviations from Ideal Party, 1968

Deviation from 1968 Ideal Party	NDP	LIBERAL	CONSERVATIVE
.2		Young-Old Left Wing-Right Wing	Left Wing-Right Wing
.3			
.4			
.5			
.6	Young-Old		
.7			Working-Middle Class
.8	Working-Middle Class	Powerful-Weak Exciting-Dull	
.9		Modern-Out of Date Working-Middle Class	
1.0			
1.1	Left-Right Wing	United-Split	
1.2			
1.3		Honest-Dishonest	
1.4			
1.5	Modern-Out of Date Honest-Dishonest	Good-Bad	Honest-Dishonest
1.6	Exciting-Dull	Competent-Incompetent	
1.7			Young-Old
1.8			
1.9	United-Split		
2.0			Competent-Incompetent Good-Bad
2.1			Exciting-Dull
2.2	Good-Bad		
2.3	Competent-Incompetent		Modern-Out of Date United-Split
2.4			Powerful-Weak
2.5			
2.6			
2.7			
2.8			
2.9	Powerful-Weak		

ranking the dimensions in descending order. In this instance, however, our approach is static and we are concerned only with the deviation in the mean score received by each party on each of the items in 1968 from the 1968 score of the Ideal party. Diagram V also ranks the dimensions examined for each party but the items are spaced vertically so as to give an indication of the relative distance between the Ideal and the actual parties.

Diagram V offers dramatic proof of the incomparably more favourable image of the Liberals, in relation to that of the other two parties. It also corrects some possible misapprehensions which can follow from a careless reading of Diagram IV. One might, for instance, conclude from the latter that the Liberals were considered by our sample to be less competent than the NDP, and particularly the Conservatives. Diagram V makes it abundantly clear that while the *rank* of the Competence dimension is lower for the Liberals than for the other two parties, their *mean score*, compared to that of the Ideal party, is still better.

The NDP appeared to do best, in 1968, in the dimensions we grouped under the heading General Orientations; the General Qualities come next, with only one exception, and the party was perceived least favourably on the Performance items. It came as a surprise to me to find that Mr. Douglas' party was found to be so youthful, particularly since the party lost .6 on this dimension from 1965 to 1968. But it will be remembered that the NDP had an enviable start here: in 1965 it was perceived to be younger even than the Ideal party!

The Conservative column in Diagram V is strongly weighted towards its lower end in the sense that only two items are to be found in its upper half and they are a good distance from the main part of the column where all the other items are closely bunched together. The Conservatives were obviously judged to be a great deal closer to the Ideal party on the class and Left-Right continua than on any of the other items, and on the latter made as good a showing as the Liberals.

It is worth noting in passing, while we are thinking of the Left-Right continuum, that *no* actual party was placed closer to the Right Wing pole than the Ideal party, an indication perhaps that all our parties appear to be more progressive (in the murky Left-Right sense) than the public might like.

Like the NDP, the Conservatives seemed to have received rather unfavourable mean scores under the Performance heading, with the Powerful—Weak pair producing their worst result. They appeared to the electors to be fairly honest, as did all three parties, with the Liberals enjoying a slight edge.

Their fourth best score was in the Young—Old dimension but with this item, as Diagram V shows, they were already farther away from the Ideal party than the Liberals on *all* our dimensions They were judged more Powerful and more Competent than the NDP, and they did better on the Good—Bad dimension. But they were deemed less united, less modern, and less exciting.

Virtually all the things said above about the Liberal party when the change in its image experienced from 1965 to 1968 was discussed apply also to its static showing in 1968. The most intriguing feature of the Liberal columns in Diagrams IV and V concerns the two lowest-ranking items. The poor showing, relatively to the other items, on the Competent—Incompetent scale is puzzling and requires additional study.

The second lowest placed, Good—Bad pair, is equally mystifying. A number of possible explanations suggest themselves, mostly turning around the lack of specificity of this item, but we had better suppress our hypotheses until we have explored the problem further in relation to data derived from other questions. At any rate, the Liberals still made a better showing, even here, than the other parties.

PARTY IMAGES OF SOME SOCIO-ECONOMIC GROUPS

So as to protect our readers from choking on a totally indigestible mass of facts, we have reduced our master tables into emaciated lists showing two sets of scores:

(1) 1968 scores of the Ideal party for the various subpopulations and the deviations from them, as assigned to the actual parties, and

(2) the changes in the scores of the Ideal party and changes in the deviations, 1965 and 1968.[12] For each socio-economic variable discussed there are thus two tables: one presenting our static and the other the dynamic measures.

Sex

Table VI shows the static difference between the party images in

PARTY	SCALE*		SCORES**	
I D E A L	(A)	G-B		M/F 1.4	
		H-D	F 1.2		M 1.3
		E-D	F 2.4		M 2.5
	(B)	M-O	M 1.9		F 2.0
		Y-O		M/F 2.9	
		W-M		M/F 3.5	
		L-R		M/F 4.6	
	(C)	P-W	F 1.9		M 2.1
		C-I	F 1.4		M 1.5
		U-S	F 1.6		M 1.7
L I B E R A L	(A)	G-B	F 1.4		M 1.6
		H-D		M/F 1.4	
		E-D	F .7		M .8
	(B)	M-O	F .7		M 1.1
		Y-O	F .2		M .3
		W-M	F .7		M 1.1
		L-R		M/F -.2	
	(C)	P-W		M/F .8	
		C-I	F 1.5		M 1.7
		U-S	M 1.0		F 1.1
P C	(A)	G-B	F 1.9		M 2.1
		H-D		M/F 1.5	
		E-D	F 2.0		M 2.1
	(B)	M-O	F 2.1		M 2.5
		Y-O	F 1.6		M 1.8
		W-M	F .6		M .8
		L-R		M/F -.2	
	(C)	P-W	F 2.3		M 2.5
		C-I	F 2.0		M 2.2
		U-S	F 2.2		M 2.4
N D P	(A)	G-B		M/F 2.2	
		H-D	M 1.5		F 1.7
		E-D	M 1.5		F 1.6
	(B)	M-O	F 1.5		M 1.7
		Y-O	M .7		F .7
		W-M	F -.7		M -1.0
		L-R	F-1.0		M -1.2
	(C)	P-W	F 2.8		M 3.0
		C-I		M/F 2.4	
		U-S	M 1.8		F 2.0

NOTE:

*The abbreviations stand for the three party aspects and ten dimensions as follows:

(A) GENERAL QUALITIES

G-B = Good-Bad
H-D = Honest-Dishonest
E-D = Exciting-Dull

(B) GENERAL ORIENTATION

M-O = Modern-Out of Date
Y-O = Young-Old
W-M = Working Class-Middle Class
L-R = Left Wing-Right Wing

(C) PERFORMANCE

P-W = Powerful-Weak
C-I = Competent-Incompetent
U-S = United-Split

**The scores for the Ideal party are mean scores; for the actual parties they represent the 1968 deviations from the scores of the Ideal party.

LEGEND:

M = Male   (50.2%)
F = Female   (49.8%)

NOTE:

The percentage for the legend refers to the total sample, including those who did not respond to the semantic differential question.

the eyes of men and women for each of our ten dimensions. The scores, as just indicated, represent the difference between the perceptions of the Ideal party in 1968 and of each of the actual parties in the same year. Table VII lists the changes in the 1965 and the 1968 deviations and, therefore, shows to what extent, and how, men's and women's perceptions of the parties changed over time.

Men and women not only differed in their 1968 perceptions of the Liberals, Conservatives and NDP but they also scored the Ideal party somewhat differently. In all but one of the six instances in which their scores were not identical, the mean score of women was lower than that of men, suggesting that they were

85

more disposed to view the Ideal party as, in a sense, "better" than men. This comment applies to all our word pairs except two: one cannot state that a lower score on the "For the Working Class— For the Middle Class", and "Left Wing—Right Wing" dimensions is better than a higher score. This depends entirely on the criteria one chooses to apply. On all the other dimensions, however, the lower pole of the scale represents the generally accepted ideal, although some might wish to argue about one or two of the items, notably the Modernity, Age and Power scales.

The ten dimensions are listed in Table VI in the same order we have adopted throughout, and we can therefore easily distinguish between the three broad aspects of party which we identified earlier. There are interesting variations in the responses of men and women, and these variations are not uniform for our three aspects. In the case of the scores for the Ideal party, for example, the party Orientation dimensions differ markedly from the other two. Three of the four instances of there being no difference in the male and female scores occurred under this party aspect, as did also the one case in which the men's mean score was lower than that of women. I am at a loss to explain this pattern at present, and must content myself with noting it and putting it on the agenda for future attention.

A look at the male and female scores for the three main parties shows that women gave the old parties better scores in 1968 than men on more dimensions than was the case with the NDP, and the Conservatives did slightly better than the Liberals. The latter obtained a higher score from men on the United—Split scale, and display three instances in which men and women ranked them equally. The Conservatives, on the other hand, failed to receive even one higher score from men and were rated by both sexes equally only twice.

Taking the ten dimensions as a whole, we find that, with respect to the NDP, the battle of the sexes (to abuse an already tired term) has ended in a draw: men and women were each "ahead" of the other four times, and they gave the party the same score twice.[13] If we distinguish between the party aspects, however, we see that the NDP was perceived more favourably by men when its general Qualities were considered but that it was rated less favourably by them on the Orientation dimensions.[14]

PARTY	SCALE*		SCORES**	
I D E A L	(A) G-B		M/F .0	
	H-D	F -.2		M .0
	E-D		M/F .0	
	(B) M-O		M/F -.1	
	Y-O	M -.2		F -.1
	W-M	M .0		F -.1
	L-R	F -.1		M .0
	(C) P-W	M -.1		F .0
	C-I		M/F .0	
	U-S	M -.1		F .0
L I B E R A L	(A) G-B	M -.4		F -.3
	H-D	M -.7		F -.4
	E-D		M/F -.9	
	(B) M-O	F -.9		M -.7
	Y-O		M/F-1.4	
	W-M	F -.2		M .1
	L-R		M/F -.1	
	(C) P-W	F -1.3		M -1.1
	C-I	F -.5		M -.4
	U-S		M/F -.8	
P C	(A) G-B	M -.2		F -.1
	H-D	M -.2		F .0
	E-D	F .2		M .4
	(B) M-O		M/F .1	
	Y-O	F -.2		M -.1
	W-M	M -.3		F -.2
	L-R	M -.2		F .0
	(C) P-W	F .1		M .3
	C-I	M -.3		F -.2
	U-S	F -.3		M -.2
N D P	(A) G-B		M/F .3	
	H-D	M .2		F .4
	E-D	M .5		F .6
	(B) M-O	F .9		M 1.0
	Y-O	M .7		F .8
	W-M	F -.2		M .1
	L-R	M .0		F 1.0
	(C) P-W	F .2		M .4
	C-I	M .3		F .4
	U-S	F .5		M .6

NOTE:

* For a full description of the listed items, see notes for Table VI.

** The figures for the Ideal party represent the changes in the mean scores of the Ideal party, 1965 to 1968; for the actual parties they represent the changes in the deviations from the Ideal party, 1965 to 1968.

LEGEND:

M = Male   (49.7%),   (50.2%)

F = Female (50.3%),   (49.8%)

NOTE:

The percentages refer to the total sample, including those who did not respond to the semantic differential questions. The first is for 1965, the second for 1968.

Turning now to the change in the deviations between the Ideal party in 1965 and 1968, we find that on the whole all parties had improved their images with men slightly and had, therefore, suffered relatively in the eyes of women. This is true also of the Ideal party in the sense that, excluding the case of the Working Class—Middle Class and Left Wing—Right Wing dimensions, men assigned a lower mean score to the Ideal party three times, as compared with only one such move towards the "better" pole for women.

The only really noteworthy comment about the improvement in the Liberal image among men concerns its location. They viewed the Liberal party more favourably than women, on the two moral dimensions of our party Quality aspect and not, as one might have expected, on the more action-oriented, party Orientation or Performance dimensions.

The Conservatives were viewed more favourably by men, relative to women, on the class dimension, and, like the NDP, on the Competence—Incompetence scale. Mr. Douglas' party also improved its male appeal on the class and the Left—Right dimensions.

Age

Another widely-held view of the 1968 Liberal victory explains the party's success partially in terms of its appeal to young voters. It is therefore instructive to examine the party images broken down by age.

Beginning again with a static view of the Ideal party, we note in Table VIII that a clear-cut generational difference exists in Canada with respect to the kind of party its citizens would like to have. Leaving aside the two dimensions which cannot, as we noted above, be ascribed a "better" or "worse" pole (the class and Left—Right scales), we observe that out of the eight remaining word-pairs, three displayed no age difference in the mean scores. On all of the remaining five dimensions our youngest age group has mean scores closest to the low end of the scale. This is perhaps hardly surprising with respect to poles like Exciting, Modern, Young, but it also holds for Competent and United. The middle aged group has either a mean score identical with that of the youngest group (Exciting—Dull, Competent—Incompetent, United—Split) or is situated between the young and old categories. The latter, composed of those aged 60 or over, has in all five cases a mean score closer to the middle of the scale.

Whatever the Liberal party's appeal to young voters may have been in the 1968 election, it is not among this group that its image is particularly favourable on our ten dimensions. Table VIII tells us that the best scores were recorded by the oldest age group, which showed the lowest deviation from the Ideal party five times, which twice shared having the best score with the youngest group and which in one instance (Left—Right) "joined" both the other age groups since all the respondents had the same mean score here. The oldest group thus registered the

PARTY	SCALE *		SCORES **		
I D E A L	(A)	G-B	A/B/C 1.4		
		H-D	A/B/C 1.3		
		E-D	A/B 2.4		C 2.6
	(B)	M-O	A 1.8	B/C 2.1	
		Y-O	A 2.8	B 3.0	C 3.1
		W-M	B/C 3.5	A 3.7	
		L-R	A 4.5	B 4.6	C 4.8
	(C)	P-W	A/B/C 2.0		
		C-I	A/B 1.5		C 1.6
		U-S	A/B 1.6		C 1.8
L I B E R A L	(A)	G-B	C 1.3	A 1.5	B 1.6
		H-D	C 1.2	B 1.3	A 1.4
		E-D	A/C .7	B .9	
	(B)	M-O	B .8	C .9	A 1.0
		Y-O	B/C .2	A .3	
		W-M	C .5	A .7	B 1.0
		L-R	A/B/C -.2		
	(C)	P-W	A/C .8	B .9	
		C-I	C 1.4	A/B 1.6	
		U-S	C .8	B 1.1	A 1.2
P C	(A)	G-B	C 1.6	B 2.0	A 2.1
		H-D	C 1.2	B 1.4	A 1.6
		E-D	C 1.3	B 2.1	A 2.2
	(B)	M-O	B 1.6	A 1.8	C 2.0
		Y-O	C 1.1	B 1.6	A 1.9
		W-M	A .4	C .6	B .7
		L-R	B -.1	A -.2	C -.4
	(C)	P-W	C 2.1	A 2.4	B 2.6
		C-I	C 1.7	A/B 2.1	
		U-S	C 1.8	A/B 2.4	
N D P	(A)	G-B	C/B 2.1	A 2.3	
		H-D	B 1.4	C 1.5	A 1.6
		E-D	C 1.2	B 1.5	A 1.7
	(B)	M-O	B 1.4	C 1.5	A 1.8
		Y-O	C .4	B .6	A .9
		W-M	B -.9	A -1.0	C -1.3
		L-R	A -1.0	C -1.1	B -1.3
	(C)	P-W	C 2.8	B 2.9	A 3.0
		C-I	C 2.1	B 2.3	A 2.4
		U-S	A/C 1.9	B 2.0	

NOTE:

* For a full description of the listed items see notes for Table VI

** The scores for the ideal party are mean scores; for the actual parties they represent the 1968 deviations from the scores of the ideal party.

LEGEND:

A = 21-39 years (44.4%)

B = 40-59 years (37.9%)

C = 60 + years (17.7%)

NOTE:

See also legend for Table VI.

best score eight times. The 21 to 39 year cohort expressed the "worst" rating the Liberals received on no less than half the ten dimensions.

The case is thus quite overwhelming, establishing that the image of the Liberal party was considerably more favourable among old than young voters. It might of course be argued by some suspicious minds that we have loaded the case by choosing a very large young category, including at the upper limit some patriarchs crowding 40. This suspicion can quickly be abandoned when the figures in Table VIII are compared with the deviations from the Ideal party recorded by first voters in 1968. This group, aged from 21 to 23, failed to score the Liberal party on the ten dimensions more "favourably" than the other age groups identified above in all but two cases.[15] The exceptions are on the Exciting—Dull and Powerful—Weak scales where the 21 to 23 year olds registered deviations from the Ideal party of .4 and .7 respectively. The scores received by the Ideal party from the first voters are generally a little higher than those recorded by our other age groups.

The relative approbation accorded the Conservative party by the oldest age group is even more striking, if perhaps somewhat less surprising, than that of the Liberals. The party's record on the Qualities and Performance items is clear cut, and in the columns of Table VIII magnificently symmetrical. The scores are everywhere lowest for the oldest age groups and then rise, indicating that the party's image is less close to that of the Ideal party, as the age of the respondents drops. This orderly progression is disturbed by only one of the six dimensions (Powerful—Weak) where the 40 to 59 year old group perceived the Conservatives in a somewhat less acceptable light than the youngest members of our sample.

Unlike the Conservative party, the NDP cannot boast a particularly symmetrical array of scores in Table VIII. The youngest voters are nevertheless concentrated, with only a few exceptions, in the extreme right-hand column and the oldest age group is to be found on the left. Older respondents thus have found the NDP more to their taste than younger ones. This applies particularly to the Performance items, and somewhat less so to the scales exploring reactions to general party Qualities.

The scores of the first voters suggest that while they rated the NDP slightly better on several items than the 21 to 39 age group, their deviations from the Ideal party were greater than those of the groups which scored the NDP most favourably in all but three cases (Working—Middle Class, Left—Right Wing, Powerful—Weak).

Age differences obviously affect the way in which voters perceive Canadian parties. On the whole, in our 1968 Survey, the older voters responded more favourably to Canadian parties than younger voters. The implications of this may be very serious for the political system and the way its institutions can perform their functions in it. There is a suggestion here that younger voters may

90

be alienated, or at least that conventional political instruments satisfy them less than they do the older citizens.

Table IX tells us that no major change occurred in the assessment of the parties between 1965 and 1968, in the sense that the overall position of any of the age groups had shifted. The youngest group still appears very much in the right hand column and the older groups on the left. In the case of the Conservative party, the gap between the Ideal party has narrowed for the youngest age group in a number of dimensions (Modern—Old, Working—Middle Class, Powerful—Weak, Competent—Incom-

TABLE IX: PARTY IMAGES BY AGE (1965-1968)

PARTY	SCALE *		SCORES **		
I D E A L	(A)	G-B		A/B/C ·0	
		H-D	A ·0	B/C .1	
		E-D	A/B ·0		C .2
	(B)	M-O	C -.2	A -.1	B .0
		Y-O	A -.2	B/C -.1	
		W-M	B/C -1.1	A -.9	
		L-R	B -.1	A .0	C .1
	(C)	P-W		A/B/C 0	
		C-I	A/B .1		C .2
		U-S	A/B -.1		C .2
L I B E R A L	(A)	G-B	C -.5	B -.4	A -.3
		H-D	B -.9	A/C -.7	
		E-D		A/B/C -.8	
	(B)	M-O	B -.9	A -.7	C -.5
		Y-O	B -1.5	A -1.4	C -1.1
		W-M	C -.4	A -.2	B ·0
		L-R	B -.1	A/C .1	
	(C)	P-W	C -1.3	A/B -1.2	
		C-I	C -.7	B -.6	A -.4
		U-S	C -1.0	B -.8	A -.7
P C	(A)	G-B	B -.3	C -.2	A -.1
		H-D	B -.3	A/C -.2	
		E-D	C ·0	A/B .2	
	(B)	M-O	A -.7	B -.6	C .4
		Y-O	C -.4	B -.2	A -.1
		W-M	A -.6	B -.4	C -.2
		L-R	C -.3	A -.2	B ·0
	(C)	P-W	A/C .1	B .3	
		C-I	A/B -.4	C -.3	
		U-S	C -.4	A -.3	B -.2
N D P	(A)	G-B	B/C .2	A .5	
		H-D	B -.1	A/C .2	
		E-D	C .3	B .5	A .7
	(B)	M-O	B .7	C .9	A 1.1
		Y-O	C .1	B .5	A .8
		W-M	B .1	A .4	C .6
		L-R	C ·0	A .1	B .2
	(C)	P-W	C .2	A/B .3	
		C-I	C -.1	B .2	A .4
		U-S	C .2	B .6	A .7

NOTE:

* For a full description of the listed items see notes for table VI.

** The figures for the ideal party represent the changes in the mean scores of the ideal party, 1965 to 1968; for the actual parties they represent the changes in the deviations from the ideal party, 1965 to 1968.

LEGEND:

A = 21-39 yrs. (43.0%), (44.4%)
B = 40-59 yrs. (38.0%), (37.9%
C = 60 + yrs. (19.0%), (17.7%)

NOTE:

See also legend for Table VII.

91

petent). The gap widened for the NDP and did so least among the oldest respondents.

An interesting pattern emerges when changes in the ratings received on some of the specific dimensions are examined. A comparison of two sets of responses is particularly rewarding. On the Young—Old scale, the Liberals have shown dramatic improvement (narrowing of the gap between themselves and the Ideal party) shared by all the age groups. The youngest cohort "improved" its score by 1.4. The Conservatives displayed a much more modest change in the same direction, with the 21 to 39 age group narrowing the gap by .1. For the NDP, however, the change was discouraging, Mr. Douglas' party slipped badly here and most among the youngest respondents who placed it further from the ideal by a substantial .8.

The gap between the Liberals and Conservatives was considerably smaller on the Modernity dimension than on most others, with respect to the middle aged and youngest cohorts (the latter showed a change of .7 for both parties) but the Conservatives suffered a deterioration of .4 in the eyes of the oldest age group. A glance at the NDP's Modernity row in Table IX reveals the serious decline the party suffered on this dimension in our respondents' eyes. The middle age group widened the gap by .7, the oldest respondents by .9 and the youngest cohort by 1.1!

Education

The images our respondents have of the parties are related to their educational background. Table X shows that with respect to conceptions of an Ideal party, while the variations were small, the best educated (in the sense that they had the most years of schooling) placed all the items under the Qualities aspect closer to the good end of the scale than those who received less formal education.

A less clear-cut pattern is discernible on the Orientation items. The ratings on the Modern—Out of Date and Young—Old dimensions display a rather curious difference in terms of the educational experience of the respondents. One would expect that generally the kind of person who preferred a Modern party would also favour a Young one. This predisposes one to assume that the same kind of educational profile would apply to the way in which the Ideal party is rated on the first two dimensions under our Orientation aspect. The two best educated groups, however, place the Ideal party closer to the Modern pole than the least educated but the reverse holds for the Young—Old dimension: here the proximity of the two least educated categories is closer to the Young side of the scale and the best educated are closer to the Old pole.

On the class and Left—Right Wing scales the best educated members of our sample register the highest scores, that is they prefer the Ideal party to be more for the Middle Class than the other age groups and a little closer to the Right Wing pole.

Looking at the deviations of the scores assigned the actual

TABLE X: PARTY IMAGES BY EDUCATION (1968)

PARTY	SCALE *		SCORES **		
I D E A L	(A)	G-B	C 1.3	A/B 1.4	
		H-D	C 1.2	A/B 1.3	
		E-D	C 2.3	B 2.4	A 2.6
	(B)	M-O	B/C 1.9	A 2.1	
		Y-O	A/B 2.9	C 3.0	
		W-M	A 3.1	B 3.6	C 4.1
		L-R	C 4.3	B 4.6	A 4.7
	(C)	P-W	A/B 2.0	C 2.1	
		C-I	C 1.3	B 1.5	A 1.7
		U-S	B/C 1.6	A 1.8	
L I B E R A L	(A)	G-B	A/B 1.5	C 1.6	
		H-D	B 1.3	A/C 1.4	
		E-D	A/C .7	B .8	
	(B)	M-O	A .8	B/C .9	
		Y-O	B/C .2	A .3	
		W-M	C .5	B .9	A 1.1
		L-R		A/B/C -.2	
	(C)	P-W		A/B/C .8	
		C-I	A 1.4	B 1.6	C 1.7
		U-S	A .9	B 1.1	C 1.2
P C	(A)	G-B	A 1.8	B 2.1	C 2.2
		H-D	B 1.4	A/C 1.5	
		E-D	A 1.4	B 2.2	C 2.6
	(B)	M-O	A 1.8	B/C 2.6	
		Y-O	A 1.4	B/C 1.9	
		W-M	C .3	B .7	A .8
		L-R	B -.2	C .3	A -.4
	(C)	P-W	A 2.2	B/C 2.5	
		C-I	A 1.7	B 2.1	C 2.4
		U-S	A 1.9	B 2.4	C 2.5
N D P	(A)	G-B	A 2.0	B 2.2	C 2.7
		H-D	B 1.5	A/C 1.7	
		E-D	A 1.2	B 1.6	C 2.0
	(B)	M-O	A 1.4	B 1.6	C 1.9
		Y-O	A/C .6	B .8	
		W-M	A 0	B -.9	C -1.8
		L-R	A -.9	B -1.1	C -1.4
	(C)	P-W	A 2.5	B 3.0	C 3.3
		C-I	B 2.3	A/C 3.0	
		U-S	A 1.8	B 1.9	C 2.1

NOTE:

* For a full description of the listed items see notes for Table VI.

** The scores for the ideal party are mean scores; for the actual parties they represent the 1968 deviations from the scores of the ideal party.

LEGEND:

A = up to 8 yrs schooling (34.7%)
B = 9-13 yrs (50.6%)
C = 13 + yrs (13.5%)

NOTE:

See also legend for Table VI.

parties from those of the Ideal party, we find a general pattern of the least educated clearly perceiving the parties as being closer to the good end of the scale and the best educated tending to take a slightly more jaundiced view. The distinctions made between the parties are rather slight but there is an unmistakable falling off in the number of favourable scores by the best educated groups as one moves away from the Liberal party, approaches the Conservatives and reaches the NDP.

When the NDP and the Conservatives are compared in terms of the actual deviations from the Ideal party, as distinct from the ranking of the educational sub-groups on each dimension, we find that the best educated assigned the NDP a better score than the Conservatives four times (Honest—Dishonest, Modern —Out of date, Young—Old, United—Split) and that the Conservatives did better in the eyes of the post-secondary school group on the remaining scales. This suggests that the NDP was rated fairly highly by those with the most years of schooling but of course not nearly as favourably as the Liberal party and a little less kindly than the Conservatives.

Assessment of the Liberal party by the groups with differing educational backgrounds, in terms of our scales, was more homogeneous than that accorded the other parties. It will be noted that the distances between the three groups is extremely close in the case of the Liberals, with only minor exceptions: the Class item and no differences being registered on the Left—Right and Powerful—Weak scales. The range for the other two parties was considerably greater suggesting that the perceptions of the educational sub-groups were more varied with respect to the Conservatives and the NDP than with the Liberals.

A comparison of Tables X and XI reveals that while the least educated groups in 1968 generally accorded all parties better scores than the most highly educated, this was even more the case in 1965: Table XI shows that generally the change in the gap between the Ideal party and the actual parties in 1965 and 1968 narrowed more for the better educated than for the less well educated or, as was usually the case with the NDP, that the widening of the gap was less great among those who had gone to school longer. The more favourable perception by those with more formal training is noticeable particularly with respect to the Liberals and the NDP.

PARTY	SCALE *		SCORES **		
I D E A L	(A)	G-B	A/B/C .0		
		H-D	A/B/C.0		
		E-D	C -.2	B 0	A .2
	(B)	M-O	C -.2	B -.1	A 0
		Y-O	B -.4	C -.2	A-.1
		W-M	C -.1	A/B .1	
		L-R	A/B/C -.1		
	(C)	P-W	B -.1	C .0	A .1
		C-I	B/C.1	A .2	
		U-S	C -.2	A 0	B .1
L I B E R A L	(A)	G-B	C -.5	B -.3	A-.2
		H-D	B -.8	C -.6	A-.4
		E-D	C-1.2	B -1.0	A-.9
	(B)	M-O	C -.8	A/B -.7	
		Y-O	A/B -1.3	C -1.1	
		W-M	A -.1	B/C 0	
		L-R	C -.2	B -.1	A .1
	(C)	P-W	C -1.4	B -1.2	A -1.1
		C-I	C -.8	A/B-.5	
		U-S	B -1.0	A -.8	C -.4
P C	(A)	G-B	B -.4	A -.3	C 0
		H-D	C -.4	B .2	A -.1
		E-D	A -.1	B .4	C .6
	(B)	M-O	A -.3	C .2	B .3
		Y-O	A -.4	C .1	B .4
		W-M	A -.4	B -.2	C -.1
		L-R	C -.1	B .1	A .2
	(C)	P-W	A -.1	C .2	B .4
		C-I	C -.8	A -.5	B -.3
		U-S	A -.5	B -.4	C -.3
N D P	(A)	G-B	A/B .3	C .5	
		H-D	B .2	A/C .3	
		E-D	A .2	B .5	C 1.1
	(B)	M-O	A .7	B/C .9	
		Y-O	C .2	A .5	B .6
		W-M	C -1.1	B 0	A .2
		L-R	B -.1	C .2	A .3
	(C)	P-W	A -.1	B .4	C .7
		C-I	C .7	B .9	A 1.0
		U-S	B -.1	A .5	C 1.1

NOTE:

* For a full description of the listed items see notes for table VI.

** The figures for the ideal party represent the changes in the mean scores of the ideal party, 1965 to 1968; for the actual parties they represent the changes in the deviations from the ideal party, 1965 to 1968.

LEGEND:

A = up to 8 yrs. schooling (33.3%), (34.7%)

B = 9-13 yrs. (51.9%), (50.6%)

C = 13 + yrs. (13.6%), (13.5%)

NOTE:

See also legend for Table VII.

We expressed some puzzlement above about the Liberal party's low rating on the Competence—Incompetence scale and the Conservatives' comparably better showing. It is useful to examine this dimension with respect to the educational background of our respondents. Table X tells us that, in 1968, the Liberals deviated from the Ideal by less than the Conservatives and that the order of the groups was the same for both: from the least educated to the most educated. Using the identifying symbols of our Table, we can summarize the parties' performance as follows:

95

| Liberal: | A 1.4 | B 1.6 | C 1.7 |
| Conservative: | A 1.7 | B 2.1 | C 2.4 |

A comparison of the change in the deviations between the Ideal and the two parties from 1965 to 1968 (Table XI) indicates that both parties narrowed the gap to about the same degree (the Liberals did a shade better as Table II shows) and that the educational breakdown was very similar:

| Liberal: | C −.8 | A/B −.5 | |
| Conservative: | C −.8 | A −.5 | B −.3 |

This suggests that the most educated group found that the *improvement* in the competence of both parties was about the same from 1965 to 1968. But they did not of course set out from the same starting line.

Religion

In the light of the well-documented relationship between religion and politics in Canada, the religious affiliation of our respondents can be expected to be related to the way in which they score the parties on our semantic differential questions. Tables XII and XIII do not disappoint our anticipation in this regard.

The mean scores assigned by the adherents of our main religious groups to the respective dimensions of the Ideal party reveal a pattern which will be of particular interest to students of Canadian political culture but which I shall merely mention without discussing either its causes or its significance. Roman Catholics produced the lowest, i.e. best, score on no less than five of the dimensions on which one can distinguish between a better and worse pole, once admittedly on the Competent—Incompetent dimension where no differences existed between the religious groups.

Much of the conventional knowledge about support for the major parties by Canadian religious groups is confirmed and possibly extended by our findings. Catholics gave the Liberal party its most favourable score on eight of the ten dimensions, Anglicans and adherents of the United Church jointly on one, and the "Other" group also on one—the Left—Right continuum. The latter group found the Liberals farthest from the Ideal party six times. It is difficult to interpret this latter pattern because the "Other" group is very much a residual category comprising everyone who did not declare himself to be a Catholic, an Anglican or an adherent of the United Church.

PARTY		SCALE*	SCORES**			
I D E A L	(A)	G-B	A 1.3	C/D 1.4	B 1.5	
		H-D	C 1.2	A/B/D 1.3		
		E-D	A/B 2.3	C/D 2.5		
	(B)	M-O	C 1.9	A/B 2.0	D 2.1	
		Y-O	C 2.7	A 3.0	B/D 3.1	
		W-M	C 3.4	B 3.5	A/D 3.6	
		L-R	A/D 4.4	B 4.5	C 4.7	
	(C)	P-W	D 1.7	C 1.9	A 2.0	B 2.1
		C-I	A/B/C/D 1.5			
		U-S	A/C/D 1.6	B 1.8		
L I B E R A L	(A)	G-B	C 1.4	B 1.7	A/D 1.8	
		H-D	C 1.2	A 1.4	B/D 1.5	
		E-D	C .6	D .7	A .9	B 1.0
	(B)	M-O	C .7	D .9	A 1.0	B 1.1
		Y-O	A/B .2	C/D .3		
		W-M	C .8	A/D .9	B 1.1	
		L-R	D .1	A/B/C .2		
	(C)	P-W	C .6	A .9	B 1.0	D 1.3
		C-I	C 1.2	A 1.7	B 1.8	D 1.9
		U-S	C .9	B 1.1	A 1.2	D 1.3
P C	(A)	G-B	B 1.8	A/D 2.0	C 2.1	
		H-D	A 1.2	B 1.3	D 1.5	C 1.6
		E-D	C 1.9	D 2.0	B 2.2	A 2.5
	(B)	M-O	B/D 2.2	C 2.3	A 2.4	
		Y-O	A/C/D 1.6	B 1.7		
		W-M	B .6	A/C/D .7		
		L-R	B .0	D .1	A .2	C .5
	(C)	P-W	B 2.2	A 2.4	C 2.5	D 2.7
		C-I	A/B 1.9	D 2.0	C 2.2	
		U-S	B 1.9	C 2.3	A/D 2.4	
N D P	(A)	G-B	B/D 2.1	C 2.2	A 2.3	
		H-D	D 1.1	A/B 1.4	C 1.7	
		E-D	B 1.3	D 1.4	C 1.6	A 1.8
	(B)	M-O	D 1.4	B 1.5	A/C 1.6	
		Y-O	D .5	A/B .7	C .9	
		W-M	C .4	D 1.1	A/B 1.2	
		L-R	D -1.1	A/B/C -1.0		
	(C)	P-W	B 2.8	A/C 3.0	D 3.2	
		C-I	B 2.2	A/D 2.3	C 2.4	
		U-S	B 1.0	D 1.9	A/C 2.0	

NOTE:

*For a full description of the listed items, see notes for Table VI.

**The scores for the Ideal party are mean scores; for the actual parties they represent the 1968 deviations from the scores of the Ideal party.

LEGEND:

A =Anglican   (12.5%)

B =United Church   (20.2%)

C =Roman Catholic (41.7%)

D =Other   (25.6%)

NOTE: See also legend for Table VI.

Our respondents, classified by their religious affiliation, scored the Performance aspect of the Liberal party in an interesting, almost perfectly symmetrical way. Catholics judged the party as more Powerful, Competent and United than the other groups, and the adherents of our residual category judged it least favourably on these dimensions. The distance between the Catholics and the next group most favourably disposed to the Liberals was not insignificant under the Performance aspect generally, and on the Competence—Incompetence scale came to .5. Catholics also assessed the Liberals better on all the items under the party Qualities aspect, but the adherents of the other religions did not produce an orderly pattern on these three dimensions.

Adherents of the United Church gave the Conservative party

97

their best score on seven of the ten dimensions. Their preference for Mr. Stanfield's party was particularly noticeable on the items under the party Orientations and Performance aspects. They, and the other religious groups, are scattered throughout section (A) of Table XII in a manner which suggests that religious affiliation had little to do with the judgements which were made here about the Qualities aspects of the Conservative party.

TABLE XIII: PARTY IMAGES BY RELIGION (1965-1968)

PARTY	SCALE*	SCORES**			
I D E A L	(A) G-B	A -.2	B/D .0	C .1	
	(A) H-D	C -.1	D .0	A/B .1	
	(A) E-D	A -.3	B -.2	D -.1	C .2
	(B) M-O	A/B -.2	C/D .0		
	(B) Y-O	A/B/D -.2	C -.1		
	(B) W-M	A/B -.1	D .0	C .2	
	(B) L-R	A/B -.3	D -.2	C .1	
	(C) P-W	D -.4	A -.2	B -.1	C .0
	(C) C-I	D .0	B/C .1	A .2	
	(C) U-S	D -.2	A -.1	B/C .0	
L I B E R A L	(A) G-B	D -.4	A/B -.3	C -.2	
	(A) H-D	A -1.0	B/D -.8	C -.4	
	(A) E-D	D -1.1	A -1.0	C -.9	B -.8
	(B) M-O	C/D -.8	A -.7	B -.6	
	(B) Y-O	A/C -1.4	B/D -1.3		
	(B) W-M	C -.2	A/D .0	B .2	
	(B) L-R	A/D -.1	C .1	B .2	
	(C) P-W	C -1.2	A -1.1	B/D -1.0	
	(C) C-I	A -.8	B -.6	C -.5	D -.4
	(C) U-S	A -.9	B/C -.8	D -.7	
P C	(A) G-B	C -.3	D -.2	B -.1	A .1
	(A) H-D	A -.4	B/C -.2	D -.1	
	(A) E-D	C .1	D .4	A/B .7	
	(B) M-O	C -.3	D .1	B .2	A .5
	(B) Y-O	C -.5	A/D -.1	B .2	
	(B) W-M	C -.4	D -.2	A/B -.1	
	(B) L-R	D -.1	B .0	A .1	C .5
	(C) P-W	C 0	B .3	A/D .5	
	(C) C-I	A/C -.4	B/D -.3		
	(C) U-S	B -.5	C -.4	A -.1	D .0
N D P	(A) G-B	C -.4	B/D .2	A .5	
	(A) H-D	D -.3	B -.1	A .1	C .4
	(A) E-D	B .3	C .5	D .6	A .9
	(B) M-O	D .7	B/C .9	A 1.0	
	(B) Y-O	D .3	A .5	B .6	C .8
	(B) W-M	C -.2	B -.1	A .0	D .2
	(B) L-R	B -.3	A -.2	C -.1	D .0
	(C) P-W	B/C .3	A .5	D .6	
	(C) C-I	A/B .0	D .3	C .4	
	(C) U-S	B .3	C .6	D .7	A .8

NOTE:

*For a full description of the listed items, see notes for Table VI.

**The figures for the Ideal party represent the changes in the mean scores of the Ideal party, 1965 to 1968; for the actual parties they represent the changes in the deviations from the Ideal party, 1965 to 1968.

LEGEND:

A = Anglican   (12.7%)
                    (12.5%)

B = United Church   (22.4%)
                    (20.2%)

C = Roman Catholic (41.9%)
                    (41.7%)

D = Other   (23.0%)
                    (25.6%)

NOTE: See also legend for Table VII.

The religious factor seems to have affected the NDP scores less than those of the older parties. United Church adherents seem to give the NDP better scores than members of the other religions, and notably on the party Qualities and Performance items and, interestingly, members of our residual category judged the NDP more favourably than any other religious group on three of the ten dimensions.

Before leaving the 1968 static deviations we must note the constraint exhibited by Anglicans in rating the parties: they have produced the best mean score for any party only five times out of thirty possibilities. Even the "other" group did a little better than this, although not much.

The most interesting feature of Table XIII is probably its message with respect to the changing Catholic perceptions from 1965 to 1968, of the Conservative party. Catholics showed the greatest improvement (or least deterioration) in their perception of the Stanfield party on seven of the ten dimensions, spread over all three party aspects. On several of our scales, the Catholic improvement was even greater with respect to the Liberal party but this does not diminish the relative change in the position of Catholics among those scoring the Conservatives. The relative "slippage" of the United Church members as Conservative supporters is equally noteworthy. They occupied the "top" position in the Conservative ratings seven times, as was noted above, but when the change from 1965 to 1968 is considered, they "headed the list" only once! Their scores showed greater improvement (or lesser deterioration) in this sense with respect to the NDP.

Ethnic Origin

A continuously perplexing problem faced by students of Canadian politics concerns the degree to which national behaviour patterns ascribed to qualities associated with Catholics are in reality linked to characteristics of French Canadians: a very large proportion of Canadian Catholics is of course French-speaking. It is therefore useful to follow our discussion of religious differences in the perception of parties by looking at the scores assigned the parties by members of Canada's main ethnic groups. We shall distinguish only between those whose origin is British, French and neither, that is, those who belong to some other ethnic group.

In indicating the kind of Ideal party they would like to see, French Canadians in Table XIV show a small preference, as compared with the other two groups, for a more moral party: their scores on the Good—Bad and Honest—Dishonest scales are slightly lower. They also prefer a more modern and a younger

PARTY	SCALE*	SCORES**		
I D E A L	(A) G-B	C 1.3	B/A 1.4	
	(A) H-D	C 1.2	B/A 1.3	
	(A) E-D	B 2.4	C/A 2.5	
	(B) M-O	C 1.8	A/B 2.0	
	(B) Y-O	C 2.6	A 2.9	B 3.0
	(B) W-M	A 2.9	C 3.4	B 3.6
	(B) L-R	B 4.4	A 4.6	C 4.8
	(C) P-W	C 1.8	A/B 2.1	
	(C) C-I	B/C 1.4	A 1.6	
	(C) U-S	B 1.3	C 1.5	A 1.7
L I B E R A L	(A) G-B	A 1.2	C 1.3	B 1.7
	(A) H-D	C 1.2	A/B 1.4	
	(A) E-D	C .6	A .7	B .9
	(B) M-O	A .7	B/C .9	
	(B) Y-O	B .2	A/C .3	
	(B) W-M	C .8	B .9	A 1.5
	(B) L-R	A/B/C -.2		
	(C) P-W	A/C .7	B .9	
	(C) C-I	C 1.3	A 1.6	B 1.8
	(C) U-S	A .9	C 1.0	B 1.5
P C	(A) G-B	B 1.9	A/C 2.1	
	(A) H-D	B 1.3	A/C 1.6	
	(A) E-D	C 1.8	A 2.0	B 2.1
	(B) M-O	B 2.2	A 2.3	C 2.4
	(B) Y-O	B 1.6	A 1.7	C 2.0
	(B) W-M	B .6	C .7	A 1.3
	(B) L-R	B .1	A -.2	C -.7
	(C) P-W	B 2.2	A 2.3	C 2.7
	(C) C-I	B 2.0	A 2.1	C 2.2
	(C) U-S	A/C 2.4	B 2.6	
N D P	(A) G-B	A 1.9	B 2.2	C 2.3
	(A) H-D	A 1.4	B 1.5	C 1.7
	(A) E-D	A 1.4	B/C 1.6	
	(B) M-O	A 1.5	B 1.6	C 1.7
	(B) Y-O	B .7	A .8	C .9
	(B) W-M	A/C .2	B -1.2	
	(B) L-R	B -1.0	A/C -1.1	
	(C) P-W	A 2.7	B 2.9	C 3.1
	(C) C-I	A 2.2	B 2.4	C 2.5
	(C) U-S	A 1.8	C 2.1	B 2.2

NOTE:

* For a full description of the listed items, see notes for Table VI.

** The scores for the Ideal party are mean scores; for the actual parties they represent the 1968 deviations from the scores of the Ideal party.

LEGEND:

A = "Other" (33.9%)

B = British (44.1%)

C = French (22.0%)

NOTE: See also legend for Table VI.

party than the British and the so-called "Others" and on these dimensions the gap separating the French is wider than is the case on the moral dimensions.

Students wishing to compare the political styles of French and English Canadians will be interested in the scores assigned by the two groups to the items under the Performance heading. The French preferred a more Powerful party than the other groups, and the British were more concerned with Unity. The two groups produced the same score on the Competence—Incompetence scale.

PARTY	SCALE*		SCORES**
I D E A L	(A)	G-B	B -.1 C .0 A .1
		H-D	B/C .0 A .1
		E-D	B -.2 A .2 C .3
	(B)	M-O	B -.2 C ·0 A .1
		Y-O	B -.3 A -.2 C ·0
		W-M	A -.5 B .0 C .2
		L-R	B -.2 A -.1 C .2
	(C)	P-W	B -.1 C ·0 A .1
		C-I	B ·0 A/C .1
		U-S	B -.5 C -.1 A .1
L I B E R A L	(A)	G-B	A -.7 C -.4 B -.3
		H-D	B -.8 A -.7 C -.6
		E-D	A/C -1.0 B -.8
	(B)	M-O	A -.9 C -.8 B -.7
		Y-O	C -1.8 A/B -1.3
		W-M	C -.3 B ·0 A .6
		L-R	A/B/C 0
	(C)	P-W	A/C -1.2 B 1.1
		C-I	C -.5 B -.4 A -.3
		U-S	C -1.2 A -1.0 B -.4
P C	(A)	G-B	C -.2 B -.1 A .5
		H-D	C -.3 A/B -.2
		E-D	C -.3 A .1 B .5
	(B)	M-O	C -.3 B -.1 A .2
		Y-O	C -.4 A -.2 B .1
		W-M	C -.3 B -.2 A .2
		L-R	B ·0 A .1 C .4
	(C)	P-W	A/C .1 B .2
		C-I	C -.4 A -.3 B -.2
		U-S	C -.2 B .1 A .7
N D P	(A)	G-B	A ·0 B/C .3
		H-D	A ·0 B .2 C .3
		E-D	A/C .4 B .7
	(B)	M-O	A .6 C 1.0 B 1.1
		Y-O	B .4 A .8 C .9
		W-M	A -.4 C .1 B .3
		L-R	B -.1 A ·0 C .2
	(C)	P-W	A .2 B .4 C .6
		C-I	B .2 C .3 A .4
		U-S	A .3 C .7 B 1.0

NOTE:

* For a full description of the listed items see notes for table VI.

** The figures for the ideal party represent the changes in the mean scores of the ideal party, 1965 to 1968; for the actual parties they represent the changes in the deviations from the ideal party, 1965 to 1968.

LEGEND:

A = "Other" (29.6%), (33.9%)
B = British (47.0%), (44.1%)
C = French (23.4%), (22.0%)

NOTE:

See also legend for Table VII.

French Canadians, as Table XIV shows, gave the Liberals more favourable scores than the other ethnic groups but the "Others" were not far behind.

A number of minute and fussy comparisons between French Canadian and Catholic scores indicate that, although there were some differences, there was considerable convergence between the two groups' respective ranking and actual scores. The differences were so small that, for the sake of economy of time and space, I shall not discuss them here. The task of disentangling the differences and causal relationships between French Canadian

101

and Catholic behaviour patterns will require more subtle analysis than we have so far applied to the semantic differential and our other data.

Table XIV shows that the way in which the Conservatives were scored by the three ethnic groups could hardly be more clear-cut. Those of British origin liked them best, French Canadians least and the "Others" were in between. This order was reversed in the Exciting—Dull dimension, varied only slightly on the class continuum and varied also on the United—Split scale. Here the French and "Others" gave the Conservatives a better score than those of British origin.

If the Liberals did particularly well among French Canadians, and Conservatives among those of British origin, the NDP was just as strongly preferred by the "Others". They accorded the party its best score on every dimension under the Qualities and Performance aspects although, for two of the three items in the latter, the "Others' " actual deviations from the Ideal party were greater with respect to the NDP than the Conservatives. Under the same aspect, the French Canadians, on the other hand, despite ranking behind the "Others", twice chalked up more favourable mean scores for the NDP than they did for the Conservatives.

Between 1965 and 1968 voters of British origin moved closer to the better end of our scales on six of the eight dimensions on which the Ideal party can be evaluated in this way; the "Others", however, placed the Ideal party closer to the worst pole on all but one of the eight dimensions. The perceptions of the Ideal party, Table XV tells us, changed very little insofar as the French-speaking respondents were concerned. I am at a loss to explain these ethnic differences in the changing expectations from our parties but find them both striking and suggestive; they warrant further extensive analysis.

It is not surprising that the image of the Liberal party should have improved generally on most of our dimensions from 1965 to 1968 but an amelioration on an even broader front in perceptions of the Conservative party among French Canadians is quite startling. French-speaking respondents registered the greatest improvement of our three ethnic groups in their perceptions of the Liberal party on seven of our ten dimensions; with respect to the Conservatives they showed greater improvement than the British and "Others" on eight! They did little to prevent the

PARTY		SCALE*	SCORES **		
I D E A L	(A)	G-B	C 1.3	A/B 1.4	
		H-D		A/B/C 1.3	
		E-D	A/B 2.4	C 2.5	
	(B)	M-O	C 1.9	A/B 2.1	
		Y-O	A 2.9	C 3.0	B 3.2
		W-M	B 3.4	A 3.5	C 3.7
		L-R	B/C 4.5	A 4.6	
	(C)	P-W	C 1.9	A/B 2.0	
		C-I		A/B/C 1.5	
		U-S	A/C 1.7	B 1.8	
L I B E R A L	(A)	G-B	C 1.4	A 1.5	B 1.6
		H-D	C 1.2	B 1.3	A 1.4
		E-D	C .7	A .8	B .9
	(B)	M-O	A .7	C .9	B 1.0
		Y-O	C .1	A/B .2	
		W-M	C .8	A/B .9	
		L-R	A -.3	B/C ·0	
	(C)	P-W	A .8	B .9	C 1.1
		C-I	C 1.5	A 1.6	B 1.8
		U-S	B .9	A 1.0	C 1.2
P C	(A)	G-B	B 1.8	A 2.0	C 2.4
		H-D	A/B 1.3	C 1.6	
		E-D	B 1.9	A 2.1	C 2.2
	(B)	M-O	A/B 2.1	C 2.9	
		Y-O	B 1.2	A 1.7	C 2.0
		W-M	A .6	B/C .9	
		L-R	A/B -.2	C .1	
	(C)	P-W	B 2.2	A 2.3	C 2.7
		C-I	B 1.8	A 2.0	C 2.6
		U-S	A 1.2	B 1.9	C 2.4
N D P	(A)	G-B	B 2.0	A/C 2.2	
		H-D	B 1.4	A/C 1.6	
		E-D	B 1.4	C 1.5	A 1.8
	(B)	M-O	A/B 1.4	C 1.7	
		Y-O	B .4	A .7	C .8
		W-M	B/C -1.3	A -.8	
		L-R	C -1.3	A/B -1.0	
	(C)	P-W	B 2.8	A 2.9	C 3.2
		C-I	B 2.2	A 2.3	C 2.4
		U-S	B/C 1.7	A 1.9	

NOTE:

* For a full description of the listed items see notes for Table VI.

** The scores for the ideal party are mean scores; for the actual parties they represent the 1968 deviations from the scores of the ideal party.

LEGEND:

A = Born in Canada (81.8%)

B = Arrived in Canada in or before 1945 (8.5%)

C = Arrived in Canada in or after 1946 (9.5%)

NOTE:

See also legend for Table VI.

deterioration of the mean scores of the NDP between the two elections; nor were they among the ethnic groups which exhibited a below normal loss of regard for the NDP on the dimensions on which their image became less attractive from 1965 to 1968.

Period of Immigration

Our data on ethnic origin are highly suggestive and obviously require that considerably more work be done on them. They should be examined in relation to the amount of time which the members of the various groups spent in Canada. While neither

PARTY	SCALE*		SCORES**		
IDEAL	(A)	G-B	A/B/C 0		
		H-D	A .0	B .1	C .2
		E-D	B -.3	A .0	C .1
	(B)	M-O	B 0	A/C .1	
		Y-O	C -.2	A -.1	B .0
		W-M	B -.2	C .0	A .1
		L-R	C -.3	B -.1	A .0
	(C)	P-W	B .1	A/C .0	
		C-I	A/B/C .1		
		U-S	A .0	B/C .2	
LIBERAL	(A)	G-B	B -.6	C -.5	A -.4
		H-D	C -1.0	B -.9	A -.6
		E-D	C -1.1	A -.9	A -.6
	(B)	M-O	A -1.0	B -.8	A -.5
		Y-O	C -1.6	A -1.5	B -1.1
		W-M	A -.1	B .0	C .2
		L-R	C -.3	B -.1	A .1
	(C)	P-W	A/B/C -1.2		
		C-I	A/B/C .5		
		U-S	B -1.1	A -.9	C -.8
PC	(A)	G-B	A/C -.2	B -.1	
		H-D	A/C -.4	B -.1	
		E-D	C .0	A .3	B .8
	(B)	M-O	A -.2	C .0	B .2
		Y-O	B -.5	A -.2	C -.1
		W-M	A -.3	B .0	C .6
		L-R	B -.2	A/C .1	
	(C)	P-W	A .0	B/C .2	
		C-I	A -.4	C -.2	B -.1
		U-S	A -1.4	C -.6	B -.5
NDP	(A)	G-B	C .1	A/B .3	
		H-D	A .0	B/C .1	
		E-D	B/C .6	A .8	
	(B)	M-O	B .6	A/C .7	
		Y-O	B .3	A .6	C .8
		W-M	A/B .2	C .4	
		L-R	B -.2	A- .1	C .1
	(C)	P-W	A .3	B/C .5	
		C-I	A .2	B .4	C .5
		U-S	B .2	A .5	C .6

NOTE:

* For a full description of the listed items see notes for table VI.

** The figures for the ideal party represent the changes in the mean scores of the ideal party, 1965 to 1968; for the actual parties they represent the changes in the deviations from the ideal party, 1965 to 1968.

LEGEND:

A = Born in Canada (80.7%), (81.8%)
B = Arrived in or before 1945 (10.8%), (8.5%)
C = Arrived in or after 1946 (8.5%), (9.5%)

NOTE:

See also legend for Table VII.

time nor space permits us to embark upon this path at present, I include the Tables which show the scores of three groups: those who were born in Canada, immigrants who arrived here before the end of the Second World War, and those who came since 1946. Table XVI and XVII contain our usual measures for the three groups; I can do little more here than just brush past them on the way to completing my description of the socio-economic variables.

The Liberals have amassed the best response in 1968 from the "New Canadians", the group which arrived since 1946, and their image was least attractive to the "old settlers", those who immigrated before 1945. Canadian born respondents were somewhat between these two groups. The "New Canadians" did not perceive the Conservatives in a particularly favourable light. Mr. Stanfield's party appeared to be about equally attractive, in terms of our dimensions, to those who were born in Canada and to immigrants who arrived before the end of the Second World War. The NDP was also viewed most favourably by this group—the "old settlers"—but found few very warm supporters among the Canadian born and fewer still among the "New Canadians". Table XVI shows that some interestingly homogeneous patterns emerged under the party Qualities aspect of our ten dimensions.

The general picture which emerges from a comparison of Tables XVI and XVII is that there was relatively little change between 1965 and 1968, with respect to the categories under dicussion here, except perhaps that the Canadian born seemed to have developed a somewhat more favourable image of all the parties in the period intervening between the two elections.

Region

Regional differences have long been considered an important key essential to the unlocking of the mysteries of Canadian politics. The two surveys support the generally-held view that there are substantial differences between Canadians residing in the different regions with respect to the images they have of Canadian politics and of Canadian parties.

Our Quebec respondents, as Table XVIII reveals, rated the Ideal party "most idealistically", that is closer than anyone else to the good pole on the two moral dimensions under our party Qualities aspect, on the Youth and Modernity dimensions, and on two of the Performance scales—Competence and Unity. They thus had a better image of the Ideal party than residents of any other region.

British Columbians, while not exactly falling overboard in their efforts to rate the Ideal party as close as possible to the good pole, did seem to have a more "idealized" conception of parties than inhabitants of some of our other regions. But when their assessment of actual parties is examined, we find, as Table XVIII shows, that they liked all the parties, except perhaps the Liberals, less than those living further East. There is a faint suggestion of alienation from political parties here which requires closer scrutiny. The inclusion of the Social Credit party in our analysis may alter the picture presented in Table XVIII.

A look at the scores received by the actual parties tells us that the Liberals did particularly well in the central provinces—Quebec and Ontario—and that their scores were least favourable in the Atlantic provinces and the Prairies. On the whole, Quebeckers found the Liberals particularly to their liking on the party Qualities and Performance items, and Ontarians on the party Orientations dimensions.

In view of Robert Stanfield's popularity in the Atlantic provinces, and of the traditional acceptance of the Conservatives there, it is not surprising that the most clear-cut regional pattern we have found in Canada concerns the extremely favourable per-

TABLE XVIII: PARTY IMAGES BY REGION (1968)

PARTY	SCALE*		SCORES**				
I D E A L	(A)	G-B	B/E 1.3	D 1.4	A/C 1.5		
		H-D	B/E 1.2	C/D 1.3	A 1.4		
		E-D	C 2.3	A/D/E 2.4	B 2.6		
	(B)	M-O	B 1.8	D/E 2.0	A 2.1	C 3.0	
		Y-O	B 2.5	A/C 2.9	E 3.0	D 3.1	
		W-M	A 2.9	B/C 3.5	D 3.6	E 3.7	
		L-R	C 4.4	E 4.5	D 4.6	A/B 4.7	
	(C)	P-W	A 1.8	B 1.9	C 2.2	D/E 2.2	
		C-I	B 1.2	E 1.4	C/D 1.5	A 1.7	
		U-S	B 1.5	E 1.6	C 1.7	A/D 1.8	
L I B E R A L	(A)	G-B	B 1.2	C 1.4	E 1.6	A/D 1.9	
		H-D	B 1.2	C 1.3	E 1.4	A/D 1.7	
		E-D	B .5	E .6	C .8	A/D 1.0	
	(B)	M-O	C -.1	B .8	A/E .9	D 1.2	
		Y-O	C .1	D/E .2	B .4	A .5	
		W-M	B .7	A/C/D .9	E 1.0		
		L-R	C/E -.1	B/D -.2	A -.6		
	(C)	P-W	C .5	B/E .6	D .9	A 1.3	
		C-I	B .5	C/E 1.6	A 1.7	D 2.0	
		U-S	B/C -.0	A/D/E 1.2			
P C	(A)	G-B	A 1.5	D 1.8	C 2.0	B 2.1	E 2.3
		H-D	A 1.5	D 1.3	B/C/E 1.5		
		E-D	A/C 1.4	B 1.8	D 1.9	E 2.4	
	(B)	M-O	D .5	A 1.3	C 1.6	B 2.4	E 2.7
		Y-O	A 1.1	D 1.5	E 1.8	C 1.9	B 2.0
		W-M	A -.4	D .4	B .6	E .7	C .9
		L-R	C/D .0	E .2	A -.3	B -.5	
	(C)	P-W	A/D 2.1	C 2.4	B/E 2.5		
		C-I	A 1.3	B 1.4	D 1.9	C 2.2	E 2.4
		U-S	A 1.8	B/C/D 2.3	E 2.7		
N D P	(A)	G-B	A/C 2.0	D 2.1	B/E 2.4		
		H-D	E 1.5	A/C/D 1.6	B 1.7		
		E-D	A/B 1.5	D/E 1.6	C 1.7		
	(B)	M-O	C .5	A 1.4	D/E 1.6	B 1.8	
		Y-O	D .4	A/E .7	C .8	B 1.0	
		W-M	A .2	B -.3	C -.9	D -1.1	E -1.2
		L-R	A .7	C -.9	B/D -1.1	E -1.3	
	(C)	P-W	D/E 2.6	C 2.9	A/B 3.0		
		C-I	A 1.9	C 2.0	D/E 2.2	B 2.4	
		U-S	D 1.5	B/C 1.8	E 1.9	A 2.0	

NOTE:

*For a full description of the listed items, see notes for Table VI.

**The scores for the Ideal party are mean scores; for the actual parties they represent the 1968 deviations from the scores of the Ideal party.

LEGEND:

A = Atlantic   (10.1%)

B = Quebec   (27.2%)

C = Ontario   (35.1%)

D = Prairies   (18.5%)

E = British Columbia   (9.0%)

NOTE: See also legend for Table VI.

ception Maritimers have of the Conservatives. They received their best scores in the Atlantic provinces on eight of our dimensions; on some—the two moral scales, for example—the deviations from the Ideal party registered by those from the Atlantic provinces were smaller for the Conservatives than for the Liberals. British Columbians, on the other hand, have generally rated Mr. Stanfield's party less favourably than residents of any other region.

The NDP made its best showing in the Atlantic provinces and the Prairies and was received least well in British Columbia and Quebec. Respondents in the latter region, interestingly, assigned the same excellent score to the Liberals and the NDP on the Exciting—Dull continuum but this is a most untypical convergence repeated on no other dimension.

Another unexpected set of responses by the Quebeckers, one

TABLE XIX: PARTY IMAGES BY REGION (1965-1968)

PARTY		SCALE*	SCORES**					
I D E A L	(A)	G-B	A/B/C/E .0	D .1				
		H-D		A/B/C/D/E .0				
		E-D	E -.1	A/C/D -.2	B .3			
	(B)	M-O	A/D/E -.1	B .1	C .4			
		Y-O	C -.3	A/D/E -.2	B -.1			
		W-M	A -.5	D -.1	C/D .1	B .2		
		L-R	C -.3	D -.2	A -.1	E .1	B .3	
	(C)	P-W	A -.5	E -.1	C/D .0	B .2		
		C-I	A/B -.1	E .0	C/D .1			
		U-S	B/E -.1	C .0	D .1	A .4		
L I B E R A L	(A)	G-B	E -.8	B/D -.5	C -.4	A .2		
		H-D	E -1.0	B -.7	C -.6	A -.2	D .4	
		E-D	E -1.5	B -1.2	C -.8	D -.6	A -.2	
	(B)	M-O	B -1.1	C/E -1.0	D -.7	A -.5		
		Y-O	C -1.7	B/E -1.5	D -1.4	A -1.0		
		W-M	A/C/D .0	E -.1	B -.3			
		L-R	C/D -.1	E .0	B .1	A .2		
	(C)	P-W	E -1.7	C -.4	D -1.2	B -1.1	A -.2	
		C-I	B -1.4	E -.9	C/D -.4	A .1		
		U-S	A -1.1	E -1.0	B/D -.9	C -.8		
P C	(A)	G-B	B/E -.3	A -.2	C/D -.1			
		H-D	B -.5	C -.2	D/E -.1	A .0		
		E-D	B -.5	C -.3	E .0	A .2	D .8	
	(B)	M-O	D -1.2	D -1.2	B -.5	A/C -.1	E .0	
		Y-O	A/B -.4	E -.2	D .0	C .2		
		W-M	B -.4	C -.3	A/D -.2	E -.1		
		L-R	E -.3	A/D -.1	C .0	B .4		
	(C)	P-W	B .3	E .1	C/D .3	A .7		
		C-I	B -1.3	E -.4	A/C/D -.2			
		U-S	A/B -.4	C/E -.3	D .0			
N D P	(A)	G-B	D -.1	C .2	A/E .3	B .7		
		H-D	E .0	A/D .2	C .3	B .4		
		E-D	B .3	A/E .6	D .7	C .8		
	(B)	M-O	C .3	A .6	D .7	B/E 1.0		
		Y-O	D .3	A/C/E .6	B .9			
		W-M	D -.4	E -.3	A/B -.1	C .0		
		L-R	A -.3	C/D -.1	E .0	B .3		
	(C)	P-W	B .0	C .3	D .4	E .5	A .6	
		C-I	C -.1	A/D .0	E .1	D .3		
		U-S	A -.2	D .0	B .4	C .6	E .7

NOTE:

*For a full description of the listed items, see notes for Table VI.

**The figures for the Ideal party represent the changes in the mean scores of the Ideal party, 1965 to 1968; for the actual parties they represent the changes in the deviations from the Ideal party, 1965 to 1968.

LEGEND:

A = Atlantic (8.3%)
         (10.1%)
B = Quebec (29.2%)
         (27.2%)
C = Ontario (38.7%)
         (35.1%)
D = Prairies (14.5%)
         (18.5%)
E = British (9.2%)
    Columbia (9.0%)

NOTE: See also legend for Table VII.

which is foreshadowed in our breakdown by ethnic origin, concerns the 1965 to 1968 change in deviations between the Conservative and Ideal parties. They provided the best score on our measure of change, as Table XIX shows, on eight of the ten dimensions. It is quite apparent, therefore, that despite the poor showing of the Conservatives in Quebec during the 1968 election, the image of the party improved more in Quebec between 1965 and 1968 than anywhere else in Canada. But it was extremely unfavourable to begin with and Mr. Stanfield, who made heroic efforts to woo Quebec in the campaign, had a very long way to go indeed to convert a hostile perception of his party into a friendly one.

Mr. Stanfield is probably one of the main reasons for the relatively small improvement of the Liberals in the Atlantic provinces. The Liberal party improved its image least there between 1965 and 1968 on four dimensions and on three others the deviation between the Ideal and Liberal parties actually increased by 1968: our respondents in the four most easterly provinces scored the Liberals less favourably on the Good—Bad, Left—Right and Competent—Incompetent scales.

The guess that the Liberals' relatively poor showing is partly ascribable to the emergence of Mr. Stanfield as the new Conservative leader is based on the assumption that the personality of the leader is a substantial factor in shaping party images. This assumption remains to be tested as part of our larger study. The fact that the changes affecting perceptions of the Liberal party follow other regional patterns cast some doubts about the explanatory power of the leader factor in this context: after the Atlantic provinces, the Liberals improved their position least in the Prairies, and the perceptions of the party improved quite noticeably more in British Columbia than in the two regions we have just discussed. These geographical aspects are not easily reconciled with some of the hypotheses one is tempted to make about the effect of leaders on changing perceptions of party images.

The NDP actually improved its position slightly on the Good—Bad scale among the Prairie respondents, who also liked the party better in 1968 on the class dimension. Quebeckers contributed more than respondents in other regions to the deterioration of the NDP image.

TABLE XX : PARTY IMAGES BY CLASS (1968)

PARTY	SCALE *		SCORES **		
I D E A L	(A)	G-B		U/M/L 1.4	
		H-D	U/M 1.2	L 1.3	
		E-D	U 2.2	M 2.4	L 2.5
	(B)	M-O	M 1.9	U/L 2.0	
		Y-O	U 2.8	M/L 2.9	
		W-M	L 3.0	M 3.9	U 4.3
		L-R		U/M/L 4.6	
	(C)	P-W		U/M/L 2.0	
		C-I	U 1.3	M 1.4	L 1.6
		U-S	U 1.5	M 1.6	L 1.7
L I B E R A L	(A)	G-B	U 1.2	M 1.5	L 1.6
		H-D	U 1.2	M 1.3	L 1.5
		E-D	U .6	M .7	L .8
	(B)	M-O	U .7	M .9	L 1.0
		Y-O	U .1	M .2	L .4
		W-M	U .1	M .6	L 1.3
		L-R	M -.2	U -.3	L -.4
	(C)	P-W	U .7	M/L .8	
		C-I	U 1.5	M/L 1.6	
		U-S	U/M 1.0	L 1.2	
P C	(A)	G-B	L 1.9	U/M 2.0	
		H-D	U/M 1.4	L 1.6	
		E-D	L 1.8	M 2.2	U 2.6
	(B)	M-O	L 2.2	U 2.4	M 2.5
		Y-O	L 1.6	M 1.8	U 2.0
		W-M	U .1	M .4	L 1.0
		L-R	U .1	M/L -.2	
	(C)	P-W	L 2.3	M 2.5	U 2.6
		C-I	L 1.9	M 2.2	U 2.4
		U-S	L 2.2	M 2.4	U 2.8
N D P	(A)	G-B	L 1.9	M 2.4	U 2.5
		H-D	U/L 1.5	M 1.7	
		E-D	L 1.3	M 1.7	U 2.2
	(B)	M-O	L 1.3	U 1.7	M 1.8
		Y-O	L .7	M .8	U .9
		W-M	L -.3	M-1.3	U-1.7
		L-R	L -.8	M-1.2	U-1.6
	(C)	P-W	L 2.6	M 3.1	U 3.2
		C-I	L 1.9	M 2.6	U 2.8
		U-S	L 1.8	M 2.0	U 2.2

NOTE:

* For a full description of the listed items see notes for Table VI.

** The scores for the ideal party are mean scores; for the actual parties they represent the 1968 deviations from the scores of the ideal party.

LEGEND:

U = Upper   (7.7%)

M = Middle   (46.4%)

L = Lower   (45.8%)

NOTE:

See also legend for Table VI.

Class

Our data can contribute a useful depth to the still ongoing discussion about the importance, in Canadian political behaviour, of social class. We are using this tricky concept in its subjective sense: our respondents were asked to place themselves into one of five stated categories. These were then collapsed into the three used in Tables XX and XXI.[16]

Class differences seem to have had no effect on the way in which our respondents scored two dimensions of the Ideal party:

109

the Left—Right and Powerful—Weak continua; they led, on the other hand, to highly divergent judgements about the degree to which the Ideal party should support (be for) the Working Class or the Middle Class. Here we observe a difference in the mean score of 1.3 between those identified with the lower class (3.0) and the upper class group (4.3). Since the mid-point on our seven-point scale is 4 we see that even the upper class members placed their Ideal party only a relatively short distance from the mid- or neutral place on the scale. Members of the lower class expressed somewhat greater class consciousness in producing a mean score one full point (1.0) from the centre of the scale towards the For the Working Class pole.

On all the remaining dimensions, except the Modernity scale, the mean scores assigned the Ideal party are lowest (i.e. closer to the good pole, if conventional [middle class?] criteria are applied) for the upper class, and highest for the lower class. The middle class group has scores in between, except on the Modernity dimension where it has rated the Ideal party as slightly closer than the two classes to the Modern pole.

None of our other Tables display the order and symmetry possessed by Table XX wich is as regular and soigné as a French garden. Every one of the Liberal scales except the Left—Right dimension exhibits the same sequence: those identifying with the upper class have produced the most favourable scores; the self-styled lower class has produced the least favourable ones. The situation with respect to the NDP produces virtually a reversed mirror image: the lower class gave Mr. Douglas' party the best score on all dimensions; the upper class failed to provide the worst score only once. It equalled the good low class rating on the Honest—Dishonest dimension and thus "banished" the middle class into the cellar: it provided the least favourable score on this one dimension.

Only the Conservative party has failed to produce a thoroughly homogeneous pattern. Here the lower class produced the best score six, and the upper class four times. The middle class placed its score between the other two in almost all instances. Members of the upper class had a penchant for extremes; they produced the least favourable score whenever they were not at the good side of the pole.

If the ten dimensions are grouped into our three party aspects,

TABLE XXI: PARTY IMAGES BY CLASS (1965-1968)

PARTY	SCALE*		SCORES**		
I D E A L	(A)	G-B	U .2	M/L 0	
		H-D	M -.1	L 0	U .1
		E-D	U -.2	M/L 0	
	(B)	M-O	M -.2	U/L .1	
		Y-O	U -.4	M -.2	L -.1
		W-M	U/M 0	L .1	
		L-R	L -.1	M 0	U .3
	(C)	P-W	M -.1	U/L 0	
		C-I		U/M/L .1	
		U-S	L 0	M .1	U .2
L I B E R A L	(A)	G-B	U -.8	L -.4	M -.3
		H-D	U -1.0	M -.7	L -.6
		E-D	U -1.1	M -1.0	L -.8
	(B)	M-O	U -1.0	L -.7	M -.6
		Y-O	L -1.4	M -1.3	U -1.2
		W-M	L -.2	U 0	M .1
		L-R	U -.2	M/L -.1	
	(C)	P-W	U -1.5	M/L -1.2	
		C-I	U -.9	M -.6	L -.4
		U-S	L -.8	U/M -.7	
P C	(A)	G-B	U -.5	M/L -.2	
		H-D	U/M -.3	L -.1	
		E-D	L .2	M .3	U .5
	(B)	M-O	U -.2	L .1	M .3
		Y-O	L -.3	M 0	U .1
		W-M	L -.3	U/M -.2	
		L-R	U -.5	M -.2	L -.1
	(C)	P-W	L .1	U .2	M .3
		C-I	M -.4	U/L -.3	
		U-S	M -.3	L -.2	U 0
N D P	(A)	G-B	L .1	U .2	M .5
		H-D	U 0	L .1	M .4
		E-D	L .3	M .7	U 1.1
	(B)	M-O	L .6	M .8	U 1.0
		Y-O	U .5	M .6	L .7
		W-M	L -.2	U/M -.1	
		L-R	L -.1	M 0	U .4
	(C)	P-W	L 0	U .4	M .5
		C-I	L -.1	U .3	M .4
		U-S	L .5	M .6	U 1.1

we find that no homogeneous pattern emerges with respect to party Qualities, Orientation and Performance.

A comparison of the deviations from the Ideal party's scores by the three classes on the individual dimensions reveals some interesting insights. Members of the lower class, for example, preferred the NDP to the Conservatives on the three dimensions of the party Qualities items on which, however, the upper class assigned more favourable scores to the Conservatives. On the whole the Liberals elicited better scores from the lower class even on the several dimensions on which that class rank was third for the Liberals and first for the NDP. This shows, of course, that the image of the Liberal party was better among the lower class identifiers than was that of the NDP, and that the reason members of the lower class appear to be so favourable to the NDP in Table XX is that those identifying with the other classes like Mr. Douglas' party even less.

Table XX thus still eloquently supports the notion that class, as defined here, is a relevant and important variable which cannot be ignored when one attempts to explain the political perceptions of Canadians. Table XXI, although not as striking as Table XX, contains data which strengthen this view.

CONCLUSION

The foregoing account of some of the results we have obtained from asking two national samples to score our parties on dimensions created by ten sets of word pairs suggested by the semantic differential technique takes us towards three areas in which some concluding remarks are appropriate. These remarks, dealing sometimes with the virtues and blemishes, sometimes with the implications of what we have done so far, will have to be agonizingly brief in relation to the terrain they try to cover. They are a series of random glosses, which speculate about what might be done in the future.

Theoretical Aspects

We suggested in the Introduction that we were concerned with exploring the ways in which the political system responds to needs, wants and demands and that we thought that the use of the concept of an Ideal party, as applied in this paper, was an apposite tool in this pursuit.

One of the several problems here is the independence of the perception of the Ideal party as a yardstick against which the achievement or shortcomings of the actual parties can be measured. We saw above that the greatest change in perception of the Ideal party occurred on the youth dimension and we considered the possibility that this reflected the youthful image of Mr. Trudeau's personal and campaign styles. Did the image of the Ideal party, in other words, change in response to the changing perceptions of the popular Liberal party? If this was the case, then we cannot consider the Ideal party as an independent measure, and although it will remain a useful concept in our studies,

112

its relevance to some of our underlying concerns will be diminished. The independence of the Ideal party concept needs to be tested, and if it is found to be low, the way in which it is affected by actual parties and other agencies, will have to be explored.

I have been intrigued by the question of whether the various party perceptions tapped by our ten dimensions, possibly augmented by others which may be relevant, cluster and cohere into a reasonably stable set of cognitive and affective characteristics which would enable us to apply them as an alternative to, and also as a refinement of, the idea of Party Identification. It is plausible to assume that an individual perceives and evaluates parties in some sort of coherent pattern which both logically and chronologically precedes the Identification with a party and the voting decision. One can postulate a three-step process (more precisely, three steps in a more complex and longer process) comprising a firming-up of party perceptions into a stable set of coherent evaluations, Party Identification and the vote itself.

If this is a valid approach, then much work needs to be done tracing the causal and time sequences involved and identifying and organizing the relevant dimensions into the appropriate perception or image pattern. One of the tasks to be undertaken, not only within the broader context just outlined but also in our own immediate study, is to discover which dimensions, if any, and in what combination, are related to the voting decision to determine, if applicable, the psychological and temporal relationship between changes in party images and in the vote.

Some Methodological Problems

Aside from the obvious fact that we have not applied the semantic differential technique in anything like its fullest and most rewarding form, some other methodological problems have posed difficulties for us. We can do little more than list them here, utilizing an almost telegraphic form of the Queen's English.

While the mean scores, as used by us, offer an effective way of handling the respondents' scores, the method, like any other, leads to some distortion. It ignores, to some extent, the nature of the distribution of the respondents among the seven-point scale. The use of the mean scores can fruitfully be supplemented by graphs, showing the percent or number of respondents scoring each "slot" on the seven-point scale, but this method poses other problems which make its use virtually unmanageable.

The differences between our mean scores are exceedingly small in many cases. The problems resulting from the narrowness of the resulting margins are obvious.

The meaning of some of the word pairs is somewhat ambiguous. Words like "young" and "good", for example, can convey a variety of meanings with respect to political parties, posing problems of interpretation.

While two of our party aspects proved to be useful, and often produced homogeneous results, this was not the case with all three. Party Qualities, particularly the two moral dimensions, formed a useful category, as did the Performance rubric. They can perhaps be related to Osgood's Evaluation and Activity factors. Our third aspect, party Orientations, proved less useful.

Depending, of course, on the purposes of future research to be undertaken, both some of the word pairs, and the party aspects into which they are grouped, should be revised.

When this has been done, attempts should be made to develop spatial models of parties which would take into account, *inter alia,* the complexity and multidimensionality of the perceptions electors have of them.[17] These models should not only account for the relationships of the various component images to one another, as they refer to any given number of parties, but should also indicate the respective positions of the various parties in a political system. We are, of course, still a very long way from being able to do this.

Political Issues

Throughout this report we have referred to a large number of noteworthy discoveries—some of them inexplicable within our present means. They form an inventory of insights and further research problems, the merit of which determines the usefulness of our application of the semantic differential type of question to recent Canadian experience. Instead of attempting to write a summary and construct a balance sheet of these items we shall turn to a selected number of general political issues which arise from the present paper and which seem to us to be of particular relevance and importance. In doing so, we must ever be alert to the fact that we are dealing with party images and not variables which *per se* can be linked *here* to the voting decision of our respondents.

The most persistent and noticeable overall pattern which emerges from our data is that which describes the immense improvement of the Liberal image from 1965 to 1968. In the light of the public interest in effective government (as indicated, for example, by the aforementioned anxiety about a Parliamentary minority), it is intriguing to find that the Liberals were viewed more favourably on every one of the other items than on their competence. This raises, in a very specific way, a point mentioned in our discussion of the Theoretical Aspects: which dimensions are most important in shaping the overall perception of parties and, furthermore, what combination of dimensions creates a party image capable of extracting the vote itself?

Literature (and life?) abounds with examples of devastatingly upright ladies choosing rotters and bounders as husbands and lovers over greatly more honourable and respectable men. Are voters also less conventional than is usually thought in prizing characteristics which might, at first glance at least, strike one as less appropriate than others? The Liberals' three worst dimensions arouse one's curiosity in this respect. Competence, goodness and honesty make a strange trio at the bottom of the party's list and suggest that we need to do considerably more work than we have done so far in sifting, finding and analyzing the most appropriate semantic differential dimensions and in relating them to the voting decision.

The improvement registered by the Liberals is matched by the corresponding dramatic loss in the favour accorded the NDP. Since the party changed very little from 1965 to 1968 one is tempted to conclude that the worsening of its image must be ascribed to the *relative* appearance of the NDP in 1968, when compared with the Liberals. This, if confirmed, suggests that a party's image is as much the function of what other parties look like as it is the consequence of its own intrinsic characteristics. The comparatively much better image of the Conservatives is interesting in this context. The perceptions the voters had of Mr. Stanfield's party was slightly better in 1968 than in 1965, suggesting that the Liberals' new image was much less harmful to it. The departure of Mr. Diefenbaker and the advent of Mr. Stanfield are likely reasons for this, suggesting that nowadays a party may

115

have to change its leading personnel frequently, if it is not blessed by a highly popular group of incumbents.

At any rate, the relative decline of the NDP needs to be analyzed and its roots bared. The problem is particularly interesting in the light of the fact that the electoral appeal of the NDP did not decline from 1965 to 1968 in anything like the degree suggested by the deterioration of the party image. In this context it is useful to re-state one of our earlier observations: the class nature of party perceptions in Canada is strongly supported by our data and was found to be of particular importance to the NDP.

One of the most surprising results of this analysis concerns the improvement in its image experienced by the Conservative party in the 1965-1968 period in the eyes of French Canadians. We have noted, also, that the party was perceived much more favourably by Catholics. The reasons for the change still elude us but the rest of our survey data should produce the required illumination. In our search for more light in this area, we shall also try to cope with the question of the connection between Catholicity and Frenchness in relation to party perceptions and the voting decision.

Finally, we have come across a number of subpopulations which seemed to have judged the Ideal party, or *all* our actual parties, less favourably than other subgroups. The young, residents of British Columbia and Anglicans, for example, seemed less inclined to produce high mean scores than older people, residents of more Easterly provinces and Catholics or adherents of the United Church.

This suggests that there are groups in our society which expect less from our parties and which therefore turn to other means of expressing political preferences or, and this would be serious, become apolitical.

On the basis of the data presented here we have only a vague idea of where the disaffection lies. When we analyze answers to some of our other questions, particularly the responses to batteries probing cynicism and a sense of efficacy, we will no doubt be able to obtain greater insight into the social, geographic, political and other areas in which parties are meeting with some disaffection. We have begun analyzing the answers to the semantic differential questions by the 1968 vote, by the cynicism and

116

efficacy scales, by degree of political partisanship and interest, by voting patterns and by postures taken towards the powers of the central government vis-à-vis the provinces. But these results begin another story.

NOTES

1. The basic works on the semantic differential technique are C. E. Osgood, G. J. Suci and P. H. Tannenbaum, *The Measurement of Meaning*, Urbana, Illinois, 1957 and J. G. Snider and C. E. Osgood (Eds.), *Semantic Differential Technique: A Source Book*, Chicago, Illinois, 1969. A modified use of it in the study of political behaviour was made by D. Butler and D. Stokes and is reported in their *Political Change in Britain: Forces Shaping Electoral Choice*, London, 1969, pp. 206 ff., 362 ff., 477. An interesting application to Canadian politics was reported upon by I. Schiffer, L. Rubinoff, J. Steiner and P. Fox, in "The Fantasy World of Voters," a paper presented to the 1969 Annual Meeting of the Canadian Political Science Association.

2. The 1965 survey was undertaken jointly by P. E. Converse, J. Meisel, M. Pinard, P. Regenstreif and Mildred Schwartz and the 1968 survey by J. Meisel. In the 1965 survey 2125 interviews were completed; the weighted N is 2721. No weighting was done in 1968 and 2767 successful interviews were completed. For a description of the sample design in 1965, see J. Meisel and R. Van Loon, "Canadian Attitudes to Election Expenses, 1965-6," in Committee on Election Expenses, *Studies in Canadian Party Finance*, Ottawa, Queen's Printer, 1966, pp. 23-26, 32-41, 143-5. The sample design

was similar in 1968. Further information about both these surveys can be obtained from J. Meisel, Queen's University.

3. The term "word pair" is evidently used loosely here, since in some instances we have employed more than a pair (two) words. For the sake of simplicity we shall nevertheless continue using the term "word pair" in this paper.

4. The question, as used in 1968, and the sheet used by the respondents, are reproduced in the Appendix.

5. A fuller account, with illustrations can be found below, pp. 74-75.

6. See particularly A. Campbell, P. E. Converse, W. E. Miller and D. E. Stokes, *The American Voter*, New York, 1960, pp. 120-167 and *passim*; and *idem, Elections and the Political Order*, New York, 1966, particularly P. E. Converse, "The Concept of a Normal Vote," pp. 9-39, and A. Campbell and H. Valen, "Party Identification in Norway and the United States," pp. 245-268.

7. Op. cit., p. 14.

8. There is also a considerable difference in the level of response achieved in the two surveys. It is likely that the lower refusal rate in 1968 resulted from a better formulated question and from a generally more effective job of constructing the questionnaire and of carrying out the interviews.

9. Butler and Stokes found that only about 5 percent of their respondents said "Don't Know" to virtually all the semantic differential type of questions presented to them, but on the "Left-wing/Right-wing scale more than one elector in five was too baffled to give any reply at all, a proportion which suggests the difficulty the public has in using these terms." op. cit., p. 206.

10. But, as we shall see below, the subjectively defined class of our respondents was clearly related to the way in which they scored the three parties on ten dimensions. See pp. 109-12.

11. Our 1968 respondents were asked to express an opinion on the importance of a number of issues which were held to have been important in the election. The strongest reaction was to the question of whether Canada should have a majority government. Two thirds of our sample said that this issue was either extremely important (32.6 percent) or very important (33.2 percent). As compared with the 65.8 percent who expressed considerable concern for a majority government, the proportion mentioning the next most frequently cited issue, economic problems, was 57.3 percent; the third most "popular" issue was the place of Quebec in Confederation, referred to by 44.0 percent of the respondents.

12. These are measures (2) and (3) as described on pp. 67-68 above. See also pp. 74-75 above.

13. It should be noted that to avoid rather awkward repetition in phrasing we may occasionally use the word "score" loosely. In virtually all instances when we are not talking about the Ideal Party,

the scores mentioned are not the weighted mean scores but the deviations from the Ideal party's mean scores, or the changes in these deviations, 1965-1968. The meaning can always be told quickly from the context.

14. A word of caution is in order here to prevent too casual a reader from misinterpreting Table VI and the others constructed in a like manner. A quick comparison of the Liberal and NDP listings in the Table might suggest that on the Young—Old scale, for example, men had a better perception of the NDP than of the Liberals: on the Liberal listing in Table VI they are placed in the right-hand ("worse") column, since women assigned the Liberals a better (lower) score. In the NDP section of the Table men are in the left ("better") column, since they scored the NDP more favourably than women. But when actual deviations are taken into account we see that the deviation between the Ideal party and the Liberals was .2, and between the Ideal party and the NDP a less favourable .7. Men saw the Liberal party as younger than the NDP. The placing of each subpopulation in our rows from left to right (from better to worse) refers to their *rank* on the dimension measured *for each given party*.

15. The Tables are not provided here. A later paper will deal with the differences recorded on our ten dimensions by subpopulations exhibiting differences in their political behaviour and attitudes.

16. The suggested classes were Upper, Upper Middle, Middle, Working and Lower.

17. For a suggestive paper see Donald E. Stokes', "Spatial Models of Party Competition", in *Elections and the Political Order*.

THE QUESTIONNAIRE

Example of Semantic Differential Type of Question

NOTE: The question is from the 1968 interview schedule and word pairs
are from the 1965 survey.

29. (TURN TO PAGE TWO ON WHITE SHEETS) Now I have a different kind of question for you.
I'm going to show you some word pairs. Each pair is separated by seven boxes like
this. For example, if you think that the particular political party is very modern,
you would put a check mark in the box on the right end of the scale. If you feel
it is very out-of-date, you would check the box on the left end of the scale.
Or you might rate it somewhere between these two extremes.

80-2

In some cases you may have only a very general idea of how to rate the
party. Even so, we would appreciate having your impression. So please
try to check a square in each line.

-a) First, we'll start with an imaginary political party - the one

you would consider the ideal for Canada.	SEE THAT RESPONDENT CHECKS A SQUARE IN EACH LINE AND COMPLETES EVERY APPLICABLE SHEET

-b) Now let's go on to some of Canada's federal parties.

MAKE SURE THAT RESPONDENT ANSWERS ON PAGES 2, 3, 4 AND 5 OF WHITE SHEETS PLUS PAGES 6 OR 7 WHERE APPLICABLE.	

9-3 (cont'd)

The Ideal Party

Out of date	□ □ □ □ □ □ □	Modern	18-
Competent	□ □ □ □ □ □ □	Incompetent	19-
Powerful	□ □ □ □ □ □ □	Weak	20-
Foolish	□ □ □ □ □ □ □	Wise	21-
For the middle class	□ □ □ □ □ □ □	For the working class	22-
United	□ □ □ □ □ □ □	Split	23-
Bad	□ □ □ □ □ □ □	Good	24-
Left wing	□ □ □ □ □ □ □	Right wing	25-
Strong-minded	□ □ □ □ □ □ □	Weak-minded	26-
Honest	□ □ □ □ □ □ □	Dishonest	27-
Dull	□ □ □ □ □ □ □	Exciting	28-
Young	□ □ □ □ □ □ □	Old	29-
Slow	□ □ □ □ □ □ □	Fast	30-

120

Postscript

In keeping with the normal practice of learned societies, the above paper on Party Images was commented upon at the Canadian Political Science Association's Annual Meeting in 1970 by a number of scholars, some enlisted to do so by the Programme Committee, others speaking from the floor. Among the former, Professor Jean Laponce made some particularly useful comments which led to a re-examination of the most effective way of utilizing the mean. The Laponce comments gave rise to a series of further analyses and considerable recomputation and in the end resulted in our conceptualizing the problem in a manner permitting a highly nuanced and realistic analysis.[1]

The deviation scores upon which the above analysis is based were computed by determining the mean sample (or sub-sample) scores for the Ideal party and the mean sample (or sub-sample) scores of the actual party, and then by calculating the difference between the two means. Thus the difference of means represents the deviation of the actual party score from the mean Ideal party score. This method of computation, as Laponce pointed out, may create difficulties in interpreting the data. Two of these possible difficulties were of particular interest to us: first, our computation leads to cancelling-out of signed discrepancies, that is, it may give the false impression that all respondents always place the actual party on the same side of the Ideal party and so may conceal a certain degree of *ambivalence* in the sample. A hypothetical case provides a dramatic illustration of the point: let us assume that twenty respondents each place the Ideal party at 3 on a seven-point Left-Right scale and that ten of these score the Liberals at

[1]Professor W. P. Irvine has been intimately involved in these and numerous (more ambitious) efforts to develop the most effective means of analyzing our data. I have also benefitted in the recomputations from the help of Grace Skogstad and John Dingwall, but would like to acknowledge particularly the contribution of Professor Irvine whose generosity went far beyond the bounds of even the best colleagial goodwill and of friendship.

TABLE I. Party Images: Percentages with "Minority"
Sign and Standard Deviation of
Total Sample for 1968 Word Pairs

PARTY		LIBERAL		CONSERVATIVE		NDP	
SCALE		Minority %	S.D.	Minority %	S.D.	Minority %	S.D.
	G-B	5	1.8	4	1.9	4	1.9
A	H-D	3	1.6	3	1.7	4	1.6
	E-D	17	1.9	8	2.3	11	2.2
	M-O	15	1.9	7	2.3	10	2.1
B	Y-O	25	1.8	7	2.1	18	2.0
	WC-MC	15	2.2	20	2.3	21	2.4
	L-R	23	1.6	25	1.9	11	2.0
	P-W	17	2.0	6	2.2	4	2.1
C	C-I	6	1.9	6	2.1	5	2.1
	U-S	9	1.9	7	2.3	8	2.2
	CW-UW	5	1.9	5	1.9	8	1.7
D*	GU-BU	4	1.8	4	1.9	4	1.9
	R-N	14	1.7	15	1.7	13	1.8

*Grouping D consists of the three dimensions probed only in 1968 and not in 1965. They are Concern for People's Welfare—Unconcern for People's Welfare (CW-UW), Good for Canadian Unity—Bad for Canadian Unity (GU-BU), and Religious—Non-religious (R-N).

1 and the other ten at 5. Averaging these scores would suggest that the sample actually placed the Liberal party at 3, in exactly the same position as the Ideal party. The mean does not indicate that half of the respondents saw the Liberals considerably more to the left of the Ideal party and the other half greatly more to the right. Second, the mean is a weak indicator of central tendency if there is considerable scatter in the distribution to which it is applied. And this problem exists whether the scatter is on only one side of the party's point on the scale or whether it straddles it. In this sense the mean fails to convey an accurate picture of the *homogeneity* or *heterogeneity* of responses.

These problems notwithstanding, the mean is still an indispensable measure and we therefore set out to refine its use for our purposes. We dealt with the difficulties mentioned above in two ways. We determined how many cases on each of our dimensions (for the total sample as a whole and for each sub-group) fell on the "wrong" side of the Ideal party, in the sense that they comprised a minority of respondents. Secondly, the degree of scatter was ascertained by computing the standard deviations of the distribution of discrepancy scores. These were identified by subtracting each individual's party rating on the various dimensions from his rating of the Ideal party.

The first column under each party in Table I gives the percentage of respondents falling on the "wrong" or "minority" side of the Ideal party and the second column contains the standard deviation; they thus show respectively the degree of ambivalence and heterogeneity.

The deviations from the Ideal party, as revealed by the means can, as the table shows, take four general forms. These can be represented graphically in Diagram I.

A convenient way of evaluating the means of the scores assigned the parties is by placing the various parties and dimensions in one of four quadrants created by the axes resulting from the

DIAGRAM I

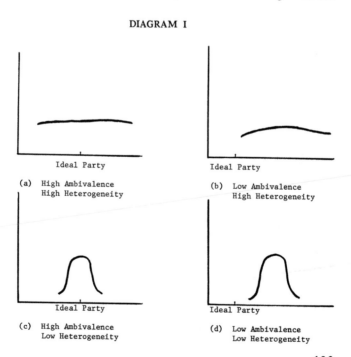

(a) High Ambivalence
High Heterogeneity

(b) Low Ambivalence
High Heterogeneity

(c) High Ambivalence
Low Heterogeneity

(d) Low Ambivalence
Low Heterogeneity

123

ambivalence-heterogeneity typology. By doing this we can see, for example, that on the For the Working Class—For the Middle Class dimension all parties fall into quadrant (a) since a fairly large minority of our sample placed each of them on the other side of the Ideal party than the majority and since the standard deviation was high, revealing considerable scatter. Almost one

DIAGRAM II

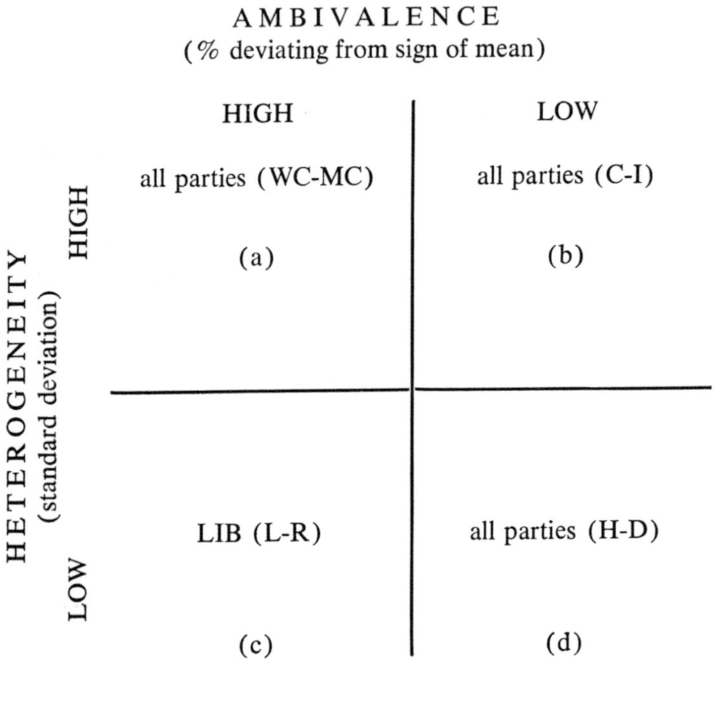

AMBIVALENCE
(% deviating from sign of mean)

	HIGH	LOW
HIGH	all parties (WC-MC) (a)	all parties (C-I) (b)
LOW	LIB (L-R) (c)	all parties (H-D) (d)

HETEROGENEITY
(standard deviation)

quarter of the sample differed from the rest in the sign of their deviations from the Ideal party, when rating the Liberals on the Left Wing—Right Wing scale, but unlike the even slightly more ambivalently judged Conservatives, the respondents clustered much more closely around the mean. The Liberal party can, consequently, be entered into quadrant (c) on the Left—Right measure. For an example of the two other kinds of spatial dispositions permitting an evaluation of the mean, we can turn to the Competent—Incompetent and Honest—Dishonest scales. In the former all parties gave rise to very low ambivalence on the part of our sample but the responses were fairly highly scattered, particularly insofar as the Conservatives and NDP were concerned. Quadrant (b) is thus the most appropriate for this dimension. The Honest—Dishonest ratings fit neatly into Quadrant (d) since both the ambivalence and heterogeneity measures were low.

Jean Laponce's comments apply particularly to cases falling into quadrant (a) and are less relevant to discrepancies in the means we would place elsewhere, particularly, of course, into quadrant (d).

The present scheme of fitting discrepancy scores into one of our quadrants is rather cavalier in its choice of cutting points between High and Low scores. A less arbitrary way, and one which can be applied not only to the total sample but also to each of the sub-groups, is to use the median in dichotomizing between High and Low. In Table I, for instance, the cutting point for the Liberal party between High and Low heterogeneity would thus be 1.9—the median standard deviation for the 39 items in the table.

The two ways examined here of adding to the eloquence of the mean are not equally useful for our theoretical purposes, however. The question of on which side of the Ideal party particular deviation may fall is not nearly as important as that concerning the degree of scatter. The reason for this lies in our assumption about the relationship between the image a voter has of a party and his voting decision. We are primarily interested in the party image because we believe that the closer a party comes to the Ideal party, on the dimensions most salient to the voter, the greater the likelihood that it will receive his vote. It is relatively unimportant, in this context, to know whether the deviation is to the left or the right of the Ideal party—the critical factor is the distance. If, in fact, in the decision-making of voters, closeness is more relevant than sign, then the signed mean is more useful than the absolute mean because in every case the latter must be larger or equal to the former. Knowledge of the degree of dispersal, on the other hand, is always necessary for a fully realistic assessment of an average.

Laponce's apposite queries about the possible dangers in using

125

the mean have led us to try several alternatives. The fact that we have in the end been compelled to conceptualize the problem in terms of "ambivalence" and "heterogeneity" has turned out to have been of considerable benefit since it has led us to recognize that the best use of the mean, particularly when discrepancy scores which may fall on either side of an ideal measure are involved, requires that it be always examined in relation to the quadrants on our axes. The analytical potential of this method of assessing party images and in relating them to the explanation of voting behaviour is extremely high.

This postscript is intended only to illustrate how we have sought to increase the effectiveness of our use of the mean. Data for comparable tables showing the ambivalence and heterogeneity on the part of various sub-groups considered in this paper, and using the 1965 responses have however also been computed and can be obtained upon request.

3

VALUES, LANGUAGE
AND POLITICS
IN CANADA

INTRODUCTION

Language as a Link to Values

THERE IS A WIDESPREAD TENDENCY TO DICHOTOMIZE THE populations of bilingual societies into sharply differentiated linguistic groups.[1] The practice conceals the fact that some citizens occupy a linguistic space between the two major language groups, so to speak, or more precisely, a dimension overlapping both. Canada, for instance, which has provided the empirical data for the present study,[2] is invariably thought of as being populated by anglophones and francophones, but a recent post-election survey shows that at least 14 percent of the electorate cannot be so classified without ambiguity. We shall examine this group of "linguistic misfits" below, as well as the more conventional language types after we have given our reasons for utilizing language as the characteristic identifying a major social cleavage which might, some would say, be equally aptly expressed in ethnic or origin terms. We are concerned with cultural differences which can be identified with language-use but which are usually measured in terms of origin or ethnicity.

A paper presented to the 7th World Congress of Sociology, Varna, Bulgaria. Session on "Social Structure and Political Alignments", September 15, 1970.

Ethnicity is a notoriously elusive concept, if one wishes to pin its meaning down or to operationalize it as an explanatory variable. Being a composite notion, usually comprising origin, language and religious background, it tends to subsume a cluster of characteristics which need to be isolated, particularly in many of the instances in which the idea of ethnic background is related to political perceptions and behaviour.

Origin, one of the components of ethnicity, is slightly less catholic but it also poses serious problems of definition. In many societies, particularly those exhibiting high rates of geographic and social mobility, significant numbers of citizens can boast ancestors collectively belonging to two or more national groups. It is difficult to know, in such cases, which is dominant or relevant. In some societies, there are in fact large numbers of the population who simply do not know their origins. It is not uncommon in Canada, for example, to encounter a paleface possessed of an unmistakably Irish name, speaking only French, who insists that his ancestors came from Canada.[3] The difficulties of defining origin precisely, and other problems associated with "origin" do not, of course, rob the concept of all its uses but they do suggest that alternate ways of defining sub-populations in heterogeneous societies might fruitfully be explored.

Language use, while not without its own problems, as we shall see, as an indicator of social cleavage and cultural differences, is one of the variables which can usefully be invoked to supplement or in some cases to replace, concepts such as ethnicity or origin in explaining social and political behaviour.

All of the above is so obvious that to mention it is almost in poor taste, even when it is done in as cursory a fashion as here. It would, in fact, be totally out of place were it it not that the points sketched above are ignored by so much of the literature on social and political cleavage and political alignments, as well as by many important general comparative studies.[4]

Two major problems confront the attempt to approach ethnic cleavage through the means of identifying the groups concerned according to the language they speak. One of these arises from the point made at the outset of this paper: the question of how linguistic groups and sub-groups are to be defined. The other relates to the nature and meaning of linguistic differences: what is it that is really represented by language use?

The second problem will detain us only briefly, not because it is unimportant but because it is much too vast to be considered here. We shall have to be satisfied with simply noting that language is a vessel which does affect its cargo. Ideas and modes of thought reflect the language in which they are formed and expressed, and vice versa. In the present context this aspect will simply be taken for granted without its nuances being explored.[5]

Language is viewed in this paper as an indicator of the degree to which various groups of Canadians are linked to the two cultures or societies comprising the country. I am using these terms in the manner defined by the Royal Commission on Bilingualism and Biculturalism, which understood by culture "a way of being, thinking, and feeling . . . a driving force animating a significant group of individuals united by a common tongue, and sharing the same customs, habits, and experiences." The Commission saw "the two dominant cultures in Canada . . . embodied in distinct societies," designating by society "the types of organization and the institutions that a rather large population, inspired by a common culture, has created for itself or has received, and which it freely manages over quite a vast territory, where it lives as a homogeneous group according to common standards and rules of conduct."[6]

Despite the fact that Canada, unlike the United States, has never espoused an aggressive "melting pot" policy with respect to its ethnic minorities, the presence of the two official languages has meant that a large proportion of the country's citizens whose origin is neither French nor English has become part of one or the other of the linguistic societies. As a result, about one quarter of those whose mother tongue is English are "immigrants" to that language, in the sense that they or their ancestors switched to it from another tongue. This applies even to those whose origin is French, since only about nine out of every ten Canadians of French origin claims French as his mother tongue. The drift *to* French is much less pronounced than to English.

The use of language as the indicator of social cleavage therefore obviously conceals the origin of many of the citizens. It is nevertheless useful since language-use tells us a good deal about the individual's day-to-day exposure to one or the other

(In percentages - N in brackets)

	Pure English	Partial English	Mixed	Partial French	Pure French	
	A	B	C	D	E	TOTAL
Total Sample	(1799)	(135)	(143)	(118)	(572)	(2767)
	65	5	5	4	21	100
ORIGIN						
British	66	18	4	4	5	(1206)
French	4	13	14	63	70	(511)
Germany, Austria	7	11	9	2	1	(160)
Italy	1	4	16	2	–	(50)
Other West European	7	15	13	6	2	(182)
Russian, Ukrainian	4	15	19	1	–	(124)
Other East European	4	15	15	1	–	(106)
Canada, U. S. A.	2	2	3	20	19	(148)
British and French	1	2	4	–	1	(38)
British plus any other	3	2	–	–	–	(62)
French plus any other	–	–	–	2	1	(16)
Other	1	4	4	–	–	(22)
	100	101	101	101	99	
Total	(1755)	(130)	(141)	(106)	(493)	(2625)
RELIGION						
Roman Catholic	19	46	62	98	100	(1153)
Other	81	54	38	2	–	(1518)
	100	100	100	100	100	
Total	(1723)	(128)	(136)	(118)	(566)	(2671)
EDUCATION						
Up to 8 years	26	34	56	43	57	(960)
9 to 13 years	60	55	33	38	32	(1406)
14 years or more	15	11	12	19	11	(374)
	101	100	101	100	100	
Total	(1791)	(131)	(138)	(116)	(564)	(2740)
AGE						
21-30	22	19	8	29	29	(639)
31-50	44	42	50	44	38	(1183)
51 and over	34	39	42	27	34	(945)
	100	100	100	100	101	
Total	(1799)	(135)	(143)	(118)	(572)	(2767)
SEX						
Male	50	64	52	59	45	(1388)
Female	50	36	48	41	55	(1379)
	100	100	100	100	100	
Total	(1799)	(135)	(143)	(118)	(572)	(2767)

of the cultures and to its values. It is thus assumed here that the English-speaking Canadian will reflect the values of the dominant, i.e. English, society and that the francophone will hold values of the minority society.[7]

But how to measure the degree of language exposure, given the fact that, as was suggested above, significant numbers of Canadians are not clear-cut French- or English-speakers?

Mother tongue is usually considered a reliable indicator of the linguistic character of populations but it has severe limitations because it "freezes" language-use in one moment of time

130

TABLE I (cont'd.)

	Pure English	Partial English	Mixed	Partial French	Pure French	
	A	B	C	D	E	TOTAL
OCCUPATION OF HEAD OF HOUSEHOLD						
Professional, Owner, Manager	21	21	13	21	18	(467)
Sales and Clerical	18	9	15	20	14	(390)
Skilled labour	37	42	44	40	39	(899)
Unskilled labour	14	16	23	13	20	(369)
Farmers	11	12	6	7	9	(231)
	101	100	100	101	100	
Total	(1549)	(118)	(120)	(102)	(467)	(2356)
LANGUAGE SPOKEN AT HOME						
English	100	70	8	3	–	(1907)
French	–	9	13	96	100	(716)
Other	–	22	79	2	–	(144)
	100	101	100	101	100	
Total	(1799)	(135)	(143)	(118)	(572)	(2767)
LANGUAGE SPOKEN AT WORK						
English	83	82	38	41	–	(1696)
French	–	6	9	32	73	(479)
Other	–	–	24	7	–	(42)
No answer*	18	13	30	20	27	(550)
	101	101	101	100	100	
Total	(1799)	(135)	(143)	(118)	(572)	(2767)
LANGUAGE SPOKEN WITH FRIENDS						
English	100	36	8	25	–	(1890)
French	–	12	1	52	100	(650)
Other	–	52	90	23	–	(227)
	100	100	99	100	100	
Total	(1799)	(135)	(143)	(118)	(572)	(2767)
LENGTH OF DOMICILE IN CANADA						
Born in Canada	82	53	34	96	99	(2264)
Arrived in 1945 or before	10	22	20	3	1	(236)
Arrived in 1946 or after	9	25	47	2	1	(263)
	101	100	101	101	101	
Total	(1797)	(135)	(143)	(118)	(570)	(2763)

*This group consists largely of housewives but it also includes some retired people. The language of work was recoded, for the purposes of this paper, so as to correspond to the language spoken at home.

and in relation to only one sphere of activity. In highly mobile societies in which political perceptions may vary considerably with the age of citizens this criterion thus leaves much to be desired: it neither takes into account the distance between the individual's original and actual languages, nor does it reflect the possibility that a person may regularly speak more than one language and thus maintain active links with two or more cultural groups.

A more revealing means of identifying the linguistic characteristics of sub-populations in heterogeneous societies is to discriminate between the areas of activity with which certain languages are associated and/or to take into account also the statuses of the individuals communicating with one another in one of several possible tongues.[8]

The Language Scale

In the present study, each respondent in the national survey was placed on a five-point language scale depending on the number of levels on which he spoke English, French or another language. Each of the 2767 persons interviewed was asked what language he or she spoke at home, at work and among friends.[9] Those who spoke French or English at all *three* levels were classed as "pure" English- or French-speakers; respondents speaking either of the major languages at any *two* of the three levels were identified as "partial" anglophones or francophones and those who spoke French and/or English at only *one*, or *no* level were placed in the middle as the linguistically "mixed" members of our sample. The following language continuum was, therefore established: pure English—partial English—mixed—partial French—pure French.

Table I summarizes some of the more relevant attributes of each of the five linguistic groups.

The reader interested in a complete and thorough profile of our five language groups could profitably spend a good deal of time tracing the similarities and differences among them, as encapsuled in the table. I shall merely draw attention to some of the most important or potentially misleading aspects.

In dealing with the section on origin, we see that two thirds of the pure anglophones, or their forefathers, come from the British Isles. The remaining third is drawn in relatively small numbers from a variety of countries, virtually all of them in western and eastern Europe. The partial English and mixed groups are a veritable Noah's Ark, if one imagines that ship to be populated by European specimens of homo sapiens, rather than animals originating throughout the world. The relatively low (70 percent) proportion of people whose origin is French, among the pure francophones, is misleading since, in addition, virtually all of the 19 per cent in this group who indicated that their ancestors came from Canada are of French origin. I estimate that only about 6 or 7 percent of the pure French are non-French in origin. Our partially francophone group is also almost completely French. This section of the table reveals an important feature of Canada's linguistic pattern—one, by the way, which greatly alarms those concerned with the survival of the French language—namely the inexorable mobility of an overwhelming proportion of all immigrants to the English language and through it into the anglophone society.

Only one, of the 566 full francophones for whom we know his religion, was not a Catholic! More surprisingly, even among the partial French-speakers, only two (2 percent) of the respondents declared their religion as being something other than Catholic. This sheds a suggestive light on the degree to which Protestants fail to become integrated, even partially, into Canada's francophone society. At any rate, the concentration of Catholics on the French side of the language continuum must be borne in mind when interpreting our data: it will be necessary to guard against ascribing to factors associated with language-use, attitudes possibly related more to the religious background of the groups concerned.

Another possible misreading of our data might follow from the failure to realize that there are significant differences in the educational experiences of our five language groups. The relevant part of Table I indicates a striking disparity in the proportion of those with only eight years or less of schooling between the pure anglophones on the one hand and the francophones and mixed group on the other. The difference between the partial French- and English-speakers is also great. The pure French-speakers and the mixed group have had the fewest number of years in school; they are followed by the two linguistically partial groups and finally by the pure anglophones whose educational opportunities were considerably better than anyone else's.

The two francophone groups are somewhat younger than the pure and partial English-speakers but it is the mixed group which stands out in the age portion of the table. They are the oldest group by far, comprising only 8 percent under thirty years of age and over 40 percent of members who have passed a half-century of life.

Little need be said about the occupational background of our five groups—it essentially reflects what we have observed about

133

their educational history, except that the occupational table suggests that in terms of jobs, at least, the inequality between French and English has been softened somewhat, although not eradicated.

A distinct disproportion between men and women exists among our two partial groups, largely, I suspect, because of the device, mentioned elsewhere in this paper, of recording the language at work of housewives to correspond in all instances to their language spoken at home. This may incorrectly have taken some partial French- and English-speaking women into the "pure" columns. This was thought to have been a necessary but the least distorting step, since it left the partial groups uncontaminated and, given the large numbers to be found in the "pure" groups, was unlikely to distort the reporting of their answers.

It is this group of housewives (which also includes widows and unemployed spinsters) which is identified in the "Language Spoken at Work" section of the table as 550 individuals giving no answer. They were originally coded as such but, as indicated, the "language at work" item was recoded for purposes of creating our language scale.

From the final section of the table we learn that the two francophone groups are by far the most indigenous Canadians and that only about a third of the mixed group was born in Canada. Almost half of these least English- and/or French-users immigrated since the end of the Second World War. A quarter of the partially English-speaking group found their way to Canada in this period, and a little over one fifth did so before 1945.

Having described the five language groups, we can at last explore the relationships we expect to find between position on the language continuum on the one hand, and political perceptions and alignments on the other.

Hypotheses: Language-use and Areas of Perception

If language use is a link to the values of cultural groups, we will expect the pure French- and the pure English-users to come closest to embodying "in the purest form" the values respectively of the majority and minority cultures in Canada. It is well-known, for example, that the Liberal party has in recent years received considerably more support from French Canadians and that Conservative allegiance was more strongly rooted among

134

voters of British origin. We therefore expect Liberal support to be substantially greater among our pure French- than among the pure English-speakers. This, as we shall see, is in fact the case and it will surprise no one.

But to understand the anatomy of political alignments it is necessary to look beyond mere partisanship and to examine a wide range of perceptions and evaluations of the electorate. Social cleavages find expression in differential responses to phenomena which range from the most private, moral sphere to the large political issues confronting society. It is therefore assumed in this paper that differences between the pure English- and French-speaking respondents will not be spread uniformly but that the two cultural groups will be fairly close to one another in some areas and that in others the distance between them will be considerable. Specifically, it is anticipated that we shall find the gap widest in areas which are the subject of controversy between them (the status of Quebec in Canada, attitudes to the Monarchy, liking of General de Gaulle); that a narrower but nevertheless clear-cut margin will be found in fields where the religious and moral values of the electors come into play (religiosity, attitudes to homosexuality, divorce, etc.); and that there will be relatively little or no difference with respect to reactions towards general public policy issues and concerns, like foreign policy questions, American influences on Canada, or the liking of L. B. Pearson.

What of the partial users of Canada's official languages? The predominantly English-speaking group can safely be hypothesized as approximating the perceptions and affects of the pure English, although I expect them in some instances to be somewhat closer to our linguistically "mixed" group, occupying the middle of the language scale. The partial English-users are, as Table I shows, individuals of diverse origins who, while generally speaking English, have retained a vestigial language which links them to the values of one of Canada's many ethnic minorities. Their political perceptions and values are therefore likely to be very close to the political culture of the English-speaking majority except that in some areas—those in which the interests of their own ethnic group may be particularly affected, for example— they may find themselves closer to our mid-point, linguistically (and therefore ethnically) least British or French category. A small proportion of them is, of course, of French descent.

The partial French group in some ways constitutes our most interesting case. Forty percent speak English at work and we are here confronting members of a large ethnic minority who are earning their living in the language of the country's dominant culture. While some of them may like this, it is a reasonable assumption that they have little choice in the matter and that many of them are simply responding as effectively as they can to the economic realities of Canada. In any event, this group, while French, maintains a continuous and probably highly meaningful link with the dominant cultural group and its values. It is possible to make two completely contradictory assumptions about the consequences of this exposure to the English-speaking world: (1) Partial submersion in the anglophone community exercises a powerful socializing effect, and the politically relevant perceptions of our partial French group will therefore approximate those of the pure English; they will at least be closer to them than to those of the pure French. (2) Constant exposure of the partially French-speakers to the dominant anglophone culture acts as an irritant by emphasizing the minority and, generally less privileged position of people of French Canada in many sectors of Canadian life. This situation thus induces in the partially French group a resentment of the dominant culture and a consequent strongly national posture towards the issues and themes of Canadian politics. The partial French will consequently be placed at least as far from the pure English as the pure French, and possibly even farther away.

It is possible to resolve, or at least blunt, the paradox posed by these two hypotheses by recalling one of our earlier expectations: the distance between linguistic groups is likely to vary depending on the area of life and politics concerned. We will thus expect the partially French to differ most from the pure and partial English-users in their perceptions of, and affects towards, items closely related to the tensions between French and English Canada but to approximate the positions of the English-speaking groups closely in matters in which the general Canadian or even American political cultures are likely to exercise a strong "ethnically neutral" influence on the individuals exposed to them.

At the risk both of dwelling on the obvious and of adding further to the complexity of our story, we must note that differential perceptions are inevitably to be observed among linguistic groups not only in relation to different phenomena but also *within* the membership of any given cluster of language users. In the present context, for example, I expect that among the partially French-speakers, the best educated, and also the youngest members are most likely to be the most nationalist, and that on questions closely relevant to the ethnic concerns of French Canada they will therefore be found at a greater distance from the anglophones than the less well-educated and the older members of their linguistic group. The same should hold for the pure French-speakers, but a little less so.

Mixed language users—the group whose members speak English and/or French at only one or none of the three levels we have used in constructing our scale—are presumably less closely identified with either the French- or English-speakers than the partial groups and their political perceptions are therefore likely to differ from either. It is to be expected, however, that this linguistically least anglicized and/or frenchified group is nevertheless likely to be socialized most by the numerically and economically dominant group in Canada—the English-speakers. Since the partial English group is very similar in the heterogeneity of its ethnic composition to the mixed group, I expect the responses of the latter to be closer to the partial than to the pure English. In spheres where the particular cultural traditions of members of the mixed group might evoke a unique response, however—respect for political leaders, for example—I expect the response of our middle group to deviate widely from the norm set by the English-users and also from those of the francophones.

A rather crude diagram can be constructed summarizing the above hypotheses concerning the relationships we expect to find between the language-use of various groups and their political perceptions. I have arbitrarily chosen to represent the position of the culturally dominant pure English-speakers as the norm against which the position of the other groups is measured. In so doing I have not tried to suggest that this position should in any way be considered as a basic norm—it would have served our purposes equally well to have chosen the pure French as our baseline, except, of course, that we expect most of the other groups to approximate them less than they do the pure anglophones.

DIAGRAM I

LANGUAGE-USE AND PERCEPTIONS OF PHENOMENA RELEVANT TO POLITICAL ALIGNMENTS

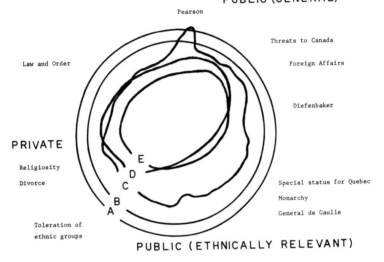

PUBLIC (GENERAL)

Pearson

Threats to Canada

Foreign Affairs

Law and Order

Diefenbaker

PRIVATE

Religiosity

Divorce

Special status for Quebec

Monarchy

General de Gaulle

Toleration of
ethnic groups

PUBLIC (ETHNICALLY RELEVANT)

A = PURE ENGLISH
B = PARTIAL ENGLISH
C = MIXED
D = PARTIAL FRENCH
E = PURE FRENCH

In the diagram the expected distance between the language groups is roughed in by means of five circles, or circular lines, which move from "Private" to "General Public" and to "Ethnically Relevant Public" areas in which the language groups perceive, and react towards, phenomena which have some relevance to their political alignments. The pure (A) and partial (B) English-speakers are represented by concentric circles in close propinquity and the middle, mixed group (C) is also nearby, somewhat less regular because of the expected influences of special "ethnic" factors. Our pure francophones (E) are most distant from the A group on political questions affecting French-English relations in Canada; they approach the anglophones somewhat in matters of private morality and come even closer to them in their perceptions and evaluations of questions of general public policy. Finally, the partial French (D) are shown as being the most distant group from the English-users in areas affecting French-English relations but they are closer to the dominant cultural group in the private values sector and also in that of general public policy.

In testing our hypotheses we shall examine each of the three areas in turn, beginning with Private Values defined quite narrowly.[10] We shall then cast a glance at some Private Values which, however, are more closely related to the General Public Policy and finally we shall consider Private Values touching on problems of Ethnic Relations in Canada. Then we shall look at the General Public Sector and finally at the Ethnically Relevant Public Sector. Throughout we shall draw freely on various questions from the 1968 post-election Canadian survey. Since this is very much an exploratory exercise, we shall select those questions or indices which are particularly useful in testing our hypotheses focusing on examples which either strongly support or question the expectations we described above. This loose method provides an admirable means of roaming freely among the available data and of seeking illuminating examples of the points raised and of finding instances confirming or challenging our expectations. It does not, however, lead to the immediate drafting of a formal theory permitting sure predictions about the relation between social structure (or its linguistic and cultural aspects) and political alignments. This may come later; the present paper is, at best, a small and halting step towards such a formalization. Its more general use will be touched upon in the conclusion.

PRIVATE VALUES

Religiosity

Our first "test" concerns the religiosity of the members of the five language groups. "Religiosity" is here conceived as being related both to the individual's exercise of religious practices and to the more social and societal aspects of religion.[11] As the enclosed chart shows, the mean scores obtained by the five language groups rise in an orderly fashion from a low of 5.3 for the pure English-users, to a high of 8.8 attained by the pure francophones. The difference between the two extreme poles is substantial. Both groups of partial users display mean scores which are less extreme than their "purer" neighbours. The distance is particularly noticeable between the partial and pure French. The linguistically mixed respondents' score places them between the anglophones and the francophones, somewhat closer to the former than to the latter.

Education, as the row of figures at the bottom of Chart I shows, has some influence on the religiosity scores within some of the language groups, particularly among the two partial users and the pure French: in each of these three cases the least educated displayed the highest degree of religiosity and the best educated the lowest. Educational background had little effect on the religiosity scores of groups A and C. But the chart makes it clear that language-use washes out the educational influence: the scores of the sub-groups corresponding to educational experience rises as we move from language group A to language group E.

The age of our respondents has had less effect even than education in offsetting the influences represented by language use. The oldest cohort, as indicated by the top row in the chart, registered a marginally higher religiosity score than its language group's overall mean in all cases but that of the pure English users and of the partial French but that is about the only relation of age to religiosity worth noting, except, of course, that language-use is an incomparably more relevant variable. In view of some observations to be made later about the middle-aged group among the partial French-speakers, we should, however, note this cohort's relatively low religiosity score among the two francophone groups.

Studies of the attitudes of Protestants and Catholics towards various aspects of religion lead us to expect "Catholic" religiosity scores to be consistently higher than those of the others.[12] As the insets in the five circles in Chart I show, this was in fact the case. The mean score of the pure Anglophone Catholics (left inset) was 6.3, that of the non-Catholics (right inset)

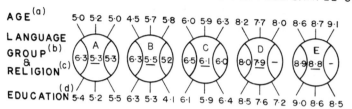

CHART I RELIGIOSITY*

(RANGE : 0-11, MEAN SCORE FOR FULL SAMPLE 6·2)

AGE (a) 5·0 5·2 5·0 4·5 5·7 5·8 6·0 5·9 6·3 8·2 7·7 8·0 8·6 8·7 9·1

LANGUAGE
GROUP (b)
&
RELIGION (c)

A 6·3 5·3 5·3   B 6·3 5·5 5·2   C 6·5 6·1 6·0   D 8·0 7·9 —   E 8·9 8·8 —

EDUCATION (d) 5·4 5·2 5·5 6·3 5·3 4·1 6·1 5·9 6·4 8·5 7·6 7·2 9·0 8·6 8·5

*NOTES

Each of the balls shows the means as follows:

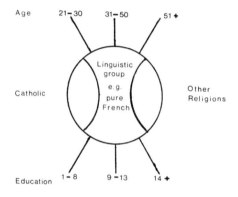

(a) *Age* The three categories for each of the language groups correspond to those in Table I. The score of the 21 to 30 year group is on the left, that of the 31 to 50 cohort in the middle and of the 51 and over group on the right.

(b) *Language* Group Pure English A; Partial English B; Mixed C; Partial French D; Pure French E. The score is underlined.

(c) *Religion* The score of the Catholics is in the left inset, that of all others in the right inset. The sample was divided into only two groups: Catholics and all others. The mean score of each of the language groups does not always correspond to that computed for the whole sample because 96 cases, whose religious affiliation is not known, had to be excluded. This explains the differences in the mean scores of Catholics and of the whole language group in D and E.

(d) *Education* The scores of those who have had up to eight years of schooling are at the left, those with 9 to 13 years of schooling in the middle, and of those with 14 years or more on the right.

5.3. The comparable figures for the partially English is 6.3 and 5.2; for the mixed group 6.5 and 6.0. There are not enough non-Catholics among the francophones to provide comparable data but the scores for the Catholics in groups D and E are significantly higher than those of the English-speaking Catholics. We see, therefore, that even when religion is held constant, the Francophone members of our sample displayed a substantially higher degree of religiosity than the anglophones and than the mixed group.

Moral Values

Very similar results obtain when we examine the reactions of our five language groups to homosexuality and divorce.[13] In both instances the two anglophone groups are more liberal (indicated by a higher score in Chart II(a) and a lower mean in Chart II(b) and the distances separating the English from the French groups are substantial. The partial francophones are slightly closer to the position of the anglophones than the pure French-speakers; the partial English have the same mean score as the pure English with respect to the treatment of homosexuals and are slightly closer to the francophones than the A group in their attitude towards divorce.

CHART II MORAL VALUES*

(a) TREATMENT OF HOMOSEXUALS (3·3)

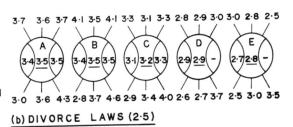

(b) DIVORCE LAWS (2·5)

142

With only minor exceptions (notably the D group's assessment of divorce laws) education is positively correlated with a liberal stand but position on the language-use continuum exerts an even stronger influence than education in enabling us to predict the attitude of our respondents to homosexuality and divorce. With respect to divorce, the mean scores of those with the lowest number of years of schooling are very close to one another in all but the pure French-speaking group. The pure English and partial French, for example, share a reading of 2.6. The differences between the language groups on the moral values dimension are generally greater among the best educated than among the other two educational categories.

No significant relationships between age and moral values are revealed in Chart II. We should, however, again note that among the partial francophones, the middle-aged group appears to be slightly more liberal than the youngest group; this pattern is not found among the pure French, however.

The difference between Catholics and non-Catholics in our total sample is greater with respect to their attitudes to homosexuals than to divorce. In the former case, the mean scores are 2.9 for the Catholics as compared with 3.5 for the others. The comparable mean scores of their attitudes to changes in the divorce laws are 2.8 and 2.3. The difference in attitudes to homosexuals must, as section (a) of Chart II shows, be ascribed almost entirely to the presence in our universe of French-speaking Catholics, since the scores for their English-speaking, and linguistically mixed coreligionists diverge only very little from those of the other religious groups, when these are lumped into one category. There is a slightly greater Catholic—non-Catholic split with respect to divorce, but even here it is small, and among the non-French groups, confined to the pure anglophones. The scores for the partial French and English Catholics are, interestingly, the same.

A comparable examination of attitudes toward the abolition of the death penalty (chart omitted) indicated that while there clearly is a difference between the five language groups, it is smaller than in the two instances discussed above. The partial French-speaking group is marginally the most liberal and the middle-aged members of the two francophone groups are, again, more liberal than the youngest group.

Our hypotheses with respect to Private Values are confirmed, when these are related rather narrowly to religiosity and attitudes on societal reactions to divorce, homosexuality and capital punishment; a substantial difference is to be observed between pure anglophones and pure francophones; members of the partial groups differ slightly from their linguistically "purer" brethren by placing themselves closer to the other language pole. The mean scores of the mixed, centrally located linguistic sub-population generally fall between the francophones and the anglophones, in somewhat greater proximity to the latter. We shall now try to discover whether we can make the same observations about moral valuations which are more directly related to questions of public policy.

Law and Order

We have selected the issue of law and order as one of our test cases and shall take two sets of snapshots, so to speak, of it: on the one hand we shall see how the language groups reacted to a number of questions in which the breaking of laws under certain stated conditions can be condemned or condoned. Some of these refer to areas of life closely relevant to the interests of the language groups. On the other hand we have obtained assessments from our respondents of the importance of, and their liking for, a number of offices and agencies concerned with maintaining law and order.

Anglophones are revealed by our index to have a distinctly higher regard for law and order than francophones.[14] The scores are as follows:

Group A	Group B	Group C	Group D	Group E
6.9	6.7	6.4	6.1	5.4

Once again the partial users of each of the two main languages are placed close to the pure users but in this instance the partial francophones are quite a long way towards the anglophone pole and are, in fact, closer to the partial English-users than to the pure French. The mixed group continues to stand between the English- and French-users, somewhat closer to the former than to the latter. It is surprising, in view of the ethnically highly relevant component of the index (the second question listed in footnote 14) that the difference between the pure language groups is not greater.

A less direct means of exploring attitudes towards law and order yields more muted results. Our respondents were asked to indicate how much they *liked* certain groups and how *important* they thought certain public offices to be. The police and the military were included among both the groups and the offices; Judges and the Supreme Court were added to the latter category.[15] While this is a clumsy and perilous way of going about our business it was judged a useful exercise for the purposes at hand.

Chart III tells us that the differences between the language groups are so small as to be meaningless. The results are in fact pointing in opposite directions: the police are rated more highly by the anglophones than by the francophones, whereas the military receive a slightly higher score from the pure French than from the pure English. This suggests that the items used are not valid indicators of attitudes to law and order but, as we shall see, they display acceptable consistency when used to assess the *importance* our respondents attach to offices concerned with maintaining law and order.

CHART III-LIKING OF POLICEMEN AND THE MILITARY*

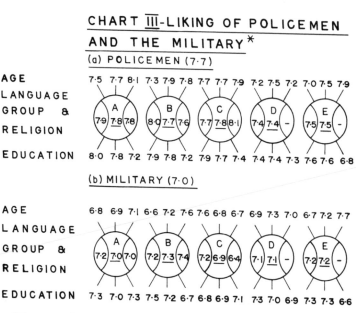

(a) POLICEMEN (7·7)

AGE	7·5	7·7	8·1	7·3	7·9	7·8	7·7	7·7	7·9	7·2	7·5	7·2	7·0	7·5	7·9
LANGUAGE															
GROUP &		A			B			C			D			E	
RELIGION	7·9	7·8	7·8	8·0	7·7	7·6	7·7	7·8	8·1	7·4	7·4	−	7·5	7·5	−
EDUCATION	8·0	7·8	7·2	7·9	7·8	7·2	7·9	7·7	7·4	7·4	7·4	7·3	7·6	7·6	6·8

(b) MILITARY (7·0)

AGE	6·8	6·9	7·1	6·6	7·2	7·6	7·6	6·8	6·7	6·9	7·3	7·0	6·7	7·2	7·7
LANGUAGE															
GROUP &		A			B			C			D			E	
RELIGION	7·2	7·0	7·0	7·2	7·3	7·4	7·2	6·9	6·4	7·1	7·1	−	7·2	7·2	−
EDUCATION	7·3	7·0	7·3	7·5	7·2	6·7	6·8	6·9	7·1	7·3	7·0	6·9	7·3	7·3	6·6

*For an explanation of the chart see Notes to Chart I.

145

The data summarized in Chart III do, nevertheless, reveal some interesting differences between our language groups. The most highly educated among the pure and partial French rate both the police and the military least favourably. With respect to age we find that in all cases except the scores of the mixed group, and interestingly, the partial French-speakers' rating of the policemen, the youngest cohort like the agents of law and order less than their seniors.

No pattern emerges when the relationship is examined between religion and language-use in the assessment of policemen; Catholics in all but one language group rate the military at 7.2. This might suggest that religion is more related to feelings towards the military than linguistic ties but the margins between the groups are so small (except in C), and the direction of the differences so inconsistent as to preclude our making any generalizations in this respect. Although we have avoided reporting on occupational differences (they were found to be generally uninteresting) it should be noted as a curiosity that whereas all other occupational groups among the pure French-users scored the police at 7.4 or 7.5, pure francophone farmers were able to muster only a mere 6.9.

It is reasonable to assume that one's attitude to law and order is related to the importance one assigns the institutions society has established to maintain them. Before turning to Chart IV, which tabulates the data, it is useful to note that francophones and anglophones ranked the agents of law and order differently, relative to the other offices about which they were questioned. All our groups thought the police to be the most important among the four law enforcement agencies but whereas both the anglophone and the mixed groups assigned them second place, immediately after that of the prime minister, the two francophone groups placed them fourth, below the provincial premiers and the federal members of Parliament. This pattern is reinforced by each of the four sections in the chart which also show that a real, although not pronounced, difference between our language groups exists in the importance they attach to the law enforcing offices and that the scores are higher among the anglophones.

The partial anglophones rate the four offices slightly more highly than the other groups; they are followed by the pure anglophones, the mixed, the partial French and finally by the pure French-users. The difference between the "neighbouring" language groups are small but consistent.

As previously, the most educated subgroups among the francophones rate the law enforcers lowest with two interesting exceptions: the educational background had no visible effect on the scores received by the judges and the Supreme Court from the pure French-users. Language-use is generally related to the scores more closely than education except in one instance

CHART IV IMPORTANCE ATTACHED TO LAW AND ORDER AGENCIES*

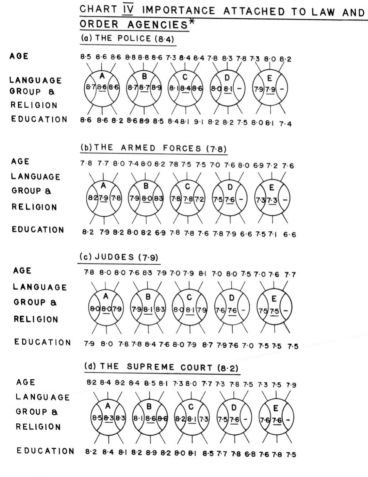

*For an explanation of the chart see Notes to Chart I.

in which the rating obtained by the armed forces from the most highly educated among the partial English-users was uncharacteristically low.[16]

The youngest cohort tends generally to rate the four offices lower than the older groups and with respect to judges and the Court respectively, displayed complete constancy in the case of both French-speaking and the mixed groups. In these cases the differences in mean scores between the language groups must be ascribed to the older generations.

Catholics among the pure anglophones and the mixed group have a slightly higher opinion of the importance of the four offices than non-Catholics but the situation is reversed among the partial English-users. The scores of the Catholics generally drop as they move from the pure English to the French poles of the continuum but this is not so in the case of the other religious groups. The higher regard for law and order among the partially English-speaking population than among the pure anglophones is in fact attributable to the higher scores received by the four offices from the non-Catholic members of the sample.

If the public's reaction to law and order, as identified above, is viewed as an extension of its private values towards some more general community values, then we can conclude tentatively that some of our hypotheses stated earlier are confirmed, while others appear less acceptable. Taking the various readings of attitudes together we find that the anglophones place law and order more highly in the scheme of things than francophones but that the difference between the linguistic groups in this area is smaller than was the case when we were considering Private Values in a narrower sense. The position occupied on the law and order index by the partial French-users—closer to the partial anglophones than to the pure French—suggests, however, that our expectation may have to be revised that in matters touching on ethnic interests the partial French would differ from the anglophone majority *more* than the pure francophones. This is a matter to which we shall return later.

The two English-speaking groups are again close together but the partial anglophones are by no means always nearer to the centre of our language continuum, as expected. The mixed group occupies its customary place between the two extremes, somewhat closer to the English pole.

The response to our probing into the degree to which law and order agents are liked casts doubt on our hypothesis that the best educated partial francophones are likely to resemble the anglophones even less than the pure francophones. We saw that the best educated among the last-named group scored the police and military much lower than the less well educated but that this was not the case among the partial French-users. The data also indicate that while generally the youngest group displayed the least affection for the officers of law and order, the mixed group and, more surprisingly, the partial francophones, failed to conform to this pattern.

We saw no reason, when formulating our hypotheses, to expect the partial anglophones to adopt "extreme" positions, in the sense of being more distant from the francophones than even the pure English-speakers. It was therefore surprising to find that they did attach more importance than their pure co-linguists to all four of our law and order offices. On the other hand, the expected behaviour of the best educated francophones and of the youngest cohort was encountered in the answers to our question about the importance of the four law and order offices, except with respect to the failure of the best educated pure French to rate the judges and Supreme Court lower than the less well educated members of their group.

Ethnic and Religious Toleration

One area in which the Private Values of individuals impinge on ethnically relevant issues in a heterogeneous society concerns how they affect their attitudes to other groups. We shall concentrate on how those belonging to our five language categories like a number of groups of different origins and religions. We shall then probe generally into the degree to which each would like to see Canada display ethnic and religious heterogeneity.[17]

Table II indicates that there are some interesting similarities, as well as differences, between the five language groups. The scores received by Americans and negroes, for example, do not vary noticeably insofar as the francophones and anglophones are concerned but, in the case of the Americans, show a perceptible difference between pure and partial language users. Differences between language groups are greater with respect to "known" or "near" groups than with the more "remote" ones

149

TABLE II: LIKING OF SELECTED GROUPS*

Selected Groups	Language Group				
	A	B	C	D	E
English Canadians	7.5	7.6	7.3	7.6	6.8
French Canadians	6.2	6.6	7.0	8.6	8.9
"Other" Canadians	6.8	7.2	7.4	6.4	6.0
Americans	6.8	7.1	6.9	7.2	6.6
Negroes	6.6	6.6	6.4	6.9	6.8
Jews	6.3	6.4	6.0	6.1	5.5
Protestants	7.5	7.2	6.6	6.9	5.9
Catholics	6.9	7.5	7.4	8.0	8.4

*For an explanation of the scores see note 15. Pure anglophones A; Partial anglophones B; Mixed C; Partial francophones D; Pure francophones E.

like negroes or Americans. For members of the "other" ethnic groups and Jews, the pure francophones report lower scores than the pure English, and the margin, while not very wide, does reveal a meaningful difference in affect. It is likely that the French-English difference in the rating of some groups and not of others is related to the proximity of the respective groups and, in some measure, to the degree to which they may be viewed as potential competitors. Americans and negroes are more remote and therefore appear less of a threat to the francophones who are likely to be particularly sensitive to the competition in the Canadian economy provided by minority groups of whose presence in Canada they are aware.

As in virtually all other cases we have examined, the partial French-users usually respond more like the English-users than the pure French and in most cases by a fairly considerable margin. Surprisingly, among the English-speaking groups the partial anglophones tend to record the higher scores.

When English- and French-speaking Canadians indicate how much they like one another, we find that the latter group is somewhat more generous: our pure anglophones give the French Canadians a score of 6.2 but the pure francophones rate English Canadians at 6.8. The partial French-users surprisingly join the partial anglophones, in assigning the highest score to English Canadians. Both francophone groups like English Canadians better than compatriots who are neither

English nor French, but the anglophones scored the latter group higher than they did French Canadians.

Although the anglophones may be less tolerant of French Canadians than vice versa, they seem to offer a somewhat more generous score than the francophones on the religious dimension (table omitted). We have already noted their higher score for Jews; when religion is held constant, we find that English-speaking protestants rate Catholics at 6.6 whereas the pure French group, which is entirely Catholic, assign the protestants a mere 5.9, as Table II shows.

While the above glimpse of the way in which the language users like or dislike various groups confirms our general hypothesis that exposure to the values of the other culture through the use of language narrows the gap between Canada's two value systems, it also presents a somewhat confused picture of the differences in their tolerance of minorities between French- and English-speaking Canadians, assuming, of course, that liking or disliking of a group can be equated with tolerance.

CHART V̲

ETHNIC AND RELIGIOUS TOLERATION*

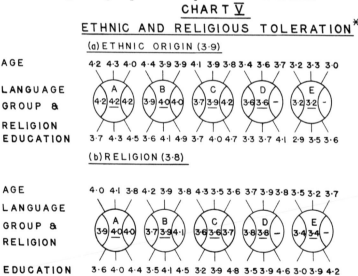

(a) ETHNIC ORIGIN (3·9)

AGE 4·2 4·3 4·0 4·4 3·9 3·9 4·1 3·9 3·8 3·4 3·6 3·7 3·2 3·3 3·0

LANGUAGE GROUP & RELIGION

A 4·2 4·2 4·2   B 3·9 4·0 4·0   C 3·7 3·9 4·2   D 3·6 3·6 –   E 3·2 3·2 –

EDUCATION 3·7 4·3 4·5 3·6 4·1 4·9 3·7 4·0 4·7 3·3 3·7 4·1 2·9 3·5 3·6

(b) RELIGION (3·8)

AGE 4·0 4·1 3·8 4·2 3·9 3·8 4·3 3·5 3·6 3·7 3·9 3·8 3·5 3·2 3·7

LANGUAGE GROUP & RELIGION

A 3·9 4·0 4·0   B 3·7 3·9 4·1   C 3·6 3·6 3·7   D 3·8 3·8 –   E 3·4 3·4 –

EDUCATION 3·6 4·0 4·4 3·5 4·1 4·5 3·2 3·9 4·8 3·5 3·9 4·6 3·0 3·9 4·2

*For an explanation of the chart see Notes to Chart I.

A clearer picture emerges when one examines the response to two statements suggesting that Canada would be a better place if it were homogeneous ethnically and religiously.[18] Chart

151

V shows that a substantial gap separates the occupants of the two poles on our language continuum, particularly on the ethnic dimension, and that the usual progression is again evident with only one exception (Groups C and D in Chart V(b)). Francophones prefer a more homogeneous Canada; anglophones are more receptive to heterogeneity. There is a faint suggestion in the chart that English-speaking Canadians find heterogeneity along ethnic lines slightly more acceptable than in the religious sphere and that the francophones display an opposite reaction: a religiously mixed Canada is a little less off-putting to them than an ethnically varied one. But the difference is very slight. The partial and pure anglophones are very close to one another here; the gap between the pure and partial francophones is more significant.

Partial French-speakers with post-secondary education are more tolerant than their pure francophone educational peers, but the gap is at least as great between some of the less educated subgroups. That education is a powerful factor is nevertheless clear: the distance in each linguistic category between the educational subgroups is considerably greater than the distance between the language groups themselves. The younger cohorts are generally more tolerant than the older ones among the anglophones and the mixed group but this pattern is not evident among the francophones. Catholics appear to be very slightly more intolerant than the other groups but the evidence here is slender indeed.

According to our expectations, the gap between the English- and French-speaking groups should be particularly wide when their private values are linked to issues touching on the relations between ethnic groups. With reference to toleration, therefore, we expected the distance between the two anglophone groups on the one hand, and the two French-speaking ones on the other, to be wider than in any other area discussed so far. We also anticipated that the best educated and youngest among the partial francophones would reveal responses substantially different from the anglophones and from less educated and older members of their own language group.

Some of these predictions were confirmed but by no means all of them. No difference between the language groups was observed in relation to the liking expressed for Americans and negroes—groups which were deemed to be largely unrelated to Canada's ethnic tensions. Considerable differences were, however, manifest when attitudes to Jews, Canadians of non-French or non-British origin were considered and particularly, and not surprisingly, when ratings were compared of French and English Canadians.

Contrary to what we anticipated, the partial French-users revealed a strong liking for the English Canadians and anglophones indicated that on the whole they did not like the French very much.

In indicating a preference between an ethnically and religiously mixed or uniform Canada, our respondents did display some of the attitudes we expected: the gap between the two dominant language groups was wider than that separating them on questions relating to divorce, homosexuality and the death penalty. We also found that the distance between anglophones and francophones was greater on the ethnic than on the religious dimensions. But the partial French-users appeared anything but the rather rabid, nationalist group we thought we might find. They were much closer to the anglophones than we expected, occupying a position mid-point between the pure French- and the partial English-users in one instance, and being even closer to the English pole in the other.

Some of our expectations clearly need to be examined more closely since they are challenged by the evidence we adduced with respect to Private Values defined narrowly at first, as related to religiosity and some moral issues, then more broadly with respect to a question in the general public area—that of law and order and, finally, in an area of some ethnic sensitivity—toleration of ethnic and religious minorities.

GENERAL CANADIAN ISSUES (PUBLIC POLICY)

Having exemplified our method of proceeding in examining differences between five classes of Canada's language-users with respect to Private Values, we can now move with greater dispatch while considering some general national issues more related to Public Policy. Again, areas of concern will be selected quite arbitrarily because they serve our current purposes and no attempt will be made to produce a microcosm of the main current Canadian preoccupations. Our attention is directed

153

towards three areas: Liking for certain leaders, perceptions of what threatens Canada, and some foreign policy questions.

Liking of Johnson, Pearson and Diefenbaker

Our respondents were asked to tell us how much they liked or disliked a number of political leaders, by giving them a score on the thermometer type question to which reference has already been made above. The three individuals scored in Table III were chosen here because one—the former President Johnson—is likely to be "ethnically" non-controversial, whereas the other two represent national leaders who had adopted quite different approaches to French-English relations. Lester Pearson was well known for his sympathetic attitude to French Canada; John Diefenbaker had failed to establish bonds of confidence with Quebec.

TABLE III: LIKING FOR JOHNSON; PEARSON AND DIEFENBAKER*

Political Figure	Group A	Group B	Group C	Group D	Group E
Lyndon B. Johnson	6.2	6.1	6.0	6.1	5.7
L. B. Pearson	6.8	7.1	7.4	6.9	6.7
J. G. Diefenbaker	6.5	6.1	6.0	5.5	5.1

*For an explanation of the scores see note 15.

With respect to President Johnson, there is no significant difference among all the groups except the pure francophones, who clearly thought less of him than the others. Mr. Pearson is liked equally well by both pure language-users and is viewed with particular favour by the mixed group. The former prime minister, Mr. Diefenbaker, is liked better than President Johnson only by the pure English and his popularity declines quite steeply as we move towards the French end of the continuum.

These scores suggest that the differences between French- and English-users can disappear when a non-controversial national personage like Mr. Pearson is evaluated, but that quite a pronounced difference occurs when an "ethnically" relevant issue is presented. This is hardly surprising but what is rather unexpected is that the differences between the partial and pure French-speakers do not vary much as we move from an ethnically "neutral" to an ethnically "sensitive" person. It is also surprising that the pure francophones should judge President

Johnson less favourably than the other language-users. Table IV, to which we turn next, suggests that this low score is not likely to be the result of greater pure francophone fear of American influences on Canada.

Perceptions of Threats to Canada

In responding to the question "Which of the following is the most dangerous to the survival of Canada?" the respondents were to choose from among the following:
- (a) Internal disunity resulting from English-French conflict
- (b) External danger of communism
- (c) An atomic war
- (d) The using up of natural resources
- (e) American economic and social domination

TABLE IV: PERCEPTION OF THREATS TO CANADA
(In Percentages)

Threat	Pure English	Partial English	Mixed	Partial French	Pure French	Total
	A	B	C	D	E	(N)
Internal Disunity	24	26	25	24	22	(608)
Communism	14	14	17	18	14	(368)
Atomic War	36	42	43	41	42	(984)
Resource Depletion	6	4	3	5	4	(138)
U.S. Domination	20	14	13	13	18	(487)
	100	100	101	101	100	
Total (N)	(1692)	(122)	(120)	(111)	(540)	(2585)

With the exception of fears of an atomic war, there were only minor differences between the two pure language groups. Not even the threat of Canada being disunited because of the French-English conflict elicited a highly differentiated response. In the case concerning the war threat the pure francophones reacted in a manner very similar to that of all the other groups except the pure anglophones who were more sanguine than everyone else about this menace.

The partial and mixed groups react somewhat differently from the pure ones to both communism and American domination. It is the partial francophones who are most concerned about communism, followed closely by the mixed group. The differences are small, but, in the case of the partial French particularly, nevertheless puzzling. One third of the mixed group has east European origins and can therefore be expected to have a somewhat stronger reaction to communism, but the same cannot be said of the members of our D category. They also share, with the mixed group, the lowest percentage of individuals fearing American economic and social domination. Here both the pure groups showed noticeably greater concern, the anglophones a shade more so.

Foreign Policy

General questions of foreign policy, when unrelated to the *Francophonie* or to Quebec's international presence, might be expected to evoke a rather similar response from anglophones and francophones in Canada and were therefore considered useful items for the testing of our hypotheses with respect to the distance likely to separate our linguistic groups in areas of General Public Policy.

There is, however, little point in trying to seek opinions on policy questions from individuals who have little or no interest in, or knowledge of, them. Our respondents were accordingly led through a gateway which allowed the more interested to be retained for further questioning and the less interested to get on to other things. A fairly wide gap separated the francophones from all others on the screen question, which sought to discover whether our respondents were extremely, fairly or not too interested in foreign affairs: [19]

Group A	Group B	Group C	Group D	Group E
3.0	3.0	3.0	3.3	3.6

The response of the partial francophones seems somewhat contaminated by their contact with the English-speaking world. Differences between our language groups assume a much finer texture, however, when we continue questioning the 1476 individuals (53 percent of the total) who passed through our gateway by stating that they were at least fairly interested in foreign policy questions.

On balance, there is more agreement than disagreement among the language groups on this battery of eight questions. Table V shows that there was a fairly impressive English-

TABLE V: ATTITUDES TO FOREIGN POLICY ISSUES*
(N = 1475)

Issues	Language Groups				
	A	B	C	D	E
a) Greater Involvement in Latin America	3.2	3.1	3.0	2.7	2.3
b) No Need for Present Level of Forces	3.5	3.5	3.3	3.4	2.7
c) Closer Relations with China	3.0	3.1	3.3	3.6	3.2
d) Reduce Foreign Aid	3.6	3.3	3.3	3.1	3.2
e) Help U.S.A. in Vietnam	4.3	4.4	4.0	4.3	4.2
f) Give U.S.A. Canadian Bases	2.2	2.4	2.5	2.3	2.6
g) Greater Independence from U.S.A.	2.1	2.1	2.1	2.4	1.9
h) Increase Immigration from Asia and Africa	3.6	3.4	3.3	3.9	3.5

*The exact wording of the question was: "Here are some of the suggestions that have been made about what Canada should do in world affairs. For each, please tell me whether you agree strongly, agree mildly, disagree mildly or disagree strongly. If you have no opinions, please say so. a) Canada should become more involved in Latin America; b) Canada does not need to maintain its present level of military forces; c) Canada should establish closer relations with Communist China; d) Canada should *reduce* its foreign aid; e) Canada should send military forces to help the United States in Vietnam; f) Canada should continue to give the United States the use of Canadian bases and air space; g) Canada's foreign policy should be more independent of the United States; h) Canada should encourage an increase in the number of immigrants from Asia and Africa." The mean scores were arrived at by adopting our usual coding scheme for this type of question: Agree Strongly 1; Agree Mildly 2; No Opinion 3; Disagree Mildly 4; Disagree Strongly 5.

French difference over the idea that Canada should become more involved in Latin America and also between the pure francophones on the one hand and all the rest on the other, with respect to Canada not needing its existing level of military forces. A modest margin separated the two pure language groups' positions on foreign aid and on Canada providing the United States with air space and bases but the difference on all other issues is so small as to be insignificant. There is, thus, something approaching agreement on all issues which are not ethnically relevant: Latin America has, for obvious reasons, been of greater interest to francophones than to anglophones and the pure francophones' posture on statement (b) may reflect French Canada's long history of opposing military involvement in Europe.[20]

The mixed group displays a curious inconsistency in adopting the most hawkish position of the five with respect to Canada's getting involved in Vietnam and at the same time indicating the second strongest opposition to Canada offering the United States bases and air space. Another arresting pattern is provided by the partial French-speakers who record the strongest disagreement with establishing closer ties with China, with Canada adopting a foreign policy more independent of the United States and with increasing immigration from Asia and Africa. These postures were perhaps foreshadowed in some of the threat perceptions (communism and American domination) but they do not seem congruent with those adopted by the same group in other areas.

Our excursion into a number of General Public Issues has confirmed our expectations about this area in at least one important respect: the distance between the language groups, particularly the pure anglophones and francophones, is narrower here than in the area of Private Values, and frequently disappears altogether. But the gap between them tends to widen (as Mr. Diefenbaker's scores and the attitudes to closer ties with Latin America indicate) as soon as the general sphere assumes some special significance, even fairly remote, to ethnic relations in Canada.

When dealing with Private Values we observed a general tendency for the partial, and to some extent also the mixed, groups to fall into a neat progression endowing most of the series on our continuum with what appears like a highly scaleable quality. This pattern is much less evident in the examples of responses to Public Issues we consulted above. The partial groups in many instances seem, so to speak, to stake out a position for themselves somewhat independent of the pure language users. The pattern observed here, however, does not confirm one of our hypotheses, namely that the partial francophones might become more extreme, nationalist and radical than their French-speaking neighbours, when they confront ethnically sensitive questions and problems. We will be able to shed more light on this aspect of our analysis when we focus fully on some issues which are of unmistakable ethnic relevance—a task to which we turn next.

ETHNICALLY RELEVANT PUBLIC ISSUES

From the plethora of examples available to us, we shall select some related to the place of the monarchy, constitutional change, to some issues specifically related to current political controversies between French- and English-speaking Canadians and to the liking of three controversial politicians.

The Monarchy and Constitutional Change

Charts VI and VII yield insights into perceptions of the monarchy by summarizing some data on how important the Queen and the Governor General were judged to be, and by recording reactions to the proposal that the monarchy be abolished in Canada.[21] In addition to the latter, Chart VII also indicates what was thought of making changes in the constitution and of enabling provincial governments to participate in international educational conferences (both currently hot issues in French-English relations).[22]

CHART VI IMPORTANCE ATTACHED TO QUEEN AND GOVERNOR GENERAL*

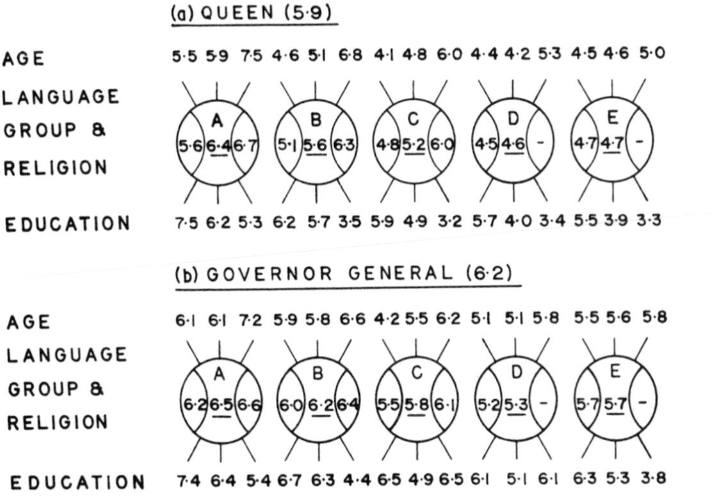

(a) QUEEN (5.9)

AGE
5.5 5.9 7.5 4.6 5.1 6.8 4.1 4.8 6.0 4.4 4.2 5.3 4.5 4.6 5.0

LANGUAGE GROUP & RELIGION
A 5.6 6.4 6.7 | B 5.1 5.6 6.3 | C 4.8 5.2 6.0 | D 4.5 4.6 - | E 4.7 4.7 -

EDUCATION
7.5 6.2 5.3 6.2 5.7 3.5 5.9 4.9 3.2 5.7 4.0 3.4 5.5 3.9 3.3

(b) GOVERNOR GENERAL (6.2)

AGE
6.1 6.1 7.2 5.9 5.8 6.6 4.2 5.5 6.2 5.1 5.1 5.8 5.5 5.6 5.8

LANGUAGE GROUP & RELIGION
A 6.2 6.5 6.6 | B 6.0 6.2 6.4 | C 5.5 5.8 6.1 | D 5.2 5.3 - | E 5.7 5.7 -

EDUCATION
7.4 6.4 5.4 6.7 6.3 4.4 6.5 4.9 6.5 6.1 5.1 6.1 6.3 5.3 3.8

*For an explanation of the chart see Notes to Chart I.

159

Distances are great between the francophones and the anglophones, particularly among the pure language-users. It is, indeed, in this cluster of responses that we find the greatest gaps occurring between Canada's language groups—a result that is hardly surprising. The mixed group generally continues to place itself in the middle. But our interest focuses specially on the partial users. Here we see a rather wide margin separating the partial from the pure anglophones, with the exception only of one dimension—(c) in Chart VII, Group A is clearly more royalist and, in the present context, more conservative. It should, however, be noted that although the pure anglophones

CHART VII ATTITUDES TO SOME ETHNICALLY RELEVANT ISSUES*

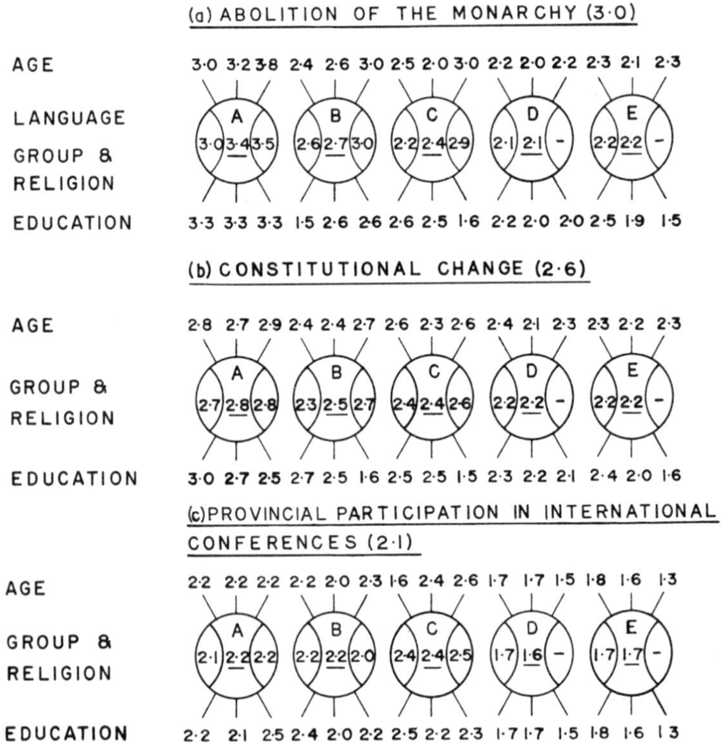

(a) ABOLITION OF THE MONARCHY (3·0)

AGE   3·0 3·2 3·8 2·4 2·6 3·0 2·5 2·0 3·0 2·2 2·0 2·2 2·3 2·1 2·3

LANGUAGE GROUP & RELIGION

A: 3·0 3·4 3·5   B: 2·6 2·7 3·0   C: 2·2 2·4 2·9   D: 2·1 2·1 –   E: 2·2 2·2 –

EDUCATION   3·3 3·3 3·3 1·5 2·6 2·6 2·6 2·5 1·6 2·2 2·0 2·0 2·5 1·9 1·5

(b) CONSTITUTIONAL CHANGE (2·6)

AGE   2·8 2·7 2·9 2·4 2·4 2·7 2·6 2·3 2·6 2·4 2·1 2·3 2·3 2·2 2·3

GROUP & RELIGION

A: 2·7 2·8 2·8   B: 2·3 2·5 2·7   C: 2·4 2·4 2·6   D: 2·2 2·2 –   E: 2·2 2·2 –

EDUCATION   3·0 2·7 2·5 2·7 2·5 1·6 2·5 2·5 1·5 2·3 2·2 2·1 2·4 2·0 1·6

(c) PROVINCIAL PARTICIPATION IN INTERNATIONAL CONFERENCES (2·1)

AGE   2·2 2·2 2·2 2·2 2·0 2·3 1·6 2·4 2·6 1·7 1·7 1·5 1·8 1·6 1·3

GROUP & RELIGION

A: 2·1 2·2 2·2   B: 2·2 2·2 2·0   C: 2·4 2·4 2·5   D: 1·7 1·6 –   E: 1·7 1·7 –

EDUCATION   2·2 2·1 2·5 2·4 2·0 2·2 2·5 2·2 2·3 1·7 1·7 1·5 1·8 1·6 1·3

*For an explanation of the chart see Notes to Chart I.

160

may appear to be considerably more devoted to the Queen and the Governor General than our other groups, they still consider them to be far less important than any of the other offices cited.

If the partial anglophones exhibit a somewhat atypical relationship with their pure co-linguists, the attitudes of the partial French-users are even more interesting. On all but one of the positions reported upon in Charts VI and VII, the partial French take a more French Canadian nationalist position than the pure French-speakers. The distance is small but it will be recalled that in virtually all previously examined cases they were *between* the pure French- and the English-speaking groups. Partial language use (or, more precisely, what is represented by it) thus appears to be conducive to the adoption of a more nationalist stance.

Educational levels achieved by the francophone respondents are not related to a more nationalist position quite in the way I anticipated. Among the pure French-users there is an unmistakable pattern of the best educated being the most nationalist but we did not find, as we had expected, that this was even more pronounced, and consistent, among the partial French-speakers. The contrary was the case. We cannot leave a discussion of the effects of education without noting that the post-secondary group in all categories but the pure English made a similar, very low assessment of the Queen's importance; only among the pure anglophones was this pattern broken, and even here the best educated groups assigned the Queen a relatively low score.

The youngest members of the francophone groups were not found to be the more nationalist. Although differences between cohorts within the francophone groups are small, such as do appear tend to reveal the middle-aged group as most radical, in this sense. Roman Catholics are distinctly more anti-royalist than the other religious groups combined, but English-speaking Catholics less so than those who speak French. On the constitutional dimension, Catholics appear a little more conservative.

Attitudes to Quebec

Some of the highly suggestive patterns, particularly in the responses of the partial francophones are not, alas, confirmed when we zero in on questions dealing specifically with the

French-English crisis. One of the bones of contention here has been the status of the province of Quebec in the Canadian federation: should it occupy a special position or should no difference be made between it and the other provinces? The response to this question is a good indicator of where an individual stands with respect to the French-English controversy. About 90 percent of our anglophone respondents wished Quebec to be treated like the other provinces but the response of the francophones was rather less clear-cut.[23]

	Group A	Group B	Group C	Group D	Group E
Treated like others	88%	90%	78%	70%	56%
Special Status	6%	7%	12%	25%	35%

Despite containing a very much larger proportion of individuals who prefer Quebec to enjoy special status, more than half of the pure francophones (Group E) support the idea that Quebec should be treated like the other provinces. The partial French-speakers, who had therefore been so much more nationalist, show themselves to be quite considerably less so on this question. For the best-educated partial francophones the corresponding percentages are even more startling (73% for equal treatment, 14% for special status, N=9) but there are too few cases to make anything of this. Among the pure francophones, the post-secondary group (N=60) divides itself equally between the two options.

Differences among the language groups with respect to the possible separation of Quebec from Canada mirror those just discussed and they make it quite obvious that even the francophones were opposed, in impressive numbers, to the establishment of a state of Quebec.[24]

Group A	Group B	Group C	Group D	Group E
4.4	4.6	4.5	4.2	4.1

The distance between the two groups at the extremes of our scale is noticeable but not very wide. The partial anglophones are most opposed to separation, followed by the mixed group. Group D, the partial francophones, instead of being more separatist than Group E as we predicted, turn out to be slightly less so and quite close to the pure anglophones in this regard. Among the mixed, and the two anglophone groups, the opposition to separation grows uniformly with years of schooling (the figures are not given). The post-secondary group among the pure French-speakers are most favourably disposed towards Quebec independence (3.9) but among the partial francophone group it is the least educated who are most nationalist and the difference between the secondary and post-secondary groups is insignificant.[25]

Liking for De Gaulle, Lévesque and D. Johnson

Since we have run into inconsistent and contradictory responses from the partial francophones, the group which interests us most here, we need at least one more look at them; we can do this best, for our present purposes, by situating them on some ethnically specially provocative terrain. We shall accordingly examine responses to three personalities who, in various degrees, have become the subjects of controversy between French and English Canadians. General de Gaulle, addressing a large crowd during a visit to Quebec, used the separatist slogan, "Vive le Québec Libre!"; René Lévesque, a former leading member of the Provincial government, became the most illustrious separatist leader; Daniel Johnson, Quebec's premier until his death, was a tough and able protagonist of Quebec in its negotiations with the federal government. The distance between the two pure language categories is, as expected, quite enormous, but what of the margins separating the pure from the partial categories, particularly on the French side?

We see in Table VI that the scores in the D column are consistently lower than in column E and that the margin, at least with respect to General de Gaulle and former Premier Daniel Johnson, is not insignificant. Among the partial francophones,

TABLE VI: LIKING FOR DE GAULLE, LEVESQUE, AND DANIEL JOHNSON*

Political Figure	Group A	Group B	Group C	Group D	Group E
General de Gaulle	3.4	3.5	4.7	5.2	5.9
René Lévesque	4.4	4.2	5.0	5.4	5.6
Daniel Johnson	5.2	5.3	5.9	6.8	7.2

*For explanation of the scores see note 15.

the best-educated liked de Gaulle least! In any event, we must conclude that in this example the partial francophones did not appear to be more nationalist and that their attitudes to the monarchy and to constitutional change cannot be taken as representative of all their postures. Little need be said about the mixed group which, as almost always, occupies the centre of our continuum not only logically but also in terms of its liking of de Gaulle, Lévesque and Daniel Johnson. The positions of the partial English is, to all intents and purposes, identical to that of the pure anglophone.

On questions which have some relevance to the relations between French and English Canadians, the distance between our two pure language groups was, of course, extremely great. This, the most obvious of our hypotheses, was confirmed. But we also predicted that the partial francophones might be more distant from the anglophone "norm" than the pure French-users, and this expectation was confirmed only partially and was, in fact, contradicted by two sets of responses. We found that the best-educated on the whole adopted the most nationalist positions among the pure francophones, but did not do so among the partial French-speakers. The middle-aged members of this language group also tended to be more nationalist than the youngest cohort. There was little difference between the two anglophone groups, although a tendency is apparent among the partial English-users of taking a position slightly farther from the French pole than the pure anglophones. The mixed group seems not to wish to budge from its central location.

POLITICAL ALIGNMENTS

Before reviewing our effort to see how perceptions and evaluations of the five groups of language-users vary, in relation to the area in which they occur, (Private Values, General Policy, Ethnically Relevant Spheres) we shall look at political alignments. To compare the partisan positions of our five language groups is, in some measure, to retrace our steps, since these alignments are obviously related to all three of the areas we have identified as influencing the distance between their views. The foregoing testing of our hypotheses will thus be supplemented by seeing to what extent the patterns observed so far are repeated with respect to the various aspects of the political alignments of the five language groups.

Even more than previously we shall present a good many data in rapid succession without attempting to exploit anything like their full meaning, except with reference to the most striking differences between the five language groups.

TABLE VII: PARTY IDENTIFICATION AND 1968 VOTE
(In Percentages)

Party		Language Group				
		A	B	C	D	E
LIBERAL	Vote	50	66	84	69	64
	Identification	48	61	81	73	68
CONSERVATIVE	Vote	33	15	12	14	20
	Identification	33	18	9	12	20
NDP	Vote	14	20	3	9	5
	Identification	14	19	6	7	4
CREDITISTE	Vote	—	—	—	8	9
	Identification	—	—	—	7	8
SOCIAL CREDIT	Vote	2	—	2	1	1
	Identification	4	2	4	1	1
		99	101	101	101	99
TOTALS		99	100	100	100	101

Table VII shows that both in terms of Party Identification and the 1968 vote, the distance between the different language users is quite immense.[26] Over 80 percent of the mixed group are Liberal, whereas the pure anglophones do not quite manage to place more than half their number in the Liberal camp. The range between the groups is much narrower with respect to the other parties of course, but the proportion of Conservative pure anglophones is in all but one case twice as great as that of the mixed or partial groups. Only the pure anglophones display anything other than a colossal margin between the proportion of their number supporting the Liberals and that identifying with, or voting for, the Conservative or any other party. The very wide margin separating the pure Liberal anglophones from the group containing the next largest proportion of Liberals might suggest that there is a deep political cleavage in Canada and that the degree of polarization is extremely high. That this is not quite the case is attested to by even the "low" pure anglophones delivering half their members into the Liberal camp. From the viewpoint of this paper, it is most interesting that the rather orderly sequence of scores moving in stately propriety from one end of our continuum to the other, which we observed in so many previous series, is totally absent here. The order of the language groups is quite atypical. Taking Liberal support as our basic dimension we can rank the groups in descending order as follows:

Vote:	C	D	B	E	A
Identification:	C	D	E	B	A

Instead of speculating at this point about the reason for, and significance of, the partisan pattern, we shall examine some related data.

TABLE VIII: DIFFERENCE BETWEEN PARTIES*

Area of Difference	Language Group				
	A	B	C	D	E
Degree of difference between Parties (2.3)	2.2	2.2	2.7	2.4	2.4
Importance of which party in Power (fed.) (2.0)	1.9	2.0	2.1	2.1	2.3
Importance of which party in Power (prov.) (1.9)	1.8	2.0	2.1	2.0	2.2

*The lower the score, the greater the difference or importance.

Our respondents were asked to state how much difference they saw between the federal parties and also how much difference it makes which party is in office in Ottawa and in their provincial capital.[27] The francophones, as Table VIII shows, are somewhat less impressed by the difference between the parties, and by the degree of difference it makes which is in office at either level of government. The gap is not great, however, and the partial groups seem, on the whole, to place themselves on these questions in the positions we saw them occupy in most cases previously. There is no difference between the pure and partial types of either language in one case, and in another (the difference at the provincial level), the partial anglophones and francophones have the same mean score. The mixed group sees the least difference between the parties. One of the most interesting features of the table is its message with respect to the similarity in the response of French- and English-speaking respondents to the importance of parties at the two levels of government. The francophones might have been expected to think that it made a greater difference which party was in power at the provincial level but the responses of the language groups here are quite similar.

After the dramatic difference displayed by the language groups in their party alignment it is curious to see such a bland response to the items covered by Table VIII. The contrast becomes even more astounding when we glance at another of our findings. After inquiring about the respondent's financial state we asked "Do you think that the way the election turned out will make any difference in how well off you are?" and received the following response:

	Group A	Group B	Group C	Group D	Group E
Yes	21%	20%	20%	11%	10%
No	66%	59%	59%	76%	79%

Although a great many of the francophones gave the Liberals electoral support, a large proportion of them did not think that the outcome of the election would affect them financially.

Very little difference was evident between the pure anglophones and francophones with respect to their numbers who found the leader or the candidate most important in their voting decision. Indeed, among all language groups, about 40 percent, as Table IX tells us, thought the leader the most important factor. The francophone groups claimed to have been influenced more than the others by the work of the parties' MPs but attached less weight to the party as a whole.

While the partial English-speaking members of our sample took the leader and the party as a whole slightly more seriously than their pure brethren, the partial francophones stood, if anything, a hair closer to the English pole of the continuum than the full French-speaking group. But the differences are so small with respect to the partial groups that the only thing that one can really say is that they did not behave in as idiosyncratic a manner as in their Party identification and vote.

167

TABLE IX: FACTORS IN THE VOTING DECISION*
(In Percentages)

Factors	Language Group					
	A	B	C	D	E	TOTAL
Leader	39	40	39	39	38	(1069)
Work of MP's	7	7	5	12	14	(229)
Candidate	16	7	10	15	16	(421)
Party as a whole	35	38	33	29	27	(906)
Do Not Know	3	7	14	5	6	(122)
	100	99	101	100	101	
Total	(1783)	(135)	(141)	(116)	(572)	(2747)

*The question read: "In deciding what you would do in this recent election, which was most important to you: the leaders, the work of the MP's, your local candidates, or the parties, taken as a whole?"

Since the leader and the party as a whole were declared the most important factors in the respondent's decision it will be well to see what the reactions were to the individual leaders and to the way in which the parties approached the major election issues. The mean scores received by the leaders of the three main parties on a thermometer type question were as follows:[28]

	Group A	Group B	Group C	Group D	Group E
Trudeau (Liberal)	5.7	6.3	6.8	6.5	6.0
Stanfield (P.C.)	4.9	4.4	4.4	4.3	4.5
Douglas (NDP)	5.0	4.7	4.4	3.8	3.4

While the distance between the language groups is not nearly as impressive as that separating them on the vote, it is interesting that the sequence in which they ranked Mr. Trudeau is the same as that which we observed with respect to their 1968 Liberal vote: C D B E A. The sequence for Mr. Stanfield is more congruent with our earlier results (although the partial French rate him slightly lower than the pure) and that for Mr. Douglas demonstrates an even, graceful descent from the English to the French poles.

The intriguing ranking of the groups, according to their rating of Mr. Trudeau, parallel to that of the Liberal party, raises the question of what, if any, causal connection there is between these results. At this preliminary stage of our inquiry we can do little more than note the problem. We should, however, recall that Mr. Pearson, the former Liberal leader, was scored quite differently, in terms both of magnitude and sequence (C B D A E), but that there is some similarity in the distance between D and E, in each case, and in the two pure groups scoring lowest, although they are not in the same order.

Our respondents were asked two sets of questions tapping their attitudes to current issues. One sought to elicit unprompted responses and simply asked what the most important problems were which the new government should tackle and then asked further that they be ranked. The second mentioned a number of election issues and asked whether each was extremely, very, fairly or not too important to the respondent. We were therefore able to construct an ordinal scale and compute mean scores indicating something of the intensity of feeling aroused by the issues.

For present purposes the most important conclusions to be drawn from these data are that a variety of economic issues were of great importance—unemployment and the cost of living being the chief among them; that the questions of whether Canada would have a majority government loomed extremely large (minority ministries had been in office since 1962); and that the constitutional position of Quebec was worrying a lot of people. The mean scores on the prompted questions dealing with these areas were:[29]

	Group A	Group B	Group C	Group D	Group E
Majority Government (2.2)	2.2	2.1	2.4	2.2	2.3
Economic Issues (2.4)	2.3	2.4	2.5	2.4	2.6
Quebec in Canada (2.7)	2.7	2.8	3.0	2.5	2.7

In response to the question of which party comes closest to the respondent's views on each of the listed issues we discovered that the Liberal party occupied a very special position in the eyes of the Canadian electorate and that on almost all issues the other parties lagged far behind. In the field of welfare the NDP and the Conservatives did appeal to some significant sections of the electorate but in all other areas the Liberals drew almost half the number of responses, even among the pure anglophones—the group least prone to support them.

TABLE X: PERCENTAGE OF RESPONDENTS FINDING LIBERAL PARTY CLOSEST ON SELECTED ISSUES

Issues	Language Group					
	A	B	C	D	E	Numbers*
Medicare	39	49	55	65	76	(347/676)
Welfare	46	44	59	59	68	(387/746)
The Economy	54	62	80	74	68	(725/1236)
Housing	47	57	75	73	68	(399/750)
Unemployment	48	56	66	84	70	(419/764)
Cost of Living	47	58	74	74	70	(541/1002)
Regional Inequality	49	61	68	71	73	(280/499)
Quebec	67	83	82	72	65	(674/987)

*The first number represents the respondents who said that the Liberal party was closest on the issue; the second gives the number of respondents who were asked the question. It was put only to those who said they were extremely or very interested in an issue.

Table X tells the story and contains the dramatic exception to the general pattern—an exception which is of critical importance to the understanding of party alignments in Canada. Leaving aside the totally deviant case of the issue of Quebec, we note that in all instances the two English-speaking groups found the Liberals most remote, the pure anglophones a good deal more so than the partial ones. On the social policy questions—medicare and welfare—there is a perfect progression from the French to the English side but this pattern is not maintained with respect to the economic sphere where the pure francophones are replaced, as the group finding the Liberals most to its liking, by the mixed and partial French groups. The pure French-speaking group (unlike the others) tends to find the Liberals most congenial precisely on those issues which they find most important.

Turning now to the Quebec issue we find a total reversal of the previous pattern: the pure anglophones place themselves into closer proximity to the Liberals than the pure French and the partial English-speakers display quite unusual exuberance vis-à-vis that party. The mixed and partial groups are, as a whole, more pro-Liberal here than the pure ones, but the partial French somewhat less so. The most significant feature of the table is that it shows that on the question of Quebec the two language groups come much closer than on any other, in finding the Liberal party most congenial. Although the gap is much wider, the second issue on which the language groups are least remote from one another (when their support for the Liberal position is taken as the yardstick) is the general question of the economy, the only other issue on which more than half the pure anglophones found the Liberals most congenial.

Two of the three key issues are thus ones in which the Liberals can draw on the most "balanced" support from the main language groups, the francophones being more Liberal on the economic side, and the anglophones on the Quebec problem. What of the third—majority government? This was a question which was of greater importance to anglophones than to the other groups. We have no survey data on how the parties were perceived in this context but there never was the slightest question, at the time of the 1968 election, that only the Liberals, as led by Pierre Trudeau, had a chance of winning a majority. The widely-shared desire of the anglophones for a majority government almost certainly contributed to their support of the Liberal party which, on these and more so on other grounds, made a strong appeal to the francophone members of the electorate.

The alignment of such large proportions of the pure French- and English-speaking voters with the Liberal party, while not of course fully explained by the above discussion, is at least perfectly plausible within it. What of the mixed and partial groups who, as we saw above, rallied to the Trudeau party in even larger proportions? Again, we cannot brave anything like a complete account explaining their pattern of behaviour but our analysis does permit us to make a contribution towards such an explanation. We saw above that the mixed group on the whole adopts positions *between* those of the two major language groups—in a sense they find themselves at the convergence of three value systems: their own traditional one and those of the anglophones and the francophones. They are, consequently, in a somewhat unstable position which, under their generally less favoured socio-economic conditions, is surmised to predispose them to seek stable, reassuring political options. The Liberal party, in this sense, offered by far the most attractive choice.

Essentially the same argument, although with less force, also applies to the partial groups. They have one foot, so to speak, in each linguistic camp, and as this paper shows, while usually near "their" majority culture, they appeared in a great number of cases somewhat closer to the centre of our continuum than their pure co-linguists. They too, are, therefore, under cross pressure, and exposed to both personal and political instability under contemporary Canadian conditions. No wonder then that the party they each prefer is one which appears most likely to establish majority government, and to be able to cope with the two sets of issues they think most important: national unity (the place of Quebec in Canada) and economic problems, particularly unemployment and inflation. The value systems to which they are linked through their linguistically dual life, and their socio-economic status thus seem to combine to predispose them towards the Liberals.

In examining the Party Identification and vote of our five language groups, and then the differences between the parties and how important it was thought which of them was in office, we discovered a rather inconsistent pattern. There was a staggering distance between the language groups in their partisan support, but the intensity of feeling about which party was in office was neither great, nor was there much difference between the language groups. The most surprising finding, however, concerned the placing of the groups vis-à-vis one another. Diagram II shows what would happen if we magnified the portion of Diagram I (page 138) to show the position of the circular lines representing the Liberal vote of the language groups.

This is a far cry from any part of Diagram I which, however, as an ideal model, served most of our other analyses tolerably well. We saw that there was relatively little difference between the language groups in the degree to which their voting decision was influenced by the two most often-cited factors—the leader

DIAGRAM II
DISTANCE BETWEEN LANGUAGE GROUPS
WITH RESPECT TO LIBERAL VOTES *

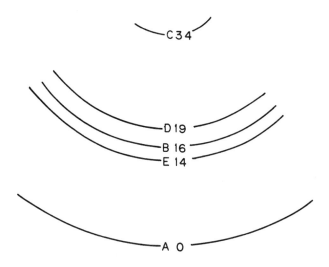

C 34

D 19
B 16
E 14

A 0

*The numbers represent the percentage points separating the language groups from the anglophones. For the actual percentages see Table VII.

and the party taken as a whole and, after examining the position the language groups took on the election issues, we decided that their deviant lineup on the all-important Liberal support was compatible with the general pattern of responses we observed in relation to the three areas of Private Values, General Issues and Ethnically Relevant Problems. But it certainly also suggests that the schema is in need of some revision.

The above effort at reconciling what appears to be something of an incongruent set of patterns between the overall effects and evaluations of our respondents on the one hand, and of their partisan alignments on the other, may strike the reader as being eccentric on at least two scores: it appears to explain partisan alignments within an excessively short-run perspective —the 1968 election—when Table VII shows that the differences between Party Identification and the 1968 vote were slight; and it fails to draw on the insights into electoral decision-making, and its antecedents, contained in the Michigan canon, the voting studies produced by the Survey Research Centre at Ann Arbor. The first impression is illusory: the short-run factors cited in connection with the 1968 election have, with the exception of Mr. Trudeau, been evident in Canada for a very long time and we simply used the vocabulary of the late sixties to describe phenomena which have essentially dominated partisan alignments, particularly Liberal support, since the depression and the advent of the Second World War, if not before.

Our explanation, although less focused than most of the work of the SRC, nevertheless is compatible with much of it. The context of the present analysis did not allow us to spell out the connection between our data and what has come to be accepted as the explanation of electoral decision-making in political settings like that of Canada. It will be necessary, when the present analysis is expanded, to examine within its framework the concepts and variables generated by the Michigan school and the growing number of scholars associated with it abroad.[30] This exercise is likely to shed further light on why some of the evaluation and affect patterns in our general discussion failed to appear in the support profile of the Liberal party. And this may in turn lead to a greater refinement and/or revision of our overall schema categorizing political perceptions into the three areas outlined above.

CONCLUSION

Review of the Schema

We have sought to gain some insight into cultural differences, particularly as related to politically relevant perceptions, by means of distinguishing between sub-populations in linguistically heterogeneous societies according to the degree to which they speak the major languages. Language-use was taken to be a link to the value systems of cultural groups and an indicator of the degree to which a linguistic sub-population had become identified with the values of one or the other of the two societies comprising Canada. It was assumed that differences would occur in the degree to which linguistic groups share the values of the major cultures, differences varying with the objects to which the values are attached.

174

Secondly, the common practice of thinking of language-use in bilingual societies in dichotomous terms was rejected in favour of a more complex pattern acknowledging the existence of partial language-users. We were thus led to establishing a language continuum, consisting of pure types at each end, of a partial group associated with each of the pure types, and of a mixed category in the middle, only weakly linked to either of the language (and therefore value) systems of their society.

The five types of language users were expected to display greater or lesser differences among themselves with respect to the way they reacted to the world around them, and particularly to its political phenomena. A number of predictions was made specifically with respect to the size of the gaps that could be expected between the five groups in relation to three areas: Private Values, General Public Policy and Policy relevant to Ethnic Relations.

Results of loosely organized exploratory tests of a schema placing the language groups into an anticipated pattern are summarized above, at the end of each relevant section. On the whole they are encouraging in that they confirm the existence of genuine differences between the five language groups on the continuum and in that they support most of the relationships we expected to find. They suggest that it is worthwhile trying to map the positions occupied by linguistic sub-groups with respect to one another in various politically relevant areas.

By no means all of our expectations were confirmed, however, both with respect to the positions taken by the pure groups (although here the results were rather impressive) and also to the order in which the five groups lined up on certain clusters of perceptions. The three areas—Private—Public—Ethnically Relevant Public—may provide too crude a grouping of categories and require considerable refinement. It is certainly necessary to depart, at least temporarily, from this kind of brazen macro-analysis and to select smaller areas of study, much as we have done, again only in a cursory and merely illustrative way, with respect to political alignments. If a series of discrete but extensive sub-analyses can fruitfully be attempted (and there is every indication that it can) it should be possible to establish finer sub-categories of the three areas. This will either lead to a more complex and finer system of classifying areas within which the relationship in the perceptions of the five language groups will permit easier explanation and possibly reasonably accurate prediction or it may even torpedo an important part of the conceptual framework within which we have developed our argument. The circular concept applied in the present analysis (see Diagram I), while useful in some respects, does impose artificial and limiting constraints which may become intolerable as the analysis becomes more acceptably refined and may in the end be abandoned for a more supple and multi-dimensional construct.

Additional work also needs to be done on the differences in perceptions between the partial and pure groups. The problem is fairly simple on the English-speaking end of the continuum. The partial anglophones do normally take positions close to the pure groups but more information is needed about the persistently recurring cases in which they adopt a more extreme stance, in the sense of being further away from the French positions than the pure English.

We were not quite sure what to expect from the partial French: on the one hand it was plausible that they should be socialized, by their exposure to English values, into attitudes and perceptions resembling those of the English-speaking majority and differing somewhat from those of the pure francophones. But it was also possible that their partial contact with English Canada might lead them to a more extreme nationalism than that displayed by their more isolated, and presumably less frequently provoked, pure French-speaking colleagues. The former was usually the case but not always. Our expectations of greater nationalism and extremism among the best-educated and youngest partial francophones were largely disappointed although among the pure French-speakers the post-secondary educational group did tend towards more forthrightly nationalist postures, than the less well-educated. In any event, there were enough deviant cases with respect to the relationship between the partial and pure groups at both ends of our continuum to warrant further studies of this problem, involving larger numbers of the relevant cases than were present in our national sample.

Implications for Theory and Political Life

Our preoccupation with establishing the use of the analysis of

176

social cleavage, in a heterogeneous society and its consequences for political perceptions, in terms of a language continuum, and our drawing on heretofore unpublished Canadian data, no doubt deflected us from some of the broader theoretical foundations of this approach. It is too late in the day to turn to this aspect of our work, but the reader will be aware of the potential relevance of the kind of analysis we wish to encourage for anyone concerned with studying the demands and supports of any given political system or interested in the whole question of system maintenance.

For those concerned more with applied politics, the way of looking at ethnically mixed societies, adumbrated above, also promises rewards. It provides a kind of warning light which can point to the presence of fissures in multilingual settings. Since it rejects both the false dichotomization of language-use and, by focusing on a wide range of perceptions, the overly-simple definition of divisions in terms of too few cleavages, it constitutes a realistic means of coming to grips with stress in multilingual and multi-ethnic polities. The present approach facilitates the identification of the areas and problems creating stress and also of the linguistic (and other) groups involved. It is, therefore, relevant to the policy-maker concerned with gaining a better understanding of the problems of his clients.

NOTES

1. The tendency applies equally to distinctions being made between linguistic families in even more multi-lingual societies but the analysis attempted here, based on only two language groups, will suffice to open up the problem.

2. The research, which started many years ago as a conventional election study, has since assumed larger proportions and is concerned with a variety of mechanisms through which inputs are converted into outputs in political systems. It is supported by a Killam Award of the Canada Council. The data for this paper are derived from 2767 interviews, of about ninety minutes' duration, with a national sample, conducted after the 1968 election. Further details

about the survey, including a description of the sample design, can be obtained from the author. I am grateful for the generous advice of W. P. Irvine and for the competent research assistance of James W. Lightbody.

3. In the aforementioned survey, no less than 27 percent answered "Canada" to the question "Please tell me from what country most of your ancestors came." When these 752 individuals were asked "And before that, where did most of your ancestors come from?" 19 percent (141) still answered "Canada."

4. Even some of the most illuminating works give short shrift to cleavages expressed in linguistic forms. Only the most scant and passing attention to this clearly relevant and in some instances critical aspect of social cleavage is to be found, for example, in Lipset and Rokkan, (eds.), *Party Systems and Voter Alignments*, or in Allardt and Littunen (eds.), *Cleavages, Ideologies and Party Systems*. In a different idiom, the papers in Merritt and Rokkan (eds.), *Comparing Nations*, similarly almost ignore linguistic dimensions. The three collections of papers cited here are singled out because they are otherwise particularly useful and comprehensive surveys of materials relevant to our present concerns and so offer striking evidence for the view that language factors have been neglected by students of the political consequences of social cleavage. A notable exception to the neglect is J. A. Laponce, "Ethnicity, Religion, and Politics, in Canada: A Comparative Analysis of Survey and Census Data," in Dogan and Rokkan, *Quantitative Ecological Analysis in the Social Sciences*, Cambridge, Mass., 1969.

5. A good introduction to the vast and rapidly growing literature is to be found in Joshua A. Fishman (ed.), *Readings in the Sociology of Language*, The Hague, 1968; J. B. Carroll, (ed.), *Language, Thought, and Reality: Selected Writings of Benjamin Lee Whorf*, New York, 1956; John B. Carroll, *Language and Thought*, Englewood Cliffs, N.J., 1968.

6. *Report of the Royal Commission on Bilingualism and Biculturalism, General Introduction, Book I, The Official Languages*, Ottawa, 1967, XXXI, XXXIII, and *A Preliminary Report of the Royal Commission on Bilingualism and Biculturalism*, Ottawa, 1965, 111. Subsequent volumes of the *Report* provide a massive analysis and unique case study of the relation between language and society.

7. Because of their numerical and economic strength, English-speaking Canadians do dominate the country as a whole. In Quebec, francophones constitute the majority culture but even here the pull of "English" values cannot always be avoided.

8. A pioneer study in the early thirties distinguished between nine "domains" of language, such as the family, the street, school (instruction and recess), church etc. See George Schmidt-Rohr, *Mutter Sprache*, Jena, 1933 and Joshua A. Fishman, "Language

Maintenance and Language Shift as a Field of Inquiry," in Fishman (ed.), *Language Loyalty in the United States,* The Hague, 1966. The following items in the aforementioned *Readings,* also edited by Fishman, are fascinating contributions to the literature on the definition of language use: Simon R. Herman, "Explorations in the Social Psychology of Language Choice," Joan Rubin, "Bilingual Usage in Paraguay," William A. Stewart, "A Sociolinguistic Typology for Describing National Multilingualism," Stanley Lieberson, "An Extension of Greenberg's Linguistic Diversity Measures;" and William F. Mackey, "The Description of Bilingualism."

9. Housewives were coded as speaking the same language at work as at home.

10. The phrase "testing our hypotheses" may, as will be seen, be too grandiose. For the sake of brevity we shall nevertheless use it occasionally. A methodologically more sophisticated analysis is projected for the future.

11. A rough and ready index of religiosity was constructed, utilizing three criteria: frequency of church (or temple) attendance; proportion of respondent's friends belonging to the same religion as he does; agreement or disagreement with a statement to the effect that too much money was being spent on churches. Details about the indices used here will be published and, in the meantime, can be obtained from the author. The highest attainable score of the religiosity index is 11, the lowest 0.

12. See, for example, G. Lenski, *The Religious Factor,* New York, 1961., particularly pp. 267-272, in the Anchor edition.

13. These reactions were obtained by asking the respondents to indicate whether they agreed or disagreed with the statements "Homosexuals should be imprisoned" and "Canada needs less severe divorce laws." The answers were coded as follows: Agree strongly 1, Agree mildly 2, No opinion 3, Disagree mildly 4 and Disagree strongly 5, and the means computed for the five language groups and within each, for the usual subgroups (education, age, religion, occupation).

14. The scores run from 0 to 9 and were created on the basis of answers to three questions: (1) "It seems to be more and more difficult always to obey the law. Some people we talk to feel that a person shouldn't be punished for breaking a law which he believes is against his religion. How about you: do you think a person *should* or *should not* be punished if he breaks a law which he believes is against his religion?" (2) "What of breaking a law going against some other deeply-felt principle but one not related to religion? A person may feel he has to break a law, for example, to assure the survival of his trade union or even of his own national group. Do you think that under these circumstances a person should or should not be punished if he breaks the law?" (3) Agreement or disagreement with the statement that "Illegal strikes should be broken up by the police."

15. The response was given by scoring each group or office with the help of a diagram of a thermometer calibrated from 0 to 100. In coding the responses scores of from 0 to 10 were assigned 1, those from 11 to 20 were coded as 2 etc. A score of 7.8, for example, thus represents a mean "thermometer reading" in the upper sixties

16. There are only 16 cases in this cell, however, and the result must therefore be treated with some caution. It is nevertheless the case that the same individuals comprise the comparable cell in the other three sections of Chart IV where the same results do not obtain. This is a good point at which to mention that, for the sake of not cluttering up the charts and text, the numbers in each cell are not shown. Where they are relevant mention is made either in the text or in the notes.

17. The degree to which the respondents liked or disliked various groups was elicited by means of a thermometer type question, similar to that described in note 15.

18. The statements are part of the battery, mentioned above, which also probed for reactions to homosexuality and divorce. Note 13, above indicates how the answers were coded. The statements are: "Canada would be a better place if all people had the same national origin," and "Canada would be a better place if all people had the same religion." It is assumed, in the full knowledge that the assumption is open to challenge that agreement or disagreement with the statements constitutes a rough indication of religious and ethnic tolerance.

19. The mean score was computed for each language group after the answers were coded as follows: Extremely Interested 1; Very Interested 2; Fairly Interested 3; Not Too Interested 4; No Opinion 5.

20. On another question, seeking a response to the statement that Canada should withdraw its troops from Europe, scored as those in Table V, the results were: A 3.4; B 3.1; C 2.9; D 2.6; E 2.6.

21. For comparable ratings of other offices see Chart IV.

22. The reactions were obtained by seeking agreement or disagreement to a battery of statements about public issues. Chart II (above) draws on other items in the battery and note 13, above indicates how the responses were coded. The full statements used in Chart VII read: (a) "Canada should abolish the monarchy." (b) "Canada's constitution should be changed," and (c) "Provincial governments should participate at international educational conferences."

23. The question read as follows: "Another question often discussed in the election concerned the relations between the governments at Ottawa and Quebec. Some people think that except for the question of language rights Ottawa should resist Quebec's demands for special status. Others say that Quebec has special needs and rights which, in addition to the use of the French language, should

180

be clearly recognized. What are your views? Do you think that Quebec should be *treated exactly like the other provinces* or that it should *occupy a special position* in the Canadian confederation?" Ambiguous and non-responses are excluded from the tabulation.

24. Almost all the interviews were conducted in the second half of 1968. The relevant question was: "There has been quite a bit of talk recently about the possibility of Quebec separating from the rest of Canada and becoming an independent country. Are you in favour of separation or opposed to it? Please tell me whether you are *strongly in favour* of separation, *slightly in favour, undecided, slightly opposed* or *strongly opposed* to separation." The mean score is based on the following coding scheme: Strongly in Favour 1; Slightly in Favour 2; Undecided 3; Slightly Opposed 4; Strongly Opposed 5.

25. The scores (with the number of cases in brackets) are: Primary 3.9 (50); Secondary 4.5 (42); Post-secondary 4.4 (22).

26. The relationship between Identification and the vote is not discussed here. The two "readings" are presented so as to enable the reader to compare what he may consider the Trudeau-dominated vote alongside a somewhat stabler measure.

27. "One of the things we are interested in is the differences which exist between our federal political parties. Considering everything the parties stand for, would you say that there is a good deal of difference between the parties, some difference, or not much difference?" "In your opinion, do you think it makes a great deal of difference, some difference, or no difference which political party is in power in Ottawa?" "Do you think it makes a great deal of difference, some difference, or no difference which party holds office in your provincial legislature?"

28. The scores were coded differently from the earlier thermometer questions. Here the relevant parts of the legend read 41-50 4; 51-60 5; 61-70 6. The question was: "How much do you like Mr. Trudeau?" etcetera.

29. Extremely Important was scored as 1, Not Too Important as 4.

30. Since the present research was organized with SCR studies very much in mind, and indeed, with the assistance of several Ann Arbor colleagues, this will not be a difficult task.

4

"CANCEL OUT AND PASS ON" A VIEW OF CANADA'S PRESENT OPTIONS

THE AUTHORS OF MOST OF THE PAPERS IN THIS BOOK DECIDED to contribute to a volume dealing with Canada's current crisis of identity on the understanding that they would write informal, off-the-cuff essays, rather than a carefully researched and fully documented final word on the respective subjects under discussion. This piece makes no claim to providing an exhaustive survey of its subject and furthermore, it is very much a personal statement on a subject which is of the greatest importance to myself in the light both of my training as a social scientist and of my reactions as a personally concerned individual.

Being neither of British nor French origin, but the son of Czech parents has given me a perspective which may explain some of the views I expound below.

Although one's personal background and professional training inevitably condition the view one takes of the relations prevailing between French- and English-speaking Canadians, many

Written for R. M. Burns [ed.], *One Country or Two?* (McGill-Queen's University Press, 1971). I am indebted to the following friends who have commented on an earlier draft of this paper: Léon Dion, Paul Fox, Peter Leslie, Hans Lovink, and Hugh Thorburn.

options are still open with respect to the general approach one can adopt. One way of looking at the present Canadian crisis is to examine the minutae and nuances of the immensely complex situation confronting us. This would take many lifetimes of work and a whole library of volumes, and is therefore quickly ruled out for this paper. Another way is to select one facet of the problem and to explore it in its infinite variety. This can be a most useful, and is indeed a necessary step, particularly if the most important features are selected for special scrutiny. Its chief limitation is that it inescapably provides only a partial picture of reality which, while perhaps being accurate in so far as it goes, may be misleading when set next to the other pieces of the puzzle.

Yet another approach is obtained by stepping fifteen paces back and by looking at the whole scene from a greater distance. This conceals many of the details but allows the broad outline to become apparent and to stand out in its stark, architectonic mass. This is what I shall do here, although occasionally I shall run more closely towards our subject to examine a given detail briefly.

The method to be adopted clearly ignores certain important features of our problem and it oversimplifies others. It may, however, reveal the quintessence of Canada's current travail— a benefit well worth the loss which it inevitably entails in terms of complexity and subtlety.

The view revealed to this distant gaze contains a few landmarks which provide the main divisions of this essay. In listing them, we shall abandon the topographical analogy. They are the general form which the accommodation between French- and English-speaking Canadians must take; the French Canadian position; the perspective of the English Canadians;[1] the conditions which must be met if both groups of interests are to be reconciled; and the prospects before us.

THE ONLY POSSIBLE SOLUTION

The whole argument of this paper follows from an axiom which, despite its cardinal importance, is often overlooked by those who claim to speak for both French and English Canada. It is this: when two or more groups of people have it in their power to survive within independent political entities, the only workable basis on which they can arrange the political relations between them is compromise. If they are to cohabit one country then each side must be satisfied that its interests are served best by this arrangement and, consequently, that no other realizable arrangement will serve it better.

The nature of the respective group interests is often the subject of acute debate and of internal divisions. In the final analysis the interests are effectively defined by those members of each group who can exercise political power. The opinion of academic observers, or even of the majority of the group's members, is less important in this context, than that of those who control the political apparatus available to each group.

It is also important to note that while constitutional and historical antecedents affect a group's attitudes, they are less important than current views. When conflicts develop between national groups politically sharing a given territory, those who advocate change tend to stress contemporary opinion and to soft-pedal historical precedents, whereas the more conservatively minded defenders of the status quo usually value the older arrangements more highly than what they deem to be more ephemeral recent whims. When differences of this sort develop, it is virtually impossible to resort to any common philosophically or religiously sanctioned values according to which the differences can be resolved; none tend to be shared, at least none to which both sides are prepared to subjugate their *national* interest. It is for this reason that political power, possibly in its extreme form—force—is the only final determinant of the arrangements to be made.

In my view, it would be lunacy to use force in settling the differences between French and English Canada and the sole basis on which the accommodation between the two communities can rest is an agreement acceptable to both. To be acceptable, it must be compatible with those things which are most highly prized by the politically effective spokesmen of each group. In the event that no acceptable basis can be found for their continued political co-existence in one country, they will have to separate, even 'though, in my view, this would lead to neither group effectively furthering its interests as they are now conceived.

185

It is much easier to give an account of "what French Canada
wants," to use the notorious, tired phrase, than to expound
the interests of English Canada.

Quebec, while more homogeneous than English Canada,
does not, of course, speak with one voice. To generalize about
its view is, in a sense, an act of monumental folly. And to
assume that what may be a consensus in Quebec is shared by
French-speaking Canadians in the other provinces dwarfs even
this colossal blunder. And yet, these incontrovertible facts notwithstanding, one can make some broadly valid generalizations
about opinion in Quebec and one can take the view that the
interests of all of French Canada are, in a sense, championed
by, and identified with that opinion and some of the policies
of the Government of Quebec.[2] There is little doubt that the
political power within Canada of the Quebec government, and
the presence in Quebec of the English-speaking minority, are
immensely important counters in the game for survival played
by francophones living in the other provinces.

It is highly questionable whether a people often knowingly
pursue a goal over long stretches of their history. And yet,
with the benefit of hindsight we can sometimes detect patterns
in historical development which indicate that, generation after
generation, a consistent course was followed by a group in a
manner which has enabled it to pursue an identifiable goal and
which has ultimately entered the consciousness of at least its
intellectuals and leaders. When this happens, the goal is articulated and becomes part of the group's self-image and of its
rhetoric. The goal which had heretofore been pursued more or
less like the acquisition of Britain's Empire—in a fit of absent-
mindedness then really does become a guideline towards which
many efforts of the group are consciously directed.

French-speaking Quebeckers, more perhaps even than the
Irish, have adopted as such a goal the survival of their group,
as a group. By this is meant, of course, the continued existence
and flourishing of the culture which evolved on Canadian soil
among the descendants of the original settlers. The two critical
components of this cultural tradition are the French language

and the Catholic religion. Together they, and institutions like the Church and a highly traditional social system, have in the past succeeded in assuring not only the survival of the small number of French-speaking immigrants who came to Canada during the hundred and thirty years before the conquest[3] but, amazingly, their growth to the present population exceeding five and a half million Canadians of French origin.

This phenomenal increase in numbers, achieved with virtually no immigration from France, indicates that the major technique, one partially related to the high birth rate (the notorious "revenge of the cradle") was the isolation of French Canada from many of the dominant trends and developments of North American life. Turning inward, preserving a traditional form of social structure, and being spared the disturbing consequences of having to absorb waves of immigrants, not to mention the menacing presence of an alien North American environment, all combined to create an identifiable and self-conscious French Canadian culture and a strongly-felt sense of national identity. Anyone who has even the scantest acquaintance with life in Montreal and Toronto, say, or Vancouver, cannot miss the rich consequence of this cultural identity for the French Canadian, as compared with the relative absence of an indigenous and unique culture of English Canada. Whether it be the simultaneously lyrical and angry songs of the Quebec *chansonniers*; the particular intellectual universe and flavour of *Le Devoir*; the staging, by several companies, of works by the prolific Quebec playwrights; or the massive output of the poets, novelists, pamphleteers and other polemicists, who have created a veritable sea of little magazines and books—these phenomena all attest to the existence of a French Canadian identity which constantly finds expression in a vigorous cultural life and an articulate national consciousness, missing in English Canada. The intensity and extent of these Quebec activities (I have merely mentioned a small sample in some of the areas in which I happen to be interested) exceed similar efforts elsewhere in Canada so strikingly that they constitute a kind of critical mass which differentiates Quebec qualitatively from the rest of Canada and establishes its culture as being *sui generis*—something which cannot be said about the culture of the English-speaking cities mentioned above.

187

The historical development which has enabled the *Canadiens* to maintain their identity as a nation in the sociological, cultural and linguistic senses, as distinct from a merely political Canadianism, which tends to characterize so much of the rest of the country, has, however, also exacted its costs. French Canada was able, in very large measure, to isolate *itself* but it was unable to *be* isolated. This seeming paradox explains much of what has recently been happening in Quebec and it points to some of the realities which will continue to confront Quebec in the future. French Canadian society evolved into its present form by successfully cutting itself off from the mainstream of American life, but the isolation was inevitably only partial. While French Canada pursued its traditional mode of life, all around it was changing and particularly the economic conditions of Quebec were responding to Canadian, North American and world developments.

The response came largely from English-speaking Quebeckers or from English-speaking "immigrants" from the other provinces, Britain or the United States. The innovators, most of whom were financiers, industrialists, entrepreneurs, and merchants, brought with them a large number of people who had the taste and technical training for activities which did not hold much attraction for many members of the more traditionally oriented French Canadian middle class. And it was these alone who, among their people, had the educational background needed for the full participation in the newer kinds of activities. Many of the large-scale commercial, mining and industrial enterprises were also fully integrated with similar ventures elsewhere and, like their successors—the present multinational corporation—they did not provide full scope for people reluctant to move frequently from one place to another and to spend their entire worklife in the English language.

Economically, therefore, French Canadians tended to provide the less-skilled and consequently the lower-paid services required by a modern industrial, and more recently, the post-industrial economy, and one of the concomitants of their isolation was, therefore, that as a group they suffered a lower standard of living than other Canadians. This was true not only throughout Canada but even in Quebec itself where most of the commercial, financial and industrial power was in the hands of English-Quebeckers or outsiders.

The reasons for the generally disadvantaged position of francophones in Canada, so depressingly but convincingly documented by the studies of the Royal Commission on Bilingualism and Biculturalism, are exceedingly complex. Only one set of responsible factors has been touched upon here. Without going into additional detail, however, it is possible to assert that some of the factors were self-inflicted (it is these which are invariably noted by francophobic anglophones) and others were imposed by others, usually quite unwittingly. It is these external causes for their economically less satisfactory state which are most frequently invoked by French-Canadian nationalists deploring the place occupied by their ethnic group in our Confederation.

Whatever the reasons, there are penalties attached to being French in Canada, and these normally take at least two forms. French Canadians have traditionally been considered less suitable for the most responsible positions in many spheres of activity and have therefore only seldom followed the promotion patterns common to anglophones. But even where opportunities might appear to be equal, the knowledge of English is considered essential, whereas ability to speak French has traditionally been deemed of lesser importance. This penalty has serious consequences for the francophone. At one of its hearings, the Royal Commission on Bilingualism and Biculturalism was given a telling description of this problem: "Everyone knows that here [Chicoutimi], where the population is 98 percent French Canadian, big business has made English the working language and anyone who wants to work his way up the plant has to use English. . . . When there are two people with the same level of education, entering one of our factories in Quebec, the English-speaking one has no need to learn a second language to earn his living, whereas the other person has to spend hours, even years mastering the second language. . . . The first one can go ahead and improve himself in the technological field and take advantage of the first promotion that comes up, whereas the other one loses time learning a second language."[4]

The other penalty concerns the constraint felt by most people who have to use a second language. Since English clearly is the language in which the most important decisions in Canada are made, whether they be in the scientific, economic or political spheres, French Canadian participants are systematically at a disadvantage in the freedom with which they can express themselves, and no doubt also with respect to the effectiveness with which they can do so. Even in those situations in which they are given every opportunity to join Canadian decision-making (and there are many worlds from which they have been and, to a lesser extent, still are excluded) they are less able than their English-speaking colleagues to translate their views and values into action.

In discussing these penalties I have departed somewhat from my resolve to deal only with our problems in the broadest outline: I am in danger of turning from monumental sculpture to fussy filigree! In reverting to the more rough-hewn style intended for this essay I can summarize the main point to be made here by noting that French-Canadians have maintained their national identity at considerable cost: that of being backward, as a group, in the sense of not being fully capable of participating in the highly technological, industrialized and commercialized world of the mid-twentieth century; the cost of being worse off than their English-speaking fellow-Canadians, enjoying comparable opportunities; and that of having their own province largely run by others, and this not only in the economic sphere but in others as well.

Until the advent of the so-called Quiet Revolution, these costs were largely unperceived or, if perceived, condoned by those who benefited from them personally either in a narrowly material sense or in having the gratification of seeing the fulfilment of the ethnically and religiously "pure" role they assigned to French Canada. The single most significant aspect of the Quiet Revolution manifested itself in the minds of French Canadian leaders who rejected the traditional form of Quebec nationalism: for a nationalism of withdrawal and rejection they substituted a nationalism of participation. What they sought and seek to participate in is not, however, necessarily a Canadian political unit but the world which provides the new rewards and opportunities made possible by the current state of scientific, technological and organizational know-how.

Two extremely important strands have combined to give this desire for the new kind of participation an enormously powerful thrust: first, the realization that the old protective mechanisms of the French Canadian identity are no longer effective; second, the sense of dynamic self-consciousness and awareness, which has filled French Canada with an unprecedented optimism and confidence in its capacity to "do its own thing" and to achieve greatness. A few words about each of these strands are in order.

Demographic analyses reveal that the birth rate in Quebec has levelled off dramatically and that it is now lower than in many other parts of Canada. The revenge of the cradle is now an obsolete weapon. To survive, French Canada must, therefore, find other means than simply population growth to offset losses through geographical and cultural emigration. Furthermore, it has now become quite obvious that the old isolationist nationalism was a potent deterrent to the full *épanouissement* of French Canada's culture and that if the latter was to flourish, and if it was to benefit from contemporary developments, it had to break out of the protective cocoon in which it had enveloped itself in the past. To continue the old way would have led to French Canada shrivelling into a quaint and picturesque folk society increasingly clinging to *dépassé* formulas out of lassitude or a desire to attract tourists seeking an escape from the monotony of the commonplace aspects of North American industrial society.

The impetus for change, now so vibrantly exuded by French Canada, is not inspired only by the negative realization that the old ways have become outmoded or that they have perhaps never really worked. There is now a flexing of muscles in Quebec because the rennaissance, which became apparent after the death of M. Duplessis, has given most Quebec leaders the sense that their society has within it the ability to participate fully in the contemporary world and to do so in a manner which can preserve and develop their own values and which can contribute something unique to it as well.

It is usually assumed that French Canadian values, having evolved somewhat in isolation of the major developments in North America, can add a less materialistic and more humane and aesthetic dimension to the post-industrial society.

There is a quixotic element of messianism in this view, held by many French Canadian nationalists—an element which I find unconvincing and unacceptable. But the presence of different values in Quebec clearly does add a significant and enriching dimension to North American ways. There *is* a French

191

Canadian style which differs from the predominant North American mode of doing things and which endows whatever it touches with a quality all its own. A comparison of the Toronto Subway and of the Montreal Métro makes the point, as did many of the best features of Expo. The preservation and growth of French Canadian culture and its lively interaction with the dominant strains of North American and English Canadian culture are, consequently, important and creative goals not only for French Canadians but for Canada as a whole.

Be this as it may (and I shall return to the point later), French Canadians, in defining themselves and their role in North America, do not think of themselves primarily as Canadians but as French Canadians or Quebeckers. The whole notion of Canadianism and of being Canadian has very little resonance among a large and politically powerful group of Quebeckers. They do not feel themselves to be Canadians as much as *Canadiens* and they are convinced, not without reason, that the rest of Canada has been quite uninterested in helping them maintain their culture. English Canadians as a whole are to them a nationally faceless group, ever willing to give up their own identity and Canadian national interests for the material advantages of becoming part of the American economy and of the Pax Americana. And while French Canada might understand and forgive the past lack of concern of the rest of the country for the survival and flourishing of French culture in Quebec, it has been keenly aware of the degree to which the other provinces have pursued policies which have inevitably led to the anglicization of their French Canadian minorities. And, as we shall see a little later, whatever the attitude was towards *past* indifference of English Canada with respect to the survival of French Canadian culture in Quebec, right now Quebec has become passionately involved with the survival of its own cultural values at home (in Quebec) and it will no longer tolerate further anglicization. It is in this context that one must look at recent efforts by the Quebec government to protect the French language through educational, immigration and other policies.

In the strong commitment of French Canadians to their own culture, and in their relative unconcern for the rest of Canada, there is not necessarily any anti-Canadian sentiment. There is

192

usually very little animosity towards the rest of the country, but rather indifference. This may be more irritating to English Canadians than outward hostility since, as is well known, nothing is as discouraging to the wooer as a response indicating a lack of interest. To English Canadians, the idea of Canada existing without Quebec has until recently been quite unthinkable, whereas many Quebeckers can tolerate the thought of their province becoming an independent state. To many, and I dare say a growing number, the possibility is in fact quite challenging and inviting. To put it at its lowest level, the idea of an independent Quebec is not appalling to a great many people in French Canada and is considered a possible alternative to the status quo because of the faith of many French Canadians in the feasibility of an independent Quebec state.

The two paramount questions about the separatist solution are whether French Canadian culture would gain or lose if Quebec were independent and whether the economic life of French Canadians could be maintained at least at the present level. Neither question can be answered without engaging in prodigious guesswork, in which one's own wishes inevitably become the mother of invention and the enemy of proof. No one has, to my satisfaction at any rate, come up with anything like convincing evidence which would lead one to make confident predictions about the likely future of French Canadian culture and of an independent Quebec's economic well-being.

No matter what the long run cultural and economic consequences of separation for the broad masses in Quebec (to which I turn later), there can be little doubt that the leaders of an aggressive nationalism and of separatism have benefited personally from the cultural, political and economic developments which have followed the Quiet Revolution and that they would do so even more in an independent Quebec. Writers and other intellectuals, musicians, artists, politicians, technocrats and civil servants, people in the communications industry— these are the individuals who not only make nationalist revolutions but who also to some extent, live off them. I am not suggesting that their nationalist commitment is insincere or that their idealism is tainted by a mercenary careerism but merely that in forecasting the future their vision and perceptions cannot but be influenced by self-interest and, more important, by the environment in which they function daily and which they unwittingly come to believe resembles the larger world more closely than is likely to be the case.

I have gone to considerable length in pursuing some of the aspects associated with the idea of a separate Quebec because the limits within which compromise between English Canada and Quebec is to be reached are immensely important to the nature of the solution to be found. And it is essential that English Canadians, who tend for their own reasons to exaggerate the evil consequences of separation, are fully aware of the degree of sanguineness with which a rupture with Canada is contemplated by a great many moderate and generous Quebeckers. Many, and some highly responsible French Canadian nationalists are certain to underestimate the difficulties and dangers of an independent Quebec and are not likely to be deterred by the spectre of a separation in pursuing their national aims. These will increasingly be pressed with the vigour and self-confidence which comes from believing that a genuine, if drastic, alternative is available.

The aims to be pursued, with the separatist alternative at the back of many Quebeckers' minds, can now be re-stated. They are closely related to one another, being in a sense merely different aspects of the same basic goal, survival of French Canadian culture.

First, French Canadians, as a group, wish to enjoy equal economic and career opportunities with other Canadians. Particularly in bilingual areas like, say, Ottawa or Montreal, they are no longer satisfied with providing primarily the nightshift— the cleaners of buildings or the operators of elevators, and with the sop of seeing a small number of their group being rewarded by means of occupying the dubious role of the negro king.[5]

Second, they wish to develop the economy of Quebec in a manner which will reflect their own priorities and their own concern for survival. One of the practical consequences of this aim is that in many spheres where the federal government has some responsibility (the location of airports, to take a recently controversial case as an example) they resent Ottawa decisions which may have far-reaching consequences for their own plans and which, while perhaps eminently sensible from the all-Canadian point of view, may conflict with policies whose aims

194

are not merely to be efficient per se, but which may also have French Canadian *national* purposes. The effect of such aims on the demands Quebec is likely to make for constitutional change in Canada is that the Quebec definition of the country is certain to be a much more decentralized federalism, resting largely on an agreement among the constituent provinces, rather than, as is the case now, on an overwhelmingly powerful central government.

Finally, French Canada insists on being *Maitre chez nous.* This resolve to wrest control from outsiders over important parts of Quebec extends not only to the areas just mentioned, like economic planning and governmental policies generally, but also to such vital areas as language use in the province of Quebec. There is no question in my mind that if it does not opt for French unilingualism, to make bilingualism a two-way street in Canada, Quebec will at least do everything in its power to make *itself* reasonably bilingual, in the sense that English Canadians will have to be able to speak French if they wish to enjoy full citizenship, just as Franco-Ontarians must now be able to manage well in English if they are to compete, on an equal footing, with their anglophone fellow-Ontarians. The present privileged position of the English minority is, consequently, going to be challenged by various measures, of which the St. Leonard crisis and the parsimonious treatment occasionally given McGill University, are probably merely tame (and clumsy) harbingers. At the heart of this assertion of French culture lies nothing as crude as revenge against the haughty and arrogant manner of some English-speaking individuals and companies but rather the stark necessity of preventing the eventual anglicization of Montreal and, with it, all Quebec.

The measures protecting the French language, which are admittedly often undertaken awkwardly and foolishly, must nevertheless be understood by non-Quebeckers to be a desperate means of coping with new demographic realities in Quebec. In wishing to become francophonic or genuinely bilingual, and in depriving English of its monopoly position in some sectors of Quebec life, the province is defending the core, or heartland of French Canada. The dramatic and highly emotional reaction of many even moderate French Canadian nationalists to the language question must be understood in these terms. For the

195

handling of this question, more even than the problem of constitutional revision in Canada as a whole, and more than the economic aspects of French Canadian nationalism, will determine whether French culture can survive in Canada or whether, as in Louisiana, it is largely to become a colourful folk-memory, to be celebrated annually by a crassly commercial Mardi Gras.

FOUR PERSPECTIVES OF ENGLISH CANADA

The aims of English-speaking Canadians are much less homogeneous than those of Quebeckers, and in a large measure they remain virtually unstated and perhaps even unperceived. Two different, but related, perspectives dominate the thoughts of English-speaking Canadians about themselves as a group and as members of a country. One leads them to a view of Canada taken as a whole, what sort of country it is and who they are as Canadians; the other concentrates more narrowly on what they conceive to be the appropriate relations between the French- and English-speaking parts of the country and, more specifically, what should be the place of Quebec in our Confederation.

Some Canadians have a strongly British conception of Canada, not only in the sense that they themselves value the British connection and its heritage but, much more important, in that they believe that the whole country must share these values. The tendency to play down these links, the gradual removal of British heraldry and of the representation of the Monarch from public places are viewed by this group as a betrayal indicative of the transformation of Canada into a rootless, polyglot entity. To many (but certainly not all) of those holding this view, the presence of French-speaking Canadians is the result of their conquest by the British. The French are tolerated, so long as they accept the essentially British nature of the country, and so long as they do not prevent the non-French majority from pursuing its ends. Most Canadians belonging to this school of thought see nothing wrong in, and often welcome, the anglicization of French Canadians. And while they deplore the loss of British elements in Canadian life, and particularly in its political culture, they do not lament the possible or actual decline of French Canadian culture.

196

According to a different, more widely held concept, Canada is a country based on its indisputable pluralism. Those who hold this view see themselves to be part of a community composed of many ethnic and cultural groups which, for better or for worse, share certain political institutions and certain problems and opportunities. There is a good deal of variation among the members of this group with respect to the degree of Canadian nationalism they display. In this they resemble the next group I will mention and it will save time if we discuss this aspect of the two groups together later. Other divergencies of opinion to be found among the "pluralists" concern their ideas about the place to be occupied in the Canadian mosaic by the French-speaking members and the degree to which the members of each of its components should be prepared to abandon their original culture. There are many Scandinavians, Slavs and others, whose families have lost their language and cultural traditions, who do not see why French Canadians should accept this kind of metamorphosis any less willingly than they did themselves, as the price of leading a safe and reasonably prosperous North American existence. This position obviously affects the way in which they react to Quebec demands for conditions required for the survival of the French language in Canada. Some do not distinguish between the French and other minorities, whereas others ascribe a special position to the descendants of the earliest *habitants*. This group resembles the third identifiable school of thought about the nature of Canada.

Like the terms of reference given the Royal Commission on Bilingualism and Biculturalism, and like the commissioners themselves, the Canadians who make this distinction assume that Canada is a partnership between two language groups. These language groups constitute two societies which share one political union. It follows from this position that both English and French occupy a special place in the life of Canada and that both languages must be accorded special and equal status in clearly identified areas. In recognizing the two principal language groups in Canada, the adherents to the country's essential dualism recognize, as I am doing throughout this essay, that people of various origins, in the process of their Canadianization, become part of one or the other of the two language

197

groups and members of one or the other of the two societies. According to this view—and it is one I accept—I am an English Canadian, despite the fact that so far as I know I cannot boast a single ancestor hailing from England.

A fourth fairly common definition of Canada by English-speaking people is more vague even than the three enumerated so far. Unlike these, it does not distinguish between various specific ethnic and cultural traditions but takes a general view of the country by seeing it as somehow different from all others. It tends not to identify anything positive which makes Canada different, but is based on its holders' belief that in numerous small ways Canada is different from other countries and that these differences give us our particular national identity. The argument, though extremely vague, is reasonably convincing, since, if casual personal observation is to be trusted, a large number of Canadians share the impression that, as a people, "we just are different" from our neighbours and from other nationalities.

It is possible to hold this view of Canada, which is not related to what the appropriate relations should be among the country's inhabitants, and belong to one of the three groups identified so far. The fourth definition gives Canada its character by comparing it with certain *external* phenomena, while the first three focus entirely on *internal* factors—the ethnic composition of the population.

It is nevertheless useful to distinguish between the four groups, even 'though they are not mutually exclusive, by determining where the priorities of various English Canadians lie. People who have *primarily* an internal, demographic perception of the country belong to one of the first three groups. The others are placed in the fourth if they subscribe to its differently-based position. The view one has of Canada's population and cultural tradition may of course affect the definition one has of the country when one compares it with others.

The schools of thought identified here can be labelled the British-Canadian, the pluralist, the dualist and the "Canada just is different" positions. The labels, like the categories themselves, are only very rough and ready identification points to four general tendencies which vary greatly from individual to individual. Their usefulness lies in permitting us to make a few comments about English Canadians who share a certain cluster of ideas about the nature of their country.

It is almost inescapable, in view of our history and origins, that Canadians should tend to define their country not so much by reference to characteristics which it possesses, as by those in which it differs from other countries. And the reference points are normally Britain and the United States with, perhaps, an occasional nod in the direction of France. Our British Canadians, ever mindful of the historical development of Canada, tend to define the country still very much in the terms which bind us to Britain and they are generally disposed to be the most active and jealous guardians of Canada's identity vis-à-vis the United States.

They are usually more nationalist than the pluralists and more strongly anti-American. In this latter trait they resemble the dualists and the "Canada just is different" group, who also tend to be fairly actively afraid of United States influences, but the groups differ from one another in the means they find most congenial to combat them. The British Canadians wish to preserve the British links, traditions and institutions. The dualists, on the other hand, are disposed to seek in the French presence in Canada a countervailing force likely to keep the Americans at bay. More precisely, they believe that a close and conscious alliance of French- and English-speaking Canadians, wishing to create out of their partnership a different kind of North American society here in Canada, can best protect us from the inroads of American culture.

The pluralists are, as a rule, the least concerned about American influences on Canada. They admire the pluralism of American society and, normally seeing no great inherent virtue in preserving British patterns in a North American setting which is radically different from the United Kingdom, nor being greatly impressed by the argument that what makes Canada unique is the French presence, they tend to think of Canada as being like the United States. As a result they are also somewhat less dismayed than the other groups by the prospect of Canada falling apart because of its inability to resolve the differences between the demands of anglophones and francophones. There are many among the pluralists who would, under these circumstances, consider without extreme anguish the possibility of

199

their province or region becoming part of the United States. This is not to say that they would particularly welcome this development but merely that they would find it somewhat less intolerable and unthinkable than the British Canadians, the dualists and the "Canada just is different" school. The consequence of this difference, from the point of view of this analysis, is that the pluralists are less disposed to compromise with the spokesmen for French Canada, than the other groups, for the sake of preserving the realm.

Their relative disinclination to compromise with French Canada is motivated by the just mentioned lesser fear of Americanization and also, of course, by the group's tendency to place a lower value on the presence of the French culture. In this they resemble the British Canadians and they differ markedly from the dualists, and also to some extent from most of our fourth group—those who sense that Canada is different, in an indefinable way, from other countries. For this reason, the two latter groups are much more willing than the British Canadians and the pluralists to see the adjustments made in Canada to accommodate the interests of Quebec.

The generalizations I have been making here about the four main strands of opinion among English Canadians are, of course, almost scandalously broad and crude. I would want to subject them to a most rigorous examination before committing myself irrevocably to them. They are, however, useful in the present context. Among other things, they are compatible with regional historical and demographic differences in Canada and they also help explain variations in regional attitudes towards the nature of the country. The so-called British-Canadian view is associated most closely with Ontario, particularly some of the rural areas, with the Atlantic provinces, and with parts of British Columbia, especially Victoria. The pluralist position is evident particularly in the Prairies, most notably among Canadians whose origin is neither British nor French, among the less British parts of British Columbia, and probably also among the inhabitants of the large Metropolitan areas. Dualists are, I suspect, most concentrated geographically in Ontario and overwhelmingly in Quebec; they are to be found in large proportion among young people and also, so far as I can tell, among leaders of national voluntary associations who have had some experience in working out compromises with articulate colleagues from French Canada. The Canadian self-consciousness which leads to an awareness of this country being different from others and therefore to a nationalism which is not necessarily related to the country's ethnic composition, is not localized in any particular region. It is most noticeable among journalists, artists, teachers and intellectuals—those, in short, whose occupatitons encourage them to define the nature of their community and to reflect upon its characteristics and problems. It is my guess that generally (and I readily concede that there must be many exceptions) nationalism among English-speaking Canadians is a middle class phenomenon. If this is so, then *taking the group as a whole,* one would find those whom I have identified as the "Canada just is different" school among the better educated, the better paid and among those with higher-ranking occupations than the average for the English-speaking group as a whole. For reasons which I have indicated above, I think that they would be particularly numerous among those with the most years of schooling and those who make their living primarily through symbolic communication.

I have devoted a fair amount of space to a somewhat hypothetical exploration of the anatomy of English-speaking opinion about the nature of the country, the place in it of French Canadians and the possible total Americanization of Canada. The detailed look at this aspect of our main problem was a necessary prelude to a consideration of the degree to which English Canadians can accommodate themselves to the needs of their French-speaking fellow citizens.

Before we turn to this question, however, it is necessary to stress two other points: one deals with the more narrowly political federal-provincial dimension, the other concerns the overall attitude of English-speaking Canadians to their country, for I believe that at least some general statements can and indeed must be made about it.

The four approaches to Canada, noted above, are essentially different clusters of opinion which are not, as such, related to any particular political option, although each, of course, predisposes the holder towards certain specific postures, *vis-à-vis* the crisis now confronting the country. The latter has a specifically political aspect which brought into being various well-defined positions advocating how we should settle our problems at the constitutional and governmental levels. The most immediate and concrete form of these political choices concerns the relations which should prevail between the federal government and the provinces, and to some extent also among the provinces themselves. What to do about revising the constitution is one important aspect of this side of our problem, as is also the appropriate fiscal relationship between the various levels of government and the means to be employed when governments at any of the two senior levels make decisions which have consequences beyond their own jurisdictions.

Whereas the four groups of definitions of Canada are largely entertained by individuals, it is primarily governments which must take political positions with respect to the nature of the country. Hence, the political options are championed by spokesmen for "Ottawa" or the various provinces, who cannot but endow their formulas and arguments with an aura of official formality. These official formulations, while unquestionably coloured by the four schools of thought considered above, tend to reflect not so much the tastes and inclinations of individuals, as the harsh economic realities interpreted by the officials and politicians serving their respective levels of government.

By and large, the poorer provinces favour a strong central government, in the hopes that the latter will engage in an extensive national redistribution of income, whereas the more affluent parts of the country, feeling their potential or actual strength, and capable of greater independent effort, tend to support a more decentralized arrangement which would enhance the powers of the provincial governments.

The position taken as the result of the economic situation of a province is either reinforced or contradicted by the views on the nature of the country prevailing among its inhabitants. Generally, the pluralists are the most centralizing group, and the dualists the most strongly committed to the idea of a system based on decentralized government by powerful, largely autonomous provinces. The British Canadians, like the pluralists, include a large proportion of centralists, partly perhaps because the addition of federal institutions to parliamentary ones tends to make for complications and may reduce the effectiveness of the latter. Another reason for their disposition to support a strong central government may be that they believe that such a government might better resist the Americanization of Canada than a number of weaker provinces. It is in part because of this last-named argument that the group of mild nationalists whom we have dubbed the adherents to the "Canada just is different" school tends to pursue a strongly centralist line. Anxiety about too much United States influence is probably least common, as I have suggested earlier, among pluralists, but is likely to be shared by virtually all Canadian politicians shaping our national and regional policies.

As for the general attitude of English-speaking Canadians to their country, there is no gainsaying the assertion often made by francophones that it has been influenced by their concern for the economic well-being of the population. This concern for maintaining a high standard of living, comparable to the maximum attained in the United States, has led most English Canadians to adopt an attitude of tolerance towards, and even encouragement of, American encroachments of Canadian sovereignty and, more important, of the Canadian mind. For American interests are allowed to permeate Canada's economy, its institutions of learning, its mass media, its world of entertainment, its voluntary associations—all its life in short—to a degree which suggests that whatever they may *say,* most English Canadians really do not care whether their country becomes indistinguishable from their neighbour.

French Canadian intellectuals who, as we have seen, are themselves enormously concerned about the survival of their identity and nation, tend to conclude that the materialistic pursuits of their English-speaking compatriots have deprived them of a will to have their country survive as an independent entity. This doubt focuses on several aspects of French-English relations in Canada, at least in so far as the intellectuals of the nationalist movement are concerned. In its general manifestation, it questions whether two groups, whose actions are motivated by so widely differing a set of priorities as appear to be dividing French- and English-speaking Canadians, can in effect continue successfully to co-exist in one state. More specifically, it questions whether a unified country, even a federal one, can function effectively when part of its population appears little willing to resist its takeover, in all but the most formal sense, by its powerful neighbour, while another important segment prizes its national survival more than anything else in the world. And finally, French Canadian scepticism is directed at the willingness of English Canadians (given their tendency to value everything in economic terms) to sacrifice anything tangible for the development and growth of a country which would afford equal opportunities to French- and English-speaking Canadians. In other words, French Canadians wonder whether English Canadians, who appear quite unwilling to make the economic sacrifices required to prevent Canada from substantial Americanization, are going to be willing to make the economic sacrifices necessary to protect their country from the disaffection of a large linguistic minority.

I find it most difficult to resist sharing these doubts. I like diversity among people and, while I see many dangers in nationalism, I do believe that Canada has been altogether too willing to permit its neighbour to make inroads into an essentially Canadian way of doing things. We have been largly unconcerned witnesses to the gradual attrition of Canada's diversity from the United States and our attachment to an ever rising standard of living may prevent us from adopting changes which may be necessary for the political survival of Canada as we know it. Those of us who take this view share, in this particular at least, the doubts of many Quebec nationalists. I believe that a dangerously large number of French-speaking Canadians nevertheless misread the way in which English Canadians see their country.

It is all too often assumed in Quebec that English Canadians are so mesmerized by the alluring dollar that nothing else matters to them and that for a high standard of living they are prepared to give up everything, including their country. This view is understandable in the light of what I have just been saying but it overlooks a point of the most critical importance: the choice before most Canadians as they make decisions compromising the country's independence and identity is not between gaining an economic advantage and preserving Canada's independence. The implications for national survival of many economic and other decisions are rarely perceived at all, and it is probably correct to say that most of the inroads into Canadian sovereignty result from individual or corporate decisions in which no thought is given to the consequences for the country as a whole. If, in the same decisions, an alternative were presented in which a choice would have to be made between damaging Canada for the sake of some material advantage, or not damaging it, the chances are that a great many Canadians would opt for the latter.

In other words, it is quite misleading to assume that, despite the absence of a strong national consciousness, and of an aggressive nationalism, English-speaking Canadians are devoid of loyalty to their country. This loyalty, often quite vigorous, is not evident in decisions affecting the Americanization of the country because so many Canadians do not see the latter as a threat to national survival. On the other hand, events like de Gaulle's *Québec Libre* speech, Quebec initiatives in diplomacy, and separatist agitation are conceived as genuine threats and provoke extremely violent responses on the part of large numbers of English-Canadians, as the perusal of even the moderate (in this context) English language press reveals at a glance.

A realistic assessment of English Canadian opinion must distinguish sharply between postures taken *vis-à-vis* the United States and those adopted in relation to what is often taken to be an internal attempt to break up the country. For many English Canadians the internal threat to the continuation of Canada is emotionally and in every other way the equivalent of the challenge to their own survival experienced by most French-Canadian nationalists. An excessively inward-looking and self-centred parochialism prevents many Quebec leaders from realizing this, and also from perceiving that the 'seventies will witness a major effort on the part of English Canadians towards reasserting Canadian interests in the face of American challenge.

Outright separatism is only the most extreme form in which English Canadians see their country's survival threatened by Quebec nationalism. There are others, and although they are less dramatic and provocative, they nevertheless arouse deep concern and anxiety among the large majority of English Canadians who worry about the future of their country. The most acute and controversial "threat" results from the desire of Quebec to make its own decisions in a wide variety of fields, many of which cannot be confined to the provincial sphere alone. Although English Canada's nationalism is not nearly so well-defined and vigorously articulated as Quebec's, it is real enough for all that, and it takes at least two clearly recognizable forms: it is based on considerable pride in Canada as a country and as a member of the international community, and it assumes that there are certain Canada-wide standards and procedures which should be common to, and shared by, all parts of the country. Quebec's occasional encouragement of, and connivance in, the slighting of Canada in the international sphere, particularly by the government of France, evokes bitter resentment in English Canada.

Secondly, and I think much more seriously, the wish of Quebec to make its own decision in fields which have ramifications far beyond education and the other areas normally under provincial jurisdiction is sometimes seen as a threat to the survival of Canadian standards. It is held that the Quebec demands for autonomous decision-making would, if acceded to without qualification, cripple the power of the central government to make decisions affecting Canadians in fields in which the interests of all parts of the country are affected. Some of the demands of Quebec are thus held to be impediments to the federal government's taking steps necessary for the well-being and equitable development of all Canadians. Even those English Canadians who strongly sympathize with the national aspirations of French Canada sometimes wonder whether the most extreme political demands arising from them may not, unwittingly perhaps, destroy Canada as a viable country, by paralyzing all attempts to make decisions in the common interests of all. No one has seriously suggested that Canada has reached the stage at which the decision-making powers of the federal government have been seriously frustrated by Quebec demands but the fear that they may be in danger will quite certainly impose one of the limits on the compromises some English-speaking provinces will be prepared to make in future negotiation about constitutional revisions and particularly the reallocation of responsibilities between the federal and provincial governments.

Our discussion has now reached the point where we can begin to look at the motivation for, and the content of, the compromise which will have to be reached between French-

206

and English-speaking Canadians if their country is to survive as a political entity. It will be recalled that the major premise of my argument has been that the only acceptable solution to Canada's current national dilemma is one which proves equally acceptable to both major language groups.

THE CONDITIONS NECESSARY FOR THE RECONCILIATION OF INTERESTS

We have seen that essentially both groups are seeking their survival—one in terms of its cultural identity and the other in terms of a political unit which also displays certain national characteristics. Since in each instance it is actually survival which is at stake, the clash of wills is animated by a profound and intense force which cannot easily be moderated and which may, in the end, sweep everything aside, including reason and enlightened self-interest.

And yet, it seems to me that accommodation between the two groups is possible if each believes that its objectives can be reached within the framework of Canada. At the present time English-speaking Canadians overwhelmingly think that this is possible but they are not particularly aware, as yet, of the adjustments they will have to make to accommodate the interests of French Canada. Francophones, on the other hand, probably understand the problems somewhat better, at least those aspects of them touching on their own survival. But many of their most articulate leaders are less convinced that their aims can be met without a drastic political realignment, possibly necessitating the disruption of Canada. The most encouraging feature of the present impasse is that substantial majorities on both sides have still not rejected a Canadian solution and that the impulse for separation is confined on both sides to numerically unimpressive minorities.[6] It is nevertheless disquieting to note that a significant minority is not opposed strongly to the separation of Quebec. In my survey, roughly 70 percent of those whose background is British, 65 percent of those whose origin is neither British nor French, and only 59 percent of French Canadians *strongly* opposed separation.

The situation is fluid and although I believe that there is still the necessary degree of will required among Canadians to make it possible for us to stay together, there is also a substantial level of uncertainty which makes the outcome unpredictable. One of the aspects which must be considered is the cost, to each group, of the disappearance of Canada as we know it. So far the emphasis in our discussion has largely been on the costs of staying together. We must now briefly examine the other side: how would the "departure" of Quebec affect the aims of the two language groups?

Canada would, of course, cease to exist in its present form and to some extent the traditional way of perceiving the world, the loyalty, pride and ambition of many English-speaking Canadians would consequently be seriously impaired. The often-heard bogey of the succession state(s) eventually being absorbed by the United States does not strike me as particularly convincing, however. There would be many very serious communication problems and much economic dislocation but on the whole it seems likely that the trauma of this experience and the exigencies of adjusting to new conditions might produce a sense of national cohesion among the English-speaking Canadians and the *élan* required to create a new state. The tragic and searing experiences which would almost certainly accompany its birth could easily generate precisely the kind of vigorous and active nationalism which is presently not very much in evidence in Canada (an absence, incidentally, which in the eyes of many who have elsewhere experienced the parochialism and inhumanity of chauvinism, bestows on Canada one of its most attractive characteristics). Such a revitalized nationalism would enable the truncated new country to overcome both the internal centrifugal forces, and the pull of the United States, which would inevitably threaten it. In any event, the United States might not wish to absorb all, or even part, of her northern neighbour.

The consequence of the split might, therefore, in a paradoxical way, make English Canada come to resemble present French Canada in some respects by giving its members a greater sense of national community and by making them more conscious of the need for intensifying the efforts required to resist the ubiquitious influences of the United States. There is little doubt that economically the English remnant could become a viable state, the standard of living of whose members would not, in the long run, be affected adversely by the new political conditions.

This speculation may, of course, be no more than a Pollyanna-like escape from reality. The various far-flung fragments of the new state may find the attraction of the United States too great to resist and the new Canada might ultimately disappear. I nevertheless believe that many of the important goals of English Canadians—a high standard of living, a peaceful and free society in the liberal democratic sense, and a high level of toleration of diversity—would survive the break-up of their present-day Canada. What would, alas, not survive, is the presence, in one country, of two major language groups, constantly interacting on one another and so creating a dynamism and cultural mix of which more homogeneous states are deprived. This would be a grievous loss to me and many other Canadians but it would not prevent most English Canadians from achieving their major goals in the new state.

I am not nearly as confident about the chances of a free Quebec realizing the goals currently pursued by most of the separatist leaders. This is not to say that I doubt the capacity of an independent state of Quebec to survive as a political unit in North America—I am sure that it could. What it might find exceedingly difficult to achieve is the fulfilment of the high aims pursued by virtually all French Canadian nationalists, namely the survival and flourishing of their culture and the opportunity of creating a life of dignity in French, without the corroding influences of the English North American culture.

There are many reasons for my pessimism. Three strike me as particularly compelling and I shall mention them, without examining them in detail. The first concerns the capacity of a new small state, beset by many problems resulting from the dislocation of long-established economic, political and social patterns, to resist the overpowering influence of the United States. Servain-Schreiber, in his *The American Challenge,* has admirably portrayed the pressure exercised by the American economy, and he has shown how difficult it is even for all of Western Europe to resist it. Is it likely that an independent Quebec might succeed, where Europe has so far failed?

It is, of course, possible to minimize American cultural and economic influence, as Castro's Cuba and Mao's China have shown. Conditions in these two countries, and those prevailing in Quebec are, however, so staggeringly different, that the parallel is totally meaningless. It is most improbable that the majority of the population in Quebec, or even a significant minority, would be prepared to pay the price required to eradicate or even seriously to reduce the outside influences which are said to threaten the survival of French culture. The policies almost certain to be adopted by an independent Quebec, to offset foreign influences would be no less inimical to Quebec nationalism than what can, if the will is there, be achieved within the present Canadian framework.

It is quite possible, in fact,—and this is my second reason for pessimism—that even fairly mild nationalistic economic and linguistic policies in an independent Quebec might lead to serious economic difficulties. The accompanying loss of employment and the lowering in living standards would probably lead to large-scale hardship and out-migration from Quebec, the latter particularly among the most skilled individuals who, for the sake of better jobs, would almost certainly be prepared to settle in any number of Canadian provinces or in the United States. This migration could lead to an even further lowering of living standards in Quebec and would defeat the often lofty and, on the face of it, plausible arguments of the separatists.

Thirdly, I am uneasy about the political reaction, in an independent Quebec, to the inevitable difficulties and hardships associated with starting a new, break-away state. Dangerous illiberal elements exist in any liberal democratic state and, for a great many reasons, the possibility cannot lightly be discounted of an authoritarianism of the right or the left developing, following serious social and economic dislocation in Quebec. It is easy to over-dramatize this kind of argument, and it has often been used in differing contexts by opponents of innovation. This unappetizing precedent notwithstanding, I detect many elements in Quebec society and politics which lead me to fear that under conditions of stress, even well-meaning leaders might resort to exceedingly dangerous means in an effort to achieve their goals and that if this were to happen, the cause of a dynamic and liberating Quebec nationalism would suffer. The creative society expected from an independent Quebec by its proponents would not be likely to emerge from an oppressive regime dedicated to compelling its people to like the controls deemed necessary by the rulers. The emergence of such a regime, while by no means inevitable, is a possibility which no one, I believe, can seriously ignore, particularly those of us—whether French-speaking Canadians or others—who value the richness of Quebec culture and who hope to continue enjoying it in the future.

It is perhaps futile to try to predict how separation would affect each of the two groups. The critical point is that, apart from depriving each of the other, it would present quite fearful perils to both French and English Canadians and that, in trying to find a settlement of their present differences, each should be acutely conscious of these. English Canadians are, I think, somewhat more aware of the costs to themselves of separation, since it is, of course, not they who are the most active and vigorous champions of a split and since, on the whole, they strongly oppose it. French Canadian separatists, on the other hand, tend to assume that the costs of independence would be small relative to the benefits bestowed by it. An acceptable compromise between the two positions will require that the adherents of each side have a reasonably accurate and complete understanding of the position of the other and that they are fully aware of its implications for day-to-day negotiations and bargaining that in fact nowadays occur continually between French and English Canada.

In the present essay it is of course impossible to be specific about the position that each group should take towards the other on every particular issue under discussion. The details have to be worked out in each case which will dictate their nature, but the accommodation has to occur within certain general guidelines which can be stated. Their generality and simplicity should not lead the reader to reject them too quickly: many profound truths are simple and may appear both trite and obvious.

For the French Canadian nationalist the main point to remember, as he re-defines his relationships with English Canada, is that he cannot have it all his way and still remain part of Canada. In a partnership, the aims and objectives, but particularly the *modi operandi*, of the participants cannot be defined in absolute terms pleasing to one group or the other. Each side must be prepared to accept a little less than it would really like and compromise is therefore essential. French Canada, if it feels that its long-term aims can best be achieved within a

Canadian state, will have to be prepared to bear in mind some of the deeply-felt ideas and strongly-held values of the anglophones and will therefore, have to be contented with accepting, *in some areas at least,* somewhat less than it might really want.

Quebec would, I believe, accept this watering of its nationalist wine if English Canadians showed a comparable willingness to be satisfied with less than they really want, if its leaders took a *really* serious and realistic view of the separatist alternative and if they had an awareness of the constraints on the freedom of action which would inescapably affect the domestic and foreign policies of an independent Quebec.

The principal guideline for English Canada is to realize that in the past French Canada has benefited substantially less than the English-speaking population from participating in the Canadian state and that, whatever the complex reasons, French Canada's underdog status is in part the result of English Canada's ethnocentrism. Secondly, English Canada will have to accept the idea that in several important areas of Canadian life, and particularly in the political one, there will have to be substantial changes made which will alter the character of Canada in some important ways. There is a widespread presumption, even among some exceedingly learned folk, that there is only one "real" federal state and that Canada is its most magnificent and perfect expression. They fail to see that there is an infinite number of possible federal arrangements and that Canada may have to depart quite substantially from the present formula and move toward a new one. In defining the "national" Canadian interest, the pre-eminence of the central government may have to be greatly diminished, as has already been implied, to make way for a continuous and elaborate scheme in which the provinces, enjoying greater autonomy than they do now, may have to reach agreement among themselves. English Canadians will have to recognize, as one of their basic guidelines, that although this may make for a less effective governmental system in some ways, the alternative might be the break-up of the country.

Accepting these guidelines, and the consequences which follow from this acceptance, would require that both sides make efforts of quite uncommon difficulty for the sake of finding a mutually satisfactory solution to their problems. Each group would have to swallow a great deal of pride; each would have to show a degree of realism scarcely ever achieved in the controversies concerning issues of nationalism and of the destiny of states; each would have to suppress a driving impetus towards being vindictive and malicious under extremely provocative conditions.

In Strindberg's *The Dance of Death*, the protagonists—a married couple—discover that while their life together is full of excrutiating tensions and hostilities, they have become dependent on one another and cannot really live separately. Strindberg's Edgar and Alice, realizing their mutual dependence, achieve a partial reconciliation after having inflicted awesome humiliations on one another—a reconciliation which they express by agreeing to "Cancel out and pass on!" Since seeing this play for the first time in Stratford, (interestingly in the present context, with Jean Gascon and Denise Pelletier, two of French Canada's finest actors, giving superb performances) I have often wondered whether this modest programme could not usefully be kept in mind by French and English Canadians trying to reconcile the differences now separating them. I realize, of course, that Quebec's motto is *Je me souviens*, and that there are many aspects of this country's past which neither ethnic group would wish to forget or cancel out. But in exploiting the many things which Canadians have going for them, as the current saying has it, it would often be highly desirable if both groups could learn to make light of some of the ways of the past in favour of passing on to what strikes me as a potentially exciting and highly promising future.

THE PROSPECTS BEFORE US

The chances of this happening are not, alas, encouraging.

There are strong vested interests and deep-rooted prejudices on both sides which stand in the way of the adoption of the kind of attitude of accommodation suggested above. The clear personal advantage, noted earlier, which inevitably accrues from an extreme nationalist Quebec position and from a *politique de mini-grandeur* to the Quebec writers, broadcasters and artists, and to bureaucrats, politicians and intellectuals generally, may make it difficult for them to think of the consequences for the general population of a rupture with Canada. In a situation where there are clear economic difficulties and

213

other serious problems it may be hard for politicians not to have recourse to a cheap but effective nationalistic demagoguery. The moderates may be defeated and swept aside by the louder and more pat politicians promising a panacea, once independence is achieved. It is not only the Bertrands and the Bourassas who may be overtaken by the extremist passions of an aroused population but also the Lévesques and the Parizeaus.

On the other side the picture is no more encouraging. While a great deal is now being done in this country by the federal government and some of the provinces to cope with the genuine needs and claims of French Canada, the overall picture is not very cheering. The reception generally given in the English language press to the Royal Commission on Bilingualism and Biculturalism, the political and media reaction to Mr. Trudeau's language legislation and, in Ontario, the way in which many school boards and other bodies have reacted to Mr. Robarts' enlightened and realistic approach to the problems of Franco-Ontarians are only some of the indicators suggesting that English Canada has not yet grasped the need for really fundamental changes if Canada is to survive. My pessimism may in part be caused by the fact that a good many English language newspapers display an underlying hostility to the French presence among us, and reveal daily that there is little editorial understanding of the issues facing us.

The key question in guessing the outcome of the present crisis is whether the leaders on both sides will have the wisdom and courage to make the adjustment to one another required to achieve the accommodation and compromise which, as I have argued, can be the only acceptable way of reaching a solution. It is my guess, admittedly based only on very general and unsubstantiated observations, that on the French side the general population is able and prepared to make the necessary adjustment in its aims and methods of achieving them but that a substantial number of leaders is incapable and unwilling to accept conditions necessary for a Canadian solution. The reverse situation seems to obtain in English Canada. Here an important number of leaders at the federal and provincial levels have shown the necessary insight and understanding but the general population appears to be lagging behind.

The outcome will depend on whether spokesmen for Quebec will reflect majority opinion or the wishes of a highly articulate and active minority and on whether the English spokesmen will be able to take enlightened and far sighted actions which, in the first instance at least, may not have the support of the English majority. There is much food for thought in this observation for anyone interested in the working and virtue of liberal democratic political systems, but this is a topic too removed from our present problem to warrant discussion here.

I fear that the chances of the Quebec spokesmen in the critical decisions being representative of the majority and of the English leaders not being so are poor and I therefore view the prospects before us with pessimism: we shall likely "cancel out" together but when it comes to "passing on" we shall not do so in the sense of moving together towards a new life.

I cannot think of anything that I have ever said which I would welcome more being contradicted by events.

NOTES

1. Throughout this paper, except where the context makes it clear, references to all of Canada which is not French will often use the adjective "English" despite the obvious misleading nature of the term in a situation in which many non-French-speaking Canadians belong to all kinds of ethnic groups.

2. The so-called "double legitimacy" problem nevertheless remains: it is possible that the Quebec voters elect a provincial government pursuing policies opposed by a federal government which has itself received, at approximately the same time, majority electoral support in Quebec. Who can, under such conditions, say what policies the voters really support?

3. The number is estimated at no more than 10,000.

4. *A Preliminary Report of the Royal Commission on Bilingualism and Biculturalism*, Ottawa, Queen's Printer, 1965, p. 77.

5. The image of *le roi nègre* is frequently invoked by French-Canadian nationalists. He is the native colonial ruler who receives rewards and honours as compensation for doing the bidding of the imperialist interests.

215

6. Respondents interviewed in a very large national survey I conducted late in 1968 overwhelmingly rejected the idea of separation. Fewer than 3 percent of the 2767 Canadians interviewed were strongly in favour, and under 5 percent said they were slightly in favour. Almost 14 percent were undecided. Ten percent of the respondents of French origin supported separation (4 percent strongly and 6 percent mildly) but 18 percent were undecided, as compared with only 11 percent "undecideds" among those whose origin is British, and 14 percent among those whose ancestors are neither French nor British.

5

HOWE, HUBRIS AND '72
AN ESSAY ON
POLITICAL ELITISM

THE IMPORTANCE OF ELECTIONS USUALLY RESIDES IN THEIR "objective" outcome: the character of the new legislature. There are rare occasions, however, when a more subjective aspect assumes almost equal significance because the subsequent interpretation of the voters' decision also vitally affects the future course of politics. The 1972 election falls into the latter category for two reasons: the outcome was ascribed by an alarming number of morning-after, bleary-minded editorialists and politicians to the rejection by English Canada of what had come to be thought of as "French power" in Ottawa; and the inconclusive nature of the result was greeted with profound dismay by many Canadians. Both of these reactions are dangerous, largely because they are prompted by a cripplingly selective and short-run consideration of the events and their causes.

In developing some trains of thought prompted by the 1972 campaign—some of them of the massive transcontinental

I am grateful to the Canada Council for a Killam Award which has given me the time required to think about Canadian politics in the long-term perspective of this paper, as well as in terms of the more immediate concerns of the other studies in this volume. My most immediate and joyous thanks, however, go to four beautiful women, whose help I value beyond all others: Joan Harcourt, Murie Meisel, Fanny Morales, and Patricia Peppin.

variety, others of the more modest dayliner type—I will try to avoid being sidetracked by the minutiae of the present; the analysis is set in the broader context of exploring the efficacy of the Canadian party system in responding to Canadian needs.

FRENCH POWER

It is not surprising that those, in both language groups, who wish or seek the destruction of Canada quickly seized on the startling difference in support received by the Liberals in French- and English-speaking communities and that others quite guilelessly saw the election results only in this perspective. The French power argument must nevertheless be rejected, as I shall demonstrate, and as some columnists have already started to do.[1] Henceforth, one will be able to invoke it only at the risk of being accused of wilfully ignoring or distorting the evidence.

An equally humiliating accusation can, however, be made against those who refuse to see, as three of the papers in the present volume dramatically show, that there are immense regional and linguistic differences in Canada, making for substantial divergence in the political culture of French- and English-speaking Canadians.[2] Quebeckers have often reacted differently to political stimuli and the gap in party attachments between anglophones and francophones was startlingly wide on October 30. To recognize this is not to ascribe to anglophones animosity towards Quebec or towards the idea that the federal government should provide a setting in which francophones can feel at home and play a full and satisfying role.

Having said this, it is still necessary to accept that anti-French sentiments do exist in English-speaking Canada and that they must have played an appreciable role in the decision of voters in some parts of the country. All the available data nevertheless show that there was hardly more than a trace of this influence except in a very few special areas. In the Ottawa region, for instance, or in Leeds (Ontario), where there was a noisy controversy about language practices in the Customs Office, a strong negative reaction to the government's bilingual policies in the public service—exacerbated by a few candidates —no doubt contributed to Liberal defeats. But even here it is quite unrealistic not to differentiate between attitudes totally rejecting policies designed to enhance bilingualism and mere opposition to the particular manner in which they were carried out. This is not the place in which to sort out this problem. While noting that even in areas of resentment toward bilingual policies there may have beeen a good deal more tolerance than is normally recognized, I fully accept the notion that in a few, perhaps five or six, constituencies, opposition to French power played an important role in the outcome and that in some others, as in the Prairies, it had a minor contributory effect. But that is all, as a look at the results and the pre-election polls confirms.

At least three aspects of the results are relevant. In the first place, the overwhelmingly English-speaking voters of New-foundland *increased* their support for the Liberals. I know that this had nothing to do with bilingualism, but those who say that fear of French power was responsible for anti-Trudeau votes elsewhere cannot have it both ways. It is no whit less plausible to assert that Newfoundlanders increased their Liberal support because they approved of the presence of a strong French contingent in Ottawa's corridors of power than it is to insist that British Columbians denied their votes to the government be-cause they opposed it. Secondly, the Liberals suffered con-siderable losses within French Canada, as the Quebec results show. As was not the case elsewhere in Canada, neither the Conservatives nor the NDP provided viable alternatives in Quebec. While this fact has some serious consequences for the Canadian political system, the loss of Liberal votes to the Social Credit party reveals dissatisfaction with the way in which the government did its work and this cannot be ascribed to French power. Finally, in Quebec the staunchest support for the Liberal party came from the English-speaking voters. This is no doubt related in part to Mr. Trudeau's tough stance towards separatism, and has nothing whatsoever to do with French power. Continued anglophone support, by inflating the Quebec Liberal vote, has thus strengthened the impression of francophone support for the government.[3]

Turning to data provided by opinion polls, we find irrefutable evidence for the importance of economic problems in the voters' decision, whether in Quebec or elsewhere. I shall argue

219

below that as much as the presence or consequences of the problems themselves, it was the Liberal approach to them which influenced the outcome, but the fact remains that when various samples were asked to identify election issues, an overwhelming proportion pointed to unemployment, the cost of living, and welfare. National unity, bilingualism, and a host of other matters agitating politicians and pundits hardly made a ripple.

Of the numerous country-wide polls conducted by the various parties, media, and research organizations, I shall refer to only two—those of the Canadian Institute of Public Opinion and of the CBC's French network. The former asked a sample of 741 adults, interviewed in person, what they thought to be the main problem facing the country. The economy, inflation, and high prices were mentioned 37 percent of the time, unemployment 34 percent, labour, unions and strikes 14 percent, and pollution 6 percent of the time. "The Government, Trudeau," which might *in part* reflect anti-French bias, came next with 6 percent, and "Relations with Quebec, Separatism," follow, having been named by 4 percent of the respondents.[4]

It can be argued that bigotry is usually underestimated in opinion surveys because people are ashamed of their prejudices and conceal them. Since a variety of surveys have demonstrated massive bias with respect to a depressing range of matters, this argument is not entirely convincing. But even assuming that surveys asking direct questions about problems underestimate responses growing out of religious or racial prejudice, we nevertheless have evidence which proves the inadequacy of the French power explanation. Radio Canada conducted two national telephone surveys, one in the first half of September (1992 interviews) and the second after the middle of October (2379 interviews).

A "problem" question, comparable to that of the CIPO, yielded similar results: 36 percent thought that unemployment was the problem requiring most discussion during the campaign, followed by the economy (15 percent); welfare (12 percent); taxes (7 percent). Pollution, Canadian unity and French-English relations, *including language problems!* came next, each mentioned by only 4 percent of the respondents. Interviewers also read out a number of specified problems and asked the respondents to indicate whether each was very important, fairly important, or unimportant. Canadian unity was considered very important by 54 percent, but this seemingly high percentage placed fifth, after unemployment (80 percent), cost of living (77 percent), pollution (62 percent), and strikes (57 percent). French-English relations were rated as very important by 40 percent, placing twelfth among thirteen items listed, followed by patronage, which was seen as very important by 23 percent. Regional breakdowns dispel the possible suspicion that these country-wide percentages conceal French-English differences reflecting greater anti-French bias on the part of the anglophones. The largest proportion of respondents who considered French-English relations very important was found among the New Brunswick francophones, no less than 60 percent of whom did so (but $N = 15$), followed by English-speaking Montrealers (57 percent), and then by French-speaking Montrealers (52 percent). Ontario was close to the Canadian average (with 41 percent) and the least Liberal-voting sections of the electorate, Prairie dwellers and British Columbians, attached much less importance to French-English relations: 31 percent of the former, and 30 of the latter thought that this was a very important problem. The corresponding figures for unemployment are 70 and 87 percent!

I would be indulging in a futile and messy exercise of overkill if I presented the details of all the other evidence from the two Radio Canada surveys, pointing in the same direction. Suffice it to note only a few additional responses: (1) When questioned which party was best suited to handle relations between English and French Canada, the Liberals were named at least twice as frequently as the Conservatives in virtually all regions. Only in Toronto, where they were still preferred, was the margin substantially narrower. This result does not reflect the generally pro-Liberal tone of pre-election polls, for the Conservatives were sometimes preferred, for instance with respect to farm policy. (2) Furthermore, when the respondents were invited to identify a problem the Trudeau government had failed to handle adequately, 22 percent mentioned unemployment, and only 4 percent French-English relations. (3) In the second survey, just before the election, only one percent thought that bilingualism had not been discussed adequately in the campaign. (4) When, at the same time, respondents were again invited to identify the party best suited to handle various specified problems, the Liberal party was accorded even higher scores than a month before, with respect to Canadian unity, and received overwhelming endorsement everywhere on its capacity to handle problems of bilingualism. These extremely impressive scores, contrasting eloquently with policy fields in which the Conservatives, and sometimes the NDP, were favoured, make the French power explanation of the vote appear quite ludicrous.

A different, much more localized but nevertheless significant survey reinforces the above data. Flora MacDonald, the successful Conservative candidate in Kingston and the Islands (Ontario), conducted massive canvasses as part of her campaign. Twenty thousand individuals were visited and asked what they thought were the campaign issues. About 8,000 of them mentioned one or more election issues, and among these, twelve referred to French-English relations, two favourably! This striking observation was reinforced by an independent, academic survey in selected areas of Kingston which yielded similar results. These findings are particularly instructive since one of Canada's earliest election studies was actually done in Kingston and showed quite noticeable anti-Catholic and anti-French prejudice with respect to Louis St. Laurent.[5] The difference in the two temporally so widely separated "readings" is an encouraging phenomenon in the otherwise rather bleak field of inter-ethnic accommodation in Canada.

If French power was not an issue in the election, what was? It is too early to attempt a definitive explanation of the surprising outcome, but one observation is quite inescapable even at the time of writing: there were a great many issues in the election which together undermined the confidence won by the Liberals in 1968. What made them cohere as they did?

THE LIBERAL RECORD: BOLD OR BUNGLED?

Three or four economic issues, as we have just seen, were of overriding importance in arousing public anxiety during the election. Unemployment, rising prices, and high taxes, as well as dissatisfaction with some aspects of welfare programs, notably the Unemployment Insurance Fund, caused pain throughout the land; in some parts it was acute and even excruciating, in others merely achingly dull. Against this common Canadian backdrop of economic malaise there were numerous other, smaller but equally gnawing issues which added complaints from particular local, demographic, or occupational groups puzzled and baffled by the choice they had to make on October 30. That the decision was particularly difficult was obvious from the unusually high proportion of undecided voters, detected by most polls, and the uncommon last-minute upturn in their numbers, from 11 to 17 percent, reported by the CIPO on the Saturday before voting day. Some of these issues were related to bold and imaginative government attempts to cope with problems and challenges, others arose from badly bungled measures aggravating, rather than alleviating, the country's difficulties. Several could be placed in both categories.

TABLE I. BOLD AND/OR BUNGLED POLICIES

BOLD	BUNGLED
Languages Act	Employment
LIP	Inflation
OFY	Penitentiaries
Capital Gains Tax	Post Office
Foreign policy	Immigration
Defence policy	Information Canada
Uganda refugees	Benson appointment to CTC
Pollution control (Arctic)	RCMP insignia
Parks policies in Alberta	Facing USA domination

BOTH

DREE policies
French language training
New parks
CDC
Tax reform
STOL aircraft

Consider, briefly, one voter's categorization of reasonably successful, more or less unsuccessful and in-between policies.

The items in Table I were selected at random and do not claim to be a complete inventory; nor do they indicate how our exemplary voter would assess the other parties' proposed alternatives, if any. Furthermore, the policies or performances listed differ widely in weight or significance. One can hardly equate the importance of taking care of one's own by appointing Edgar Benson to the Canadian Transport Commission, at a time when Parliament was not in session (an act invoking unhappy memories of Mr. Pickersgill, as Minister of Transport, creating the position just in time to occupy it himself) and, say, the erroneous judgements made in efforts to cope with inflation and unemployment. But despite the obvious inadequacies of our table, we can use it as a basis for discerning why the Liberals were found wanting by so many Canadians. Five types of evaluation will be sketched.

The government's performance in some fields, for instance, foreign policy, seemed to be intelligent, competent, and innovative. A reassessment of Canada's role in the world, and reorganization of its foreign, commercial, consular, and diplomatic representation and back-up services was badly needed. Initiatives like the UN- and Canada-supported Stockholm World Conference on the Human Environment were perhaps lacking in dramatic appeal but added up to exactly the kind of competent and contemporary performance one would have expected from the Trudeau government. Secondly, more impressive (because they were more daring) projects like the Secretary of State's Local Initiative and Opportunities for Youth programs were widely criticized because, as was inevitable, some misfired and were abused. On balance, however, while these creative departures from normal governmental stodginess undoubtedly prompted much more criticism than praise, they strike me as worthwhile attempts to adjust to new circumstances. Had they been better explained and more forcefully justified, they could in the long run have developed into widely admired model projects. They became an electoral liability not so much because of what they were but because they were not made acceptable, and were thus permitted to contribute to the impression many had of the government as an inefficient organization spending public funds on the mindless, wasteful, and even dangerous schemes of young and/or irresponsible

224

people, possibly threatening the survival of generally accepted Canadian values.[6]

Other government programs were ill-conceived. Take the Canadian Development Corporation. This has been turned into an instrument designed to achieve ends which must ultimately clash with one another. On the one hand the Corporation is to encourage Canadians to invest in Canadian enterprises; on the other it is to support daring and developmental projects. Is one body likely to perform both functions successfully? Among its earliest acquisitions was the Connaught Laboratories, Canada's sole manufacturer of insulin. By placing this formerly publicly owned, nonprofit enterprise into the hands of a company which is supposed to attract private investment, the government has made it inevitable that in the long run the price of insulin will respond to the appetite for profit, which alone can justify nonpublic investment in the CDC. This is a failure to sort out the respective purposes of development, investment, and publicly owned pharmaceutical manufacturing organizations and to create adequate structures for carrying them out. One umbrella corporation for all is certain to run into trouble, thereby not only defeating a number of worthwhile ends but also further eroding trust in public enterprises. The story of the CDC is probably just another example of the government starting out with innovative zeal and ending with compromises incorporating the views of those, usually in the business community, who might be adversely affected by the original proposals. This kind of compromise occurred in relation to the White Paper on Taxation, the Labour Code, the Companies Act, and presumably the Prices and Incomes Commission.

Some excellent government policies aroused hostility because of the manner in which they were introduced. Even strong environmentalists found fault, for instance, with the government's announcement, during the campaign, of new national park projects in cities like Toronto, in a way which not only made them election goodies but which also precluded consultation with local planning and other authorities. Failure to work out plans jointly with relevant provincial and local governments confirmed the idea held by many people, particularly those close to these "lower" jurisdictions, that Ottawa had not yet learned a lesson on which provincial premiers and others had been harping—that, in a federal state, the central government must learn to consult the other levels *during* the evolution of policies, not after they have solidified.

Finally, a fifth type of federal policy was seen simply as an error. As in the other categories discussed here, individual judgements about which policies should be so characterized vary. The Post Office mess is a good example, or decisions affecting the location of airports. Much more important, ill-prepared changes in the penitentiary service demoralized prison staffs and, in the long run, may have retarded penal reform. Electorally, the outcomes in at least two constituencies in the Kingston area were affected by the policies of Mr. Goyer.

This selective review of policies and the reactions to them is intended to serve two purposes: first, to show that in addition to the much discussed major problems—unemployment, inflation, taxes, and welfare—a host of lesser issues brought forth a richly textured and nuanced set of responses. Secondly, that these seemed to be related as much to the manner or style with which the government approached problems, as to the policies themselves. Acceptance or rejection of a government, in other words, depends not only on what it does (or ignores) but also on how it presents and defends its policies.

Liberal ministers were no doubt convinced that they had done enough to explain, justify, and make acceptable the government's various programs; that debates and replies to questions in Parliament, speeches throughout the country, and other information supplied by the ministries should have been enough, had the country only been prepared to listen. An analysis of the election results leaves little doubt, however, that not only vast sections of the public, but even many civil servants, were not convinced that the government's activities deserved their support. How are we to explain this verdict?

In the absence of appropriately designed surveys our explanation must be tentative and fragmentary. Some indications are nevertheless to be found by looking at Canada before the election and at the national wake and post-mortem which followed it. So as to avoid an annoying repetition of disclaimers and warnings about the guesswork involved, I shall here record one general qualification about the fragmentary character and inconclusive nature of the analysis which follows and then plunge right into it, adopting a tone which would be better suited to one who really thinks that he has all the answers.

LIBERAL STRATEGY: "THE LAND IS STRONG"

When announcing the election, the government exuded confidence and placed the campaign on a high, general level. The issue, according to Mr. Trudeau, was to be national integrity, whatever that meant. The campaign was not to deteriorate into a battle between the government and the opposition parties (Parliament, according to Mr. Trudeau, is the appropriate site for such pugilism) but was to be a dialogue between the public and the ministers in which the latter would hear how Canada responded to the many fine things the government had done. The Liberal slogan, superbly encapsulating the government's self-satisfaction, was "The Land is Strong." Rather than admit that any serious problems existed, that some errors had been committed, and ought to be explained, or that the government was concerned about the way some of its policies were developing, ministers generally compared Canada favourably with other countries. Playing down the number of unemployed, they argued that Canada had created more new jobs than any comparable country in the world. The opposition parties in the meantime hammered at the government, dramatizing its shortcomings and failures. However, except for Mr. Lewis's adroit focusing of public attention on the privileges enjoyed by the so-called corporate bums, and Mr. Stanfield's success in publicizing the enormous drain on the Unemployment Insurance Fund, the opposition attack seemed to have relatively little impact. Liberal strength, according to the September polls, was substantial and increasing; Mr. Stanfield personally was not much of a hit. He consistently trailed his party in popularity while Mr. Lewis led his, but without being able to attract many of those who admired his campaign into NDP voting ranks. Mr. Caouette made a very slow start and his party was thought to be entering a decline. The undecided vote, as noted earlier, was exceptionally high. During the second half of the campaign, coinciding with the publication of reports by Statistics Canada which indicated that both unemployment and prices had risen to unusually high levels, a disenchantment with the Liberals set in.

227

The last Gallup poll reported a substantial drop in Liberal support which probably continued between the CIPO sounding and election day.

I think what had happened since 1968 was that at first the great expectations evoked by Mr. Trudeau persisted in a general belief that he, and his government, while having problems, could and would cope with them at least as well as anyone else. The opposition succeeded in identifying and discussing a large number of difficulties which beset the country. They suggested various alternative policies, without at first being taken seriously. But as the campaign progressed, a growing feeling developed that not only were the Liberals responsible for many of the ills afflicting Canadians but (and this impression resulted from their campaign strategy) that they did not or would not recognize the seriousness of the situation. Increasingly, their over-confidence, their persistent refusal to acknowledge weaknesses and seriously to debate opposition charges made people wonder whether they understood or cared about what was happening to Canada. The government, appearing aloof, unconcerned, even arrogant, forfeited support to all three other parties in their various strongholds, and particularly to the Conservatives.

To what extent can one ascribe these shifts in voting intentions to the campaign, notably to the attacks of the opposition and to the offhand response of the government? The relevant literature, which is derived from studies outside Canada, is inconclusive.[7] It seems that both the campaign attacks on the government and the cavalier response to them were important. This was the case not so much because they created a new image of the government and of the opposition in the minds of many voters, but because they activated and reinforced partly suppressed or forgotten old impressions of the government party and of its leader. I am assuming that a large proportion of the voters who abandoned the Liberals between 1968 and 1972, or who voted for the first time for the opposition parties (particularly for the Conservatives), were moved as much to *oppose* the Liberals as to *support* the other parties. Many of those, in other words, who shifted away from the Liberals did so in a two-step process: first, abandoning the Liberals, and then deciding whom to support. My main concern here is to explore the reasons for the flight from the Liberals rather than the attracttion of the other parties.

LIBERAL DEFEAT: FRAGMENTATION OF THE TRUDEAU IMAGE

It is always difficult to assess the respective influences on the outcome of particular election issues, events, long-standing party attachments, personalities of candidates and leaders, but the Liberal victory of 1968 and the party's 1972 stumble can be explained largely in Trudeau terms. His was the victory and his the fall. The extraordinary initial appeal of the Liberal leader persisted long into his first term of office and was still evident in the 1972 campaign. But for a growing number of people it underwent a slow metamorphosis leading to the emergence of a double image—one showing an attractive, exciting, resolute thinker-doer, the other a proud, temperamental, and impatient ruler. The latter appeared increasingly unable to suffer not only fools, but also critics, gladly. Many were unable to retain affection for both Trudeaus and, as the assessments of some journalists showed, the shining armour of the 1968 knight slowly turned into tarnished dross by the dawn of the seventies. Scathing imputations of stupidity directed wholesale at opposition MPs; rude words and gestures both inside and outside Parliament; the calling of civil-liberties-minded critics "weak-kneed bleeding hearts"; repeated invitations to the public to throw him and his government out of office if it did not like them, offended and alienated a large number of Canadians. On the other hand, there was still much that was attractive in an able and forthright man now and then provoked into an intemperate outburst, excesses of this kind being interpreted in some quarters as signs of strength. As the campaign started, therefore, the attitude of many Canadians toward the Prime Minister was ambivalent. Liking his undoubted qualities and both attracted to and put off by his failings, many were unconsciously of two minds in their response to his pride and peccadilloes.

As the campaign unfolded and concern about major problems and minor irritations grew, the negative assessment became more dominant. The public needed a sense that effective action would be taken, and the way in which Mr. Trudeau and his colleagues conducted the campaign did not reassure them

229

on this score. Early campaign expectations of many that the Liberals would be better able than the opposition parties to do something about the various problems troubling the nation were dispelled by a sense that the Liberal government was not troubled enough.[8] Failure to recognize and debate issues, and the well-held pose that nothing was seriously wrong, convinced majorities, particularly west of the Ottawa river, that Mr. Trudeau was somehow too far from them, too aloof to deserve renewed support. The haughty, impetuous, and arrogant half of his image—always lurking in the back of the mind—came to the fore and, as the result of the leader's campaign, became paramount. Instead of emphasizing and trading on their assets, the Liberal party and its leader conducted a campaign which permitted the opposition to exploit their major liabilities. How was it that an intelligent leader and a party full of intelligent men were so misled and so deceived in taking stock of the conditions and circumstances around them? The answers are many and complex. One of the principal explanations may lie in the combination of the general style of the government party with the particular style of its leader. The *hauteur* of Mr. Trudeau fused with traditional Liberal arrogance and the two, reinforcing one another, led to a loss of public trust.

LIBERAL STYLE: HOWE AND *Hubris*

"Style" must rank high among the weasel words we use when trying to describe a phenomenon we vaguely understand but find hard to define precisely. It is nevertheless often resorted to, usually quite ambiguously, by social scientists and critics in the arts—not to mention those dabbling in *haute couture*, either as producers or consumers. In keeping with the impressionistic and intuitive approach of this paper, I have decided to adopt it. When I speak of a party's style I have in mind the general atmosphere which envelops its activists, and particularly its leaders. The things they consider most important and how they rank them; the ways in which they approach them; the methods they use in arriving at decisions; whom they consult; the degree to which peripheral members are encouraged to influence those at the centre of the innermost circle; the proportion of professionals to amateurs—these and other factors go into imposing

230

a style on a party. Imagine that you are entering a room in the Parliament Buildings occupied by a dozen men wearing masks. They speak perfect English, betray no regional accents, and are engaged in an abstract discussion which reveals a consuming interest in politics but does not show whether they are on the government or opposition side. The party leaders are absent from the room. Even if your acquaintance with Ottawa is not intimate, you will quickly be able to tell whether you are among Trudeau, Stanfield, or Lewis colleagues. In the sixties you could have with equal ease distinguished between members of the Pearson, Diefenbaker, and Douglas teams. In both cases your identification would have been made on the basis of the parties' styles.

The Liberal style, as found by Mr. Trudeau when he first became actively involved with the party in the early 1960s (some aspects of which he had previously castigated mercilessly in *Cité Libre*)[9] was composed of many strands. These have not yet, alas, been displayed in their full glory by historians and this is not the place to do so. A few aspects will have to be touched upon, however, since they are part of our story. The modern Liberal party, as fashioned by Mackenzie King and his principal colleagues, became a competent administrative party in which the role of politicians and bureaucrats had become almost indistinguishable.[10] It had developed high standards of excellence and an outstanding civil service, the upper echelons of which were motivated by a great sense of dedication. The closest interaction between officials and politicians, as well as the coming of age, so to speak, of the King–St. Laurent party, occurred during the Second World War and its aftermath. The simultaneous advent to Ottawa of two new phenomena left an indelible mark on the Liberal party: Keynesian economics and temporary recruits from the private sector who, orchestrated by C. D. Howe, helped create Canada's prodigious industrial war effort and postwar growth. These developments gave the Liberals, and particularly Mr. Howe, a vast network of close contacts with the technocratic and managerial elites in industry.

The Liberal party thus emerged from the war years conscious, to be sure, of the need to be re-elected (it had been badly scared by a CCF–comforting wartime Gallup poll) but nevertheless greatly sensitive to its administrative responsibilities. It prized competence, predictability, efficiency—the creation, in short, of conditions favouring the continued growth of an economically stable country. The approach to most problems was businesslike and orderly, resting on a mildly sceptical optimism which assumed that while perfection was never quite within man's reach, the well-regulated efforts of decent men would lead to the gradual improvement of the lot of those who were insufficiently favoured by circumstances. While not allowing the CCF to stampede it into socialist experiments, the party nevertheless adopted a general stance promoting the slow expansion of the welfare state. The Liberal style was thus gently interventionist: the party leaders were apprehensive of wild-eyed men wishing to change things too fast but at the same time were receptive to modest change, provided it was introduced by suitably responsible leaders, preferably themselves.[11]

There was something inescapably patrician about this posture. As the years rolled by, the civil servants and Liberal politicians imperceptibly came to believe that they had acquired special gifts qualifying them to make the important decisions required to enhance the public good. Associated with this view was the feeling (it was usually not much more than that) that others—opposition politicians, provincial governments, leaders in countries with different political systems—could not quite be trusted to make correct decisions.

This lofty assumption reached its zenith during the period preceding the 1957 election. It became increasingly associated with C. D. Howe, a minister known to have many friends in the corporate board rooms, and notoriously impatient of Parliament and its insistence on what clearly struck him as largely counter-productive talk. As so often happens, a vague style was given concrete expression by some of Mr. Howe's infelicitous and impolitic statements which epitomized, for a growing number of Canadians, the Liberal arrogance. Howe's performance during the famous pipeline debates of 1956, and that of many other members of the Liberal front bench including ultimately the Liberal Speaker himself, led to a widespread conviction that the Liberal party had become afflicted by *hubris*—an overweening pride and insolence which would ultimately and inexorably lead to its downfall. The reckoning came in 1957

232

when, just as in 1972, the voters withheld support from the Liberals in quite unexpected numbers.

What, you may ask, does all this have to do with Mr. Trudeau and 1972? A good deal, in my view, since I believe that social institutions, political parties included, have a continuing life of their own. There is, in other words, a link between the party of St. Laurent, Howe, Pickersgill, Garson, and Chevrier and that which Mr. Trudeau took over in 1968, despite the intervening passage through the wilderness and the reign of the unostentatious, gentle Lester Pearson.[12]

It may at first glance seem surprising that the Liberal party's smug paternalism had not dissipated itself during the years of defeat following the 1957, 1958, and 1962 elections, and of their minority governments from 1963 to 1968, particularly since Mr. Pearson was an unassuming leader. But parties do not live in a vacuum. The humbling treatment meted out by the electorate did little to change the close professional and social contacts of the Liberal establishment with senior civil servants, leading members of the business community, some academics, and old party cronies. It is true that Mr. Pearson was able to attract a new and impressive crop of candidates who gave the party a fresher look in Ottawa, but even they were drawn largely from the urban or urbanized, successful, managerial layers of society. There was much empathy between the newer men and the old-established friends of the party in business and industry and the faithful public servants who were, or had been, generally uncomfortable under the direction of the Diefenbaker cabinet. A process started by Mr. King had in fact continued, bringing the Liberal party and the bureaucracy more closely together. A surprising proportion of ministers in the St. Laurent and then the Pearson cabinets was drawn from the ranks of former public servants, thus institutionally reinforcing the already strong congruence of views between the administrative party and the professional administrators. In the world of business, and also among the country's universities, Liberal contacts were lively, continuous, and close. All this did little to change the party's elitist tendencies and did much to make Mr. Diefenbaker and his colleagues suspect that they were the victims of an establishment conspiracy to drive them out of office. While Conservative fears were exaggerated, and their

233

isolation was partly self-induced, there was nevertheless some reason for their sense of grievance. They were not always given the benefit of the doubt, and tended to be held responsible for a variety of ills which, to say the least, were only partly of their own making. Their inexperience, geographic base in rural regions and the West, and the failure of the party to win the confidence of the business and academic establishments gave the Conservatives a shaky, ill-fitting presence in Ottawa. Combined with Mr. Diefenbaker's populism, old-fashioned, revivalist oratorical style, and sometimes idiosyncratic view of the world, these characteristics made Conservative cabinet ministers appear as aliens among the mandarinate. The NDP was not strong enough to come within reach of forming a government.

All this made the Liberals think that the years following 1957 were simply a brief interregnum in which the country would soon learn who, alone among the parties, was fitted to govern effectively. Mr. Pearson, whose political manner encouraged considerable decentralization and delegation, presided over a number of colleagues minding their own fiefdoms who, under the protective cloak provided by a modest and popular leader, continued to view the world as if it were waiting to be delivered by them from the incompetence of the Conservatives. After coming to power, in 1963, they thought that as soon as they could rid themselves of the embarrassments of a minority government and the unreasonable tactics of the Opposition, they would again slide snugly into the mantle of undisputed leadership. The unnecessary calling of the 1965 election is a good example of this expectation that the country was simply waiting to return to Liberal rule. The decision to seek a mandate in 1965 was, of course, Mr. Pearson's, but it is well known that he was counselled in this matter by some of his leading political advisors, who represented the new elements of the Liberal party.

Thus, when Mr. Trudeau came to be chosen leader, he took over a party which had not cleansed itself of the earlier overconfidence and belief in its self-evident right to rule. It is interesting and extremely suggestive that Mr. Pearson, despite his own style which was warm and in no way arrogant, was unable to change that of his party. The failure may have been caused by his own priorities and/or characteristics but it is also possible that we have a lesson here in the degree to which even a highly regarded leader can fail to alter the physiognomy and stance of his party.[13] In any event, in Mr. Trudeau the Liberals found a leader vastly different in outlook and style from any one occupying the position before him. Much more even than his two predecessors. both of whom had also been invited to seek political careers and were offered cabinet posts at the time, Mr. Trudeau had to be persuaded to seek election in 1965. An intellectual of exceptional stature, varied talents, and independent means, he had much to give up, upon entering the federal House and cabinet. He had much to gain as well, of course, and as subsequent events proved, came to enjoy the agonizing challenges which face a contemporary prime minister. But he had not been involved in electoral politics before and increasingly gave the impression that he found the cajolery, patience, and compromise required of a party leader among the least attractive features of his new job. It is paradoxical, within the context of the present analysis, that more than any other person occupying his position, Mr. Trudeau has tried to free himself of the traditional influences of the Liberal establishment, both outside Ottawa and within the public service itself.[14] It is not easy to say how well he has done this but he has obviously not succeeded in freeing himself of the *hubris* visited upon his party. Because he himself is impatient of criticism, overly confident, reluctant to recognize his own errors, and because he chose to campaign accordingly, he blew the election. His patrician style, combined with the party's arrogance, forfeited national support at a time when the country would, I believe, really have preferred to give it.

DEVELOPMENT OF THE LIBERAL STYLE: THE GROWTH OF ARROGANCE

It is no doubt audacious to attempt to explain an electoral outcome in terms of *hubris*. But even those unwilling to accord it the central place I have given it will recognize that it played an important part in the result. For this reason, if no other, it will be useful to pursue the theme further.

One might ask why the Liberal party should have fallen

victim to the sin of pride. Is there something about Liberals which encourages this? Is there a Liberal *Weltanschauung* which contains it? Is it the consequence of the kind of support the party has been receiving from various regions and segments of society? I think that the last-named point has a lot to do with it, but more important even than the party's base is the historical context in which it found itself in office. The Liberal style as we have here described it "congealed" in the period from the consolidation of Liberal power in the middle thirties to the second St. Laurent election in 1953. The party, as was briefly noted above, was in office throughout the whole of the Second World War and the reconstruction period. The war itself called for decisive and unprecedented action and effort. Despite deep and searing political cleavages, too well known to require exhumation here, the King government succeeded in performing well both during the war and immediately afterwards. To carry out the new tasks, the government attracted, as we also saw earlier, an impressive group of public servants and other peripheral advisers[15] who developed the habit of making a great many decisions under enabling legislation, without the cumbersome need to justify everything in Parliament. It was not only the war, however, which contributed to the emergence of the alliance in Ottawa between the Liberal party and the public service mandarinate. The period under discussion saw the acceptance by almost everyone of the need for heretofore unprecedented government participation in the economic and social spheres and the simultaneous recognition that this required specially trained and outstandingly competent public servants. A vastly expanded merit system, and the recruitment of people with exceptional talents, brought an influx of unusual personalities into close contact with ministers. The challenge of the war and subsequently of developing social policies suited to Canada's unique circumstances, provided a stimulating setting in which officials and party people worked for long and arduous hours, often under cohesion-inducing crisis conditions. No wonder they developed a common viewpoint and a relationship which created strong and lasting bonds between them.

Another contributing factor was probably the link, imposed by Canada's history and social structure, with the United King-

236

dom. Many of Canada's leading public servants, academics, and politicians of the period were partly educated in the United Kingdom.[16] They were consequently imbued with many of the values and attitudes of the British upper middle class, and particularly with that part of it which was prominent in Oxbridge and influential in Whitehall. While many of the British traits were clearly rejected (Canadians returning from the UK were often nationalists imbued with anti-British sentiments), others unwittingly rubbed off. This is apparent in many Commonwealth citizens who did their stint in the various institutions through which the British establishment has recruited the lesser breeds, whether of domestic or foreign origin. Among the consequences of the exposure to UK influences was a tradition of public service among university graduates and a certain smugness about the capacity of a group of efficient public servants, working with similarly trained politicians, to provide good government. I remember as a boy being greatly impressed by one of the things my universally anglophile friends used to say about the Englishman: He does not boast about the fact that the British are best, he merely admits it. Something of the same attitude, I think, was adopted by many of Ottawa's British-trained public servants in relation to their own and their coterie's performance in Canadian public life.

The slightly caricatured picture I have sketched provides a realistic description of an extremely capable, successful, and somewhat self-satisfied group of public servants and politicians, sharing many exciting experiences, who have done much to shape the style of the Liberal establishment. The fact that the ministers happened to be Liberal was, of course, largely an accident of history, but its consequences were real enough for all that.

One reason for the Liberal assumption that their party was the only one capable of governing in Canada was not prompted by accident, however, but by party attitudes, postures, and past stands. Ever since the hanging of Riel, and particularly since the conscription crisis of 1917–18, the Conservative party has been unable to attract anything like widespread support in Quebec (except in 1958), leaving the ground clear to the Grits. From 1935 to 1953, for instance, the Conservatives on no occasion elected more than five MPs in Quebec. This encouraged Liberal politicians to think that theirs was the only national party in Canada, drawing significant support from both language groups. They can hardly be faulted for holding this view and it must be admitted that the capacity to represent both French– and English–speaking Canadians in the House is an exceedingly important prerequisite for a lengthy and effective tenure in Ottawa.

THE LIBERAL STYLE AND QUEBEC: NATIVE SONS AND
DEFERENCE

The special relationship between Quebec and the Liberals requires additional comment and calls for a short digression, particularly since the question has become acute again in 1972. We must add to the historical reasons for the lack of Quebec support for the Conservative party, the Tory stand on conscription in the Second World War and the failure of Mr. Diefenbaker to develop viable bonds with French Canada. But these are not the only factors creating a situation which suggests that Quebec is more or less on permanent loan to the Liberals. Others include the Union Nationale in effect becoming the provincial Conservative party (or vice versa), thus displacing the Conservatives on the provincial scene and, of course, the fact that only the Liberals, among national parties, have chosen French Canadian leaders. Although there is no survey evidence available on this score, insofar as I know, the deviation of Quebec from national patterns in 1957 and in 1972 almost certainly was related in part to the Liberals on both occasions being led by a native son.

Another, much more speculative reason, and one also with somewhat lower explanatory power, is nevertheless immensely interesting. Until the 1960s at least, and to some extent even beyond, Quebec society has generally been more deferential than most of English Canada. Authority patterns in Quebec have for a long time placed the traditional elites in positions of special trust and respect. The Church, local dignitaries, mayors, deputies, members of the professions—all have tended to be accepted as legitimate leaders whose judgement was to be trusted on many questions of public policy.[17] Although there has no doubt been a considerable attrition of this authority

238

pattern in recent years it is likely that among significant segments of the population there still is some acceptance of the traditional politics according to which the leadership of certain well-defined groups is acknowledged. It is possible that the Liberal party has continued to profit from this tradition and that some of the reasons for which it was rejected in 1972 in English Canada—lack of concern, taking the public's acceptance for granted, for instance—were therefore less operative in Quebec than elsewhere. This was no doubt a less compelling reason for voting Liberal than the native-son status of Mr. Trudeau and the feeble alternatives presented by the Conservatives and the NDP. But this approach to political authority should not be ruled out entirely as having contributed to the difference between Quebec's behaviour and that of the rest of the country, any more than the French power argument should be eliminated entirely as one of the factors on the other side, so to speak.

To return to the Liberals' style, a principal, if not *the* principal cause, which has already been implicitly recognized, is that the party had held power for so long. Much has been written about the effects of this kind of longevity but even so we do not yet know enough about specific consequences which follow from enjoying an extended tenure in office under differing circumstances. Some parties, under these conditions, become less honest, others careless, over-confident, or ossified. The question before us is not really whether their hegemony contributed to the Liberals' particular style, but why *hubris* should have been the principal consequence of their repeated electoral successes and whether another party, say the Conservatives, would have been influenced in much the same way.[18]

GOVERNMENT AND OPPOSITION: DIFFERENCES IN RECRUITMENT

An intriguing conjecture presents itself in this context, of an admittedly speculative kind. If some of the interpretations offered so far in this paper involve me in skating on rather thin ice, then what follows is sustained by no ice at all, merely the tensile strength of the water's surface. It is plausible to assume that parties which appear to be well entrenched in office attract candidates with an interest in governing and that they are more successful in mobilizing potential leaders and ministers than parties given little chance of forming a government. Many examples leap to mind but none is more apposite than the contrast between Mr. Pearson's success in persuading the Three Wise Men—Messrs. Trudeau, Marchand, and Pelletier—to seek Liberal nominations (and, of course, accept cabinet posts) and Mr. Stanfield's failure, despite persevering attempts, to put together a strong team of Quebec candidates. Since before the election only a slim chance was given Mr. Stanfield of becoming prime minister, he encountered problems in recruiting outstanding candidates even in English Canada, although some highly qualified potential cabinet ministers did present themselves. Parties with long governmental records and expectations of continued success thus accumulate more managerial and power-seeking candidates and members than those likely to remain out of office.[19] Candidates who are particularly attracted to ministerial parties are likely to exhibit certain elitist tendencies. In some respect this is probably true for most individuals seeking electoral office but I believe it to be more common among those attracted to government parties. When I say that they are elitist I do not mean merely that they display leadership qualities, but also that they are exceptionally aware of the manner in which they differ from a great many other people.

The areas in which they think they deviate from the average vary, since there are many elites and many kinds of elitism. They may be elitist in their approach to making and taking responsibility for decisions, in the way they work with other people, in their conviction of how the country should be run, in their devotion to public service, in their independence of meaningless fashions, and so on. Elites, in other words, differ from the majority of the population in a variety of ways. One of these, and it is here that the tensile strength of the water is being most sorely tested, concerns the life styles of members of elites who exhibit a tendency to gravitate towards governmental parties. By life styles, in this context, I do not necessarily mean their incomes, although these are no doubt related, but something much more pervasive and more closely related to their values, dreams, and view of life.

Without minimizing the relevance of income and class distinctions and of the presence in our political parties of economic elites in this sense, I wish to isolate an important and seldom discussed life-style difference that exists even among those who would, in class terms, be placed at the upper end of the scale, and moreover, among those occupying elite positions at this level. I have in mind the difference, within political elites, of those who have elite tastes and those who have mass tastes.

ELITE TASTES AND MASS TASTES

Now these terms are infinitely difficult to define precisely and it is also hard to escape the charge when using them, of making invidious distinctions which are totally subjective at best and odiously snobbish at worst. Yet it is obvious that even among those who share important conditions of life (members of the middle and upper income groups, for instance), there are persistent and patterned differences in values and tastes when it comes to aesthetics, literature, preferred ways of spending one's leisure, and so on.

If, for the sake of attaching *some* kind of label to each group, we identify them as those with elite tastes, and those with public tastes, we can, by way of illustration, draw up a quick sample list of preferences associated with each. The former would rather go to Stratford than watch "Bonanza", they prefer ballet to baseball, Bergman to *Love Story,* cross-country skiing to snowmobiles, European wines to beer, bird-watching to bird-shooting, the CBC to private stations, the Group of Seven to Norman Rockwell, Northrop Frye to Northcote Parkinson, the *Saturday Review* to the *Financial Post,* and *Saturday Night* to the *Saturday Review* (for nationalist reasons). They are environmentalists and not litterbugs, they approve of publicly subsidized theatres and sometimes even go to them, they support local planning boards and revile most developers, they prefer bicycles to cars and Morrises to Mustangs. The list could, of course, be extended indefinitely, no doubt bringing my readers into ever more explosive states of apoplexy. Relax, gentle reader, and note that no one person is likely to fit fully even this fragmentary list of elite– and public–taste characteristics. The preferences of most of us cross-cut any such list and I am claiming only that members of one or the other of the two groups would display a larger cluster of them on one side than on the other. There are, nevertheless, vast differences between the two poles and between the styles of individuals occupying positions close to one or the other extreme. The Liberal party, during the years from 1935 on, had become increasingly hospitable to various elites, including that just identified, and could be distinguished in this respect particularly from the Conservative party in the Diefenbaker era. I am of course fully aware that even if there were *pure* elite–taste and public–taste types of people, there would be some of each kind in all parties. It is a question of more or less. The Liberals, although harbouring their share of yahoos, simply had a large enough concentration of elite–taste leaders to affect their party style. The Conservatives, for their part, did not. What were the political consequences?

I have already indicated that I thought many of the Liberal policies were desirable and their execution sometimes impressive. This can be ascribed to a number of factors, some of which were noted above. It is almost tautological but necessary to say that the strong presence in the party of various kinds of elites was responsible for much that was particularly outstanding about its performance in fields like foreign policy; some economic areas; social policy (although here the CCF and NDP were important contributors), and what we might term cultural and creative leisure policies. Into this latter category I place items like the establishment of the Canada Council; the encouragement given Ottawa's Capital Commission, the Film Board, and more recently to Canada's budding film industry; the creation of the National Arts Centre; the use of armouries as hostels for travelling youngsters; the extension of national parks and so on.

These and other projects were introduced although there was little if any mass demand for them or any electoral pay-off in sight but because the government thought that they were useful or necessary. And it had no doubt been persuaded by its members with elite tastes. This points to two of the latter group's common characteristics: a fairly sure sense of what is good and desirable in areas of particular concern to them and a strongly held view that the things they value should be made as widely available as possible. There is, in short, a commitment to

242

improve the world, akin, albeit in a lower key, to that displayed by most social reformers. The argument can best be illustrated by an analogy from the field of broadcasting. Our elite believes that large numbers of Canadians would learn to love and derive pleasure from the very best kind of high-quality programming of which the CBC is capable. The reason that this does not happen is that an enveloping flood of musical and verbal mush, produced by private broadcasters, has debased the public taste. It is not only bad money that drives out good; bad taste also drives out good, and the state has responsibilities for both kinds of degradation. The elite further believes that it must do everything in its power to enable everyone to learn to enjoy the best and to resist the dulling artistic and intellectual pacifiers of rapacious interests in the media. Those who "know better" have a responsibility to help less enlightened citizens, and public resources ought to be allocated for this purpose. It is difficult to dissociate from this position a somewhat paternalistic conviction. Although no sense of superiority may consciously be implied, those who espouse it assume that the general public does not know, nor care enough about these things; it needs to be led, even if reluctantly, to a fuller aesthetic enjoyment of life. I need not elaborate the close relationship between this view and what I described above as the Liberal style or at least that part of it which led to government efforts not being fully defended, justified, and made convincing during the election campaign. The parallel is obvious.

The lesson to be drawn from it is equally obvious: one of the toughest challenges facing a political party aspiring to greatness is to learn how to attract and utilize the skills and motivations of societally useful elites, while not letting some hard-to-prevent byproducts of elitism isolate it from the mass public. Both the Liberals and Conservaties have, during the present era, in different ways, failed to meet this challenge.

ELITIST TENDENCIES IN THE CANADIAN CONTEXT

Our discussion so far has offered a number of reasons why the Liberals, more than the other parties, should have developed a style leading towards electoral arrogance. It is intriguing

243

to speculate about whether Canadian conditions encourage or inhibit the kind of development we saw among the Liberals. Without becoming involved too deeply in unravelling this monstrous conundrum one can raise a number of suggestive questions. Is a country with a colonial background or, more precisely, two distinct kinds of colonial backgrounds, and with a pioneering past, more likely to develop elites which become excessively dominant? What are the consequences of the population being scattered over an immense terrain, in which only the long, thin southern fringe, neighboured by an economic and cultural colossus, approximates the density found in most industrial countries? Does the presence of two major linguistic groups require a special role for elites, of the kind described in the literature on consociational democracy and if so, in what way does Canada differ from countries displaying similar cleavages?[20] Is elitism, not only in politics but in other spheres as well, more apparent in Canada because within each of the two societies the number of leaders is so small that they almost all know one another and thus form cohesive, and therefore effective, groups? Has the British heritage and the proximity of the United States (and more recently of France) set standards of professionalism and informed leadership, which a sparsely populated and fragmented Canada could only emulate by creating an exceptionally competent and unduly influential group of administrative and political leaders? Has the existence of federalism led to a long-standing (though no longer tenable) and unwitting division of labour, i.e., have parochial, client-oriented, only moderately competent administration and politics been tolerated at the provincial level, permitting the development in the federal field of a loftier, more "statesmanlike" perspective and style? One could keep adding intriguing questions of this sort, suggesting subtle influences on Canada's political culture. Since to define and examine each would take a fair amount of original research, and several additional papers, I can do no more for the present than express the opinion that every factor mentioned has had some influence on the relationships in Canada between the general public and the various elites, whether we think of politics, education, business, the arts, science, sports, or any other aspect of life. And the total effect of these and other factors has been to make Canadians less deferential than the British, and more so than the Americans.

DIFFERENCES IN DEFERENCE PATTERNS

One of the consequences of Canada's continuing dependence on, and sensitivity to, influences from outside the country may have been a differential rate of change in the deference patterns of its population. The elites may be more receptive to British and French traditions and trends, whereas the mass public may respond much more strongly to United States influences. Public taste is generally formed by, and follows, that of trend-setting elites but this is not always the case, as both the architects and victims of revolutions usually discover. Canadian political elites, one can plausibly argue, and particularly that combination of their members which has been dominant in the Liberal party, were in the sixties and seventies entertaining unjustified expectations about the uncritical way in which the public was still prepared to accept their good intentions and performance. The public, on the other hand, may have been increasingly Americanized in the sense of, among other things, becoming less deferential. Margaret Atwood's fascinating thesis culled from literature, of Canadians seeing themselves primarily as victims, may articulate a major premise of its elites but not of the masses.[21] The government, in 1972, was thus led to underestimate how much of the public's confidence it had lost and the extent to which they had forfeited the credit Canadians have normally given the ruling party.[22] It is revealing, in this context, that for the first time in the present era, Liberal losses were particularly telling in the cities.[23] Furthermore, regional differences in the magnitude of Liberal losses may in part be related to regional differences in deference patterns: Mr. Trudeau's party did best in areas in which deference is greatest.[24]

CONSEQUENCES OF THE ELECTION OUTCOME

Since the principal characteristic of the shift in votes between 1968 and 1972 was the flight from the Liberals, rather than a stampede towards any one party, the 1972 election has brought Canada back to the "normal" minority government condition of

1957–58 and 1962–68. The outcome is serious for all parties except perhaps Social Credit. The Liberals suffered devastating losses in English Canada, particularly in the West. Mr. Stanfield's efforts to re-establish his party in Quebec failed dismally and the NDP, even in an election marked by profound economic anxiety and despite Mr. Lewis's brilliant campaign, failed to make any substantial advance in the proportion of votes polled. The revival of the Créditistes may be extremely important from the viewpoint of the future of Canada's party system: the more well-entrenched regional parties there are, the more difficult it is for any party to obtain an overall majority in the House. The prospects for majority government in the near future turn entirely on the capacity of the Liberals to re-establish themselves in English Canada or of the Conservatives to develop a provincial organization, now that the Union Nationale is gone, providing a base for sustained support in Quebec. Mr. Wagner has his work cut out for him. Even if he succeeds, the task is certain to take a longer time than will be available to him before the next election.

In the meantime, Canada is again served by a minority government, continuing a pattern which has existed for fifteen years, and which will go on for quite a long time: minority and majority governments will alternate, the duration of each depending on its popularity, the width of the gap separating the two largest parties, and the strength and support patterns of the third parties.[25] One of the consequences of this situation is that it acts as a corrective to the possible perpetuation of certain established elite values and biases which may deserve to be challenged. If two parties, in the North American setting, always divide the cake between themselves, they become very much alike and tacitly (and no doubt unconsciously) exclude certain ideas or a concern for interests which may appear to affect only minorities but which can in the long run be of critical relevance to the whole society. Minority governments make all parties exceptionally sensitive to minority views and interests, and in this sense more responsive to needs that may otherwise go undetected or at least unresponded to. By rewarding all parties less richly than they would like, minority elections tend to test each, and act as a corrective to the kind of arrogance which all parties are in danger of developing and

246

which, as I have tried to show here, has afflicted some parties more than others. But minority governments obviously also pose immense problems. Are these so great that we must, at all costs, try to return to a permanent majority system, or should we learn to live with and make better use of minority governments? The fact is that we really do not know, and this seems to me to be the point which needs to be stressed above all others at the present time.

The inconclusive 1972 result was met, as I suggested at the outset, by consternation in many quarters. This reaction was concerned in part with the extent to which the vote was split on language lines, and this could become most serious, if it persists. But it may be a timely warning to those who wish to see Canada survive, that too wide a divergence in political responses between Quebec and the rest of the country can be dangerous and needs to be watched. Some, although not all, of the causes need to be attacked with vigour, persistence, and finesse, including the language policy question itself. The 1972 outcome has also sounded another alarm: politicians and students of politics have been told once again by the voters that they must examine the relative virtues and weaknesses of majority and minority governments. A qualitative and quantitative evaluation of the outputs of each is badly needed,[26] as well as an exhaustive look at conditions favouring minority and majority elections. Furthermore, as I have suggested elsewhere, parliamentary procedures and conventions may have to be adjusted drastically to facilitate the better functioning of Parliament during periods of minority governments. Some of these changes may have to be quite fundamental, touching on even such system-critical traditions as, for instance, unfailing party loyalty in the legislature. Studies are needed which simulate diverse conditions and predict the consequences of various changes. The electoral system also requires more intensive assessment. This is an area which has benefited from a number of useful explorations in recent years but their results need to be followed up by additional work and imaginative experiments.[27]

It is of course possible that the role of Parliament itself is in question. Does it need to be supplemented in some respects by other bodies permitting the greater participation of citizens in government? Mr. Trudeau and his advisers may have had this in mind when stressing the greater need for participatory democracy or when devising activities and innovations in the Offices of the Privy Council and the Prime Minister, such as the regional desks. But whatever the ultimate future of Parliament, and possibly of related bodies, the most immediate task must be to make such changes in its present operation as may be required to maximize the efficiency of a minority government. Although the reforms called for here may then create conditions favouring minority elections by taking the horror out of them, they are essential. The inconvenience and fear of minority governments felt by the political and academic elites are understandable but will not stop the general public from producing inconclusive results. The Radio-Canada pre-election polls cited earlier show, in fact, that a large and growing proportion of Canadians expected the return of a minority Liberal government. Since this obviously failed to frighten a great many of them from voting for parties other than the Liberals, or from abstaining, it seems that the fear of minority governments had diminished substantially between 1968 and 1972.[28] This shift in opinion suggests that the public generally may have come to accept minority government more readily than most politicians, academics, and editorialists. In any event, the people have the right to demand the most effective and efficient accommodation to the alternating majority–minority electoral system by those placed in the position of servicing that system.

In this paper I have presented many speculative statements and have been selective in the topics chosen for emphasis. This may lead to a serious misunderstanding about my aims. Obviously, I have not tried to produce a complete explanation of the outcome of the 1972 election and am deeply conscious of the fact that many issues, not touched upon here, were important. The quality of the government's particular policies, for instance, is immensely relevant, but I have said little about this. The emphasis on *hubris* and related themes stems from a conviction that this is a critical area badly in need of exploration. Lest it be thought that this byway has led dangerously far from the main path to an understanding of the 1972 election, I should like to invoke one of Mother Nature's better maxims: Behold the turtle, it makes progress only when its neck is out.[29]

248

NOTES

1. See particularly Ramsay Cook, " 'Racial Backlash' Theory Does Not Stand Up," *The Montreal Star*, 4 November 1972 and Claude Ryan, "Un vote anti-Quebécois ou anti Trudeau?" *Le Devoir*, 3 November 1972. Claude Ryan's piece is a characteristically courageous and honest exercise in entertaining second, revisionary thoughts, modifying an earlier position. See also Dominique Clift, "Separatist Contradiction," *The Montreal Star*, ibid; Ann Charney, "Many Quebeckers Say Vote Was Anti-French," *The Toronto Star*, 4 November 1972; Claude Lemelin, "Les perils de l'économisme électoral," *Le Devoir*, 7 November 1972, which attacks Cook; and Jean Pellerin, "Les improbables du scrutin," *La Presse*, 1 November, 1972.

2. For more fully argued and supported analyses of this aspect of Canada's complexity, based on my 1968 survey, see supra, pp. 127–81; my "Political Styles and Language-use in Canada," a paper prepared for the IPSA Round Table on "Multilingual Political Systems: Problems and Solutions" (Quebec City, March 1972), forthcoming; and Richard Simeon, "Regional Political Cultures in Canada: Involvement, Efficacy and Trust," forthcoming.

3. Note François-Albert Angers' "La 'panique' des anglophones à l'origine de la force de Trudeau au Québec," *Le Devoir*, 2 November 1972.

4. The percentages exceed 100 because some individuals cited more than one item. See Gallup Poll of Canada, "People Say Main Problems Are Economy, Job, Labour," *Toronto Daily Star*, 4 November 1972.

5. John Meisel, "Religious Affiliation and Electoral Behaviour: A Case Study," *Canadian Journal of Economics and Political Science*, XXII, 4 (November 1956)

6. For an interesting criticism of these programs, from the political Left, see Lorne Huston, "The Flowers of Power: A Critique of OFY and LIP Programmes," *Our Generation*, VIII, 4 (1972)

7. See. for instance, D. Butler and D. Stokes, *Political Change in Britain* (London, 1969), pp. 428-31, and W. J. Crotty, "Party Effort and Its Impact on the Vote," *American Political Science Review*, LXV, 2 (June 1971).

8. The resort to brazenly offering (relatively) cheap election goodies here and there must have dramatized the government's casualness for quite a number of electors.

9. See, for instance, "Pearson ou l'abdication de l'esprit," XIII (April 1963). The article is not only an apposite Exhibit "A" for the present paper but, because its analysis in many respects closely parallels my own, provides an important complement to it.

10. This aspect has received a good deal more attention than some of the other themes I shall mention. See J. E. Hodgetts, "The Liberal and the Bureaucrat," *Queen's Quarterly*, LXII, 2 (Summer 1955); idem, "The Civil Servant and Policy Formulation," *Canadian Journal of Economics and Political Science,* XXIII. 4 (November 1957) and my "The Formulation of Liberal and Conservative Programmes in the 1957 Canadian General Election," *Canadian Journal of Economics and Political Science*, XXVI, 4 (November 1960) and my *The Canadian General Election of 1957* (Toronto, 1962), chap. 3.

11. See also supra, p. 56.

12. There were, of course, some highly tangible links, which straddled the eleven years between the St. Laurent defeat and the Trudeau victory. These were Messrs. Winters, Hellyer, and Martin, as well as others, no longer in federal politics, like Messrs. Pickersgill and Lesage, and Mr. Sinclair who was to become Mr. Trudeau's father-in-law.

13. An interesting contrast is presented when a similar question is posed about the Conservative parties under Messrs. Drew, Diefenbaker, and Stanfield.

14. No other Liberal leader has made as determined efforts as he to obtain additional advice to that reaching him through the regular public service channels; none has surrounded himself with as many newcomers to Ottawa; none has been as much "his own man" as he, in terms of being free of the usual political debts. He was undoubtedly sincere when he sought to increase participatory democracy. His performance, as a result, is particularly fascinating. This is, however, not the place to review it for, as I have argued above, the election turned on how he approached his task much more than on what he was actually trying to do.

15. Consider only the talent assembled on the eve of the war in the preparation of the Rowell-Sirois Report. It would in fact, be useful to attempt a study of the contributions made to Canadian public life, both in policy and political partisan terms, of the large numbers who have served on Royal Commissions. Among this group one would find an important component of the Liberal establishment's intellectual power.

16. See the relevant chapters in John Porter, *The Vertical Mosaic* (Toronto, 1965).

17. This is an aspect of political culture which differs substantially from concern with law and order, as discussed in chapters 1 and 3 above.

18. It is suggestive in this context that whatever other consequences may have followed for the Ontario Conservatives from their solid entrenchment in Queen's Park, the Liberal kind of arrogance did not seem to have been one of them.

19. An intriguing theory exploring the differences in orientations among activists in Canada's three major parties is developed by George Perlin in a study of the Conservative party, *The Permanent Minority* (forthcoming).

20. See Arend Lijphart, *The Politics of Accommodation: Democracy and Pluralism in the Netherlands* (Berkeley. 1968) and ibid., "Cultural Diversity and Theories of Political Integration," *Canadian Journal of Political Science*, IV, 1 (March 1971) which also contains useful additional footnote references.

21. Margaret Atwood, *Survival: A Thematic Guide to Canadian Literature* (Toronto, 1972).

22. See, supra, pp. 58-9.

23. See W. P. Irvine, "The 1972 Election: The Return of Minority Government," *Queen's Quarterly*, LXXIX, 4 (Winter 1972).

24. Deference is, of course, seen here as an intervening, not an independent variable. For analyses of deference within Newfoundland and New Brunswick, see George Perlin, "Social Change: The Mobilization of Electoral Support and Political Development in Newfoundland," in A. P. Cohen and Cato Wadel (eds.), *Community Aspects of Political Development in Newfoundland*, forthcoming, and Patricia Peppin, "New Brunswick Politics: A Crisis of Confidence" (forthcoming).

25. For extensive explorations of this aspect of Canada's party system, which also complement the general analysis of the present paper, see my "The June 1962 Election: Break-Up of Our Party System?" *Queen's Quarterly*, LXIX, 3 (Autumn 1962); "The Stalled Omnibus: Canadian Parties in the 1960s," *Social Research,* XXX, 3 (Autumn 1963); "Canadian Parties and Politics," in Richard H. Leach, *Contemporary Canada* (Durham, N.C., 1967); and "Recent Changes in Canadian Parties," in Hugh G. Thorburn, *Party Politics in Canada* (Scarborough, Ontario, second ed., 1967).

26. David J. Falcone and Michael S. Whittington are to be congratulated for having made a start in this direction, although their interests were broader than what I have in mind here. See

their "Output Change in Canada: A Preliminary Attempt to Open the 'Black-Box'," paper presented to the CPSA (Montreal, 4 June 1972).

27. See particularly Alan C. Cairns, "The Electoral System and the Party System in Canada, 1921-1965," *Canadian Journal of Political Science*, I, 1 (March 1968), J. A. A. Lovink, "On Analyzing the Impact of the Electoral System on the Party System in Canada," ibid., III, 4 (December 1970) and Cairns' reply in ibid. See also T. H. Qualter, *The Election Process in Canada* (Toronto, 1970).

28. See, also, supra pp. 18–19.

29. Cited by Barbara Froom, *Ontario Turtles* (Toronto, 1971).

6

BIZARRE ASPECTS OF A VANISHING ACT: THE RELIGIOUS CLEAVAGE AND VOTING IN CANADA

> *The mackerel run as freely into a Catholic's or Baptist's net as to any other, and I naturally enough asked myself why as a legislator I should make distinctions which God in His own good providence has not made.*
>
> Joseph Howe

FOR STUDENTS OF INTEGRATION AND CLEAVAGE-MANAGEMENT Canada is a cornucopia of intriguing anomalies, problems, and solutions. Because of their potentially explosive character, French-English relations have attracted particularly searching attention, usurping energies which, from the analytical point of view, might have been as fruitfully applied to other fields. One of these concerns the closely related controversies between the

This paper was prepared for the International Political Science Association's Round Table on Political Integration, held in Jerusalem, September 1974. The research of which it is a part is supported by a Killam Award of the Canada Council. I gratefully acknowledge this assistance and also that of Patricia Peppin (who not only looked after the analysis of the data but provided the epigraph), W. P. Irvine, Ralph Joyce, Murie Meisel, and Fanny Morales.

two largest religious groupings—Catholics and Protestants—who comprise about ninety-five percent of the population. The manner in which this cleavage has evolved and has been handled is not only interesting in its own right but also invites cross-cultural comparisons.

One classic response to intergroup conflict is the emergence of political parties championing the main opposing interests. The pattern is usually either for particular parties to espouse the demands of specific groups or for each of several parties to try to encompass all the major groups. In the former case it is the whole party system, in the latter individual parties, which normally mitigate or reconcile the major sources of friction by working out compromises expected to contain disruptive tensions within manageable bounds. The nature of disunity changes in response to the compromises which may either exacerbate or attenuate conflict. In the latter case the very source of dissension may ultimately disappear, leading to what, presumably, most observers would consider the successful integration of sub-groups into a system capable of embracing them all. So orderly a course of events is, however, exceedingly rare. Usually, only partial adjustments occur and the level of accommodation takes place somewhere between the two extremes of total breakdown or perfect resolution. This means that institutional responses to cleavages fluctuate according to the success or failure of efforts to meet the needs of conflicting groups. The relationships among these groups and political parties thus become an important indicator of the capability of the system to respond to stresses within it, resulting from long-term group alignments.

It is a curious and neglected phenomenon of political behaviour that a considerable time-lag seems to affect the response of groups to the way in which political parties have dealt with problems of concern to them. Angus Campbell and his associates note that the

> association of the Republican Party with economic depression was one of the strongest features of the picture the public held of that party at the time of [their] 1952 study. Through . . . twenty years out of office the Republican Party could not erase the memory that lingered in

many minds of the hardships of the Depression nor rid itself of the onus of responsibility for them.[1]

Religious voting in some communities provides another instance of the tendency of certain issues to linger on in the memories and voting patterns of the electorate even after they have ceased to be politically relevant.

The survival of vestigial issues of this type is important because it affects the manner in which parties and legislatures can deal with current problems and because the latent and possibly unperceived consequences of earlier crises provide situations conducive to the flaring up of new tensions. Philip Converse, for instance, in an article elegantly demonstrating "that religion played a powerful role in shaping voting behavior in the 1960 [Kennedy-Nixon] election," concludes that "the spontaneous burst of hostility which greeted the simple fact of other-group membership is . . . a warning that in the mass electorate the potential for social friction . . . is far from dead." He reaches this conclusion after observing that "whatever bitter religious struggles have been moved to the political arena to plague pluralistic democracies, the 1960 election in the United States was of another order. In a sense, it was at most a flash of lightning which illuminated, but only momentarily, a darkened landscape."[2] It is my contention that such chiaroscuro tableaux occur only when a polity is possessed of underlying residual elements of a former acute cleavage or, in Converse's felicitous image, when the darkened landscape is present.

Canada provides an outstanding example of a situation in which a formerly explosive political issue has gradually been defused but where partisan preferences still powerfully reflect the alignment occasioned by the issue. It may seem paradoxical but it is nevertheless the case that religious issues or questions strongly linked to religion do not separate Canadian parties at the federal level but that religious affiliation is still the best predictor of voting available, insofar as the Liberals and Conservatives are concerned.[3]

255

Canada owes much of its present character to having emerged in the eighteenth century as the product of Anglo-French rivalry in North America. After the Treaty of Paris in 1763 the British became masters of a vast terrain populated almost exclusively by native peoples and, on the shores of the St. Lawrence, by French settlements. Contacts with France were cut, particularly after the Revolution, and the ever-accelerating new immigration came, during the first period at least, from the British Isles. Virtually all the French were Catholic and, isolated and almost leaderless as they were in North America, their faith and Church became the dominant factor in their family, social, and national life and for a time also in politics. The overwhelming proportion of British immigrants were Protestant and the never-ceasing tension and conflict between the two "founding peoples" in Canada contained not only ethnic but also strong religious strains. Ultramontane elements dominated the Quebec Church and exercised an extremely conservative influence on the life of French Canada while, at the same time, maintaining close relations with the secular powers in London and Quebec City and, after Confederation in 1867, with the federal politicians in the national capital. Any party aiming at a majority in Parliament needed a reasonable level of support in Quebec—support which, until fairly recently, was almost impossible to obtain in the face of determined opposition by the Church. The political power of the ecclesiastical authorities was therefore immense, and since the bishops were vitally interested in a wide variety of policy areas, Canadian governments had to be intensely sensitive to Catholic interests, as defined by the hierarchy.

For the first thirty years after Confederation the francophone population strongly supported the Conservative (bleu) party and, influenced by the Church, was suspicious of the anticlerical Rouges—the precursors of the Liberals. The latter, however, chose a magnetic French Canadian as their leader in 1887 and, benefiting from numerous troubles which had beset the Conservatives, won the election of 1896.[4] The Liberals under Laurier not only remained in office for the subsequent fifteen years but, more important from our present point of view, won the seemingly unshakeable electoral support of French Canada which is to this day a critical element in the operation of Canada's party system.

Important though they were, however, Catholics and French Canadians constituted a minority of the population, except in Quebec, and in the other provinces there were not only Protestant majorities but also large, well-organized, anti-Catholic and anti-French movements and organizations. Some of these—the Orange Order, for instance—knew that they could make and unmake governments if they became too pliant vis-à-vis the "enemy." National leaders and national parties have, therefore, been able to fashion majorities only so long as they have maintained at least a tenuous foothold within both major religious groupings.[5]

While the parties could not avoid taking positions on the sometimes extremely bitter religious controversies, they successfully avoided becoming irrevocaby and exclusively associated with any one religious group. Denominational cleavages were thus never politically institutionalized, as they have been in so many European countries. Specific parties did become more attractive to one religious group or another, but they strove vigorously and unceasingly to prevent their electoral base from being confined to any of the major religious groupings. Constant pressure was and is brought to bear on the most extreme partisans and activists to moderate their views with respect to controversies having religious overtones. The fact that none of the parties became sectarian, that they have all enjoyed support from a wide spectrum of religious adherents, and that religious issues have to all intents and purposes disappeared from the federal scene attest to the success of this strategy.

Canada's federal character has provided a setting which has facilitated the parties' efforts to avoid becoming too closely tied to any one religion. By confining the most sensitive issues—education, for instance—to the provincial level, the federal framework has enabled national parties to dissociate themselves from some acute religious controversies. This has been encouraged by the loose structure of national parties which are, in some ways, highly decentralized alliances of provincial organizations.[6] While there is a predisposition on the part of voters to support the same party at both levels, this is by no

257

means always so and it is quite common in Canada for a party to enjoy strong support in a given area at the provincial level, and to do quite badly there federally. Federalism, the nature of party structure, and voting habits have therefore made it possible for federal parties to protect themselves from embroilment in some of the religious-political controversies agitating Canadians.

The non-ideological, somewhat opportunistic nature of the dominant values[7] which is reflected in the party system also makes it easier for the intensity of some issues—even those relating to religion—to be contained or deflected by various quid pro quos, compromises, or simply patronage politics. The premium placed on private (as distinct from public) goods, and the generally low level of politicization of issues, characteristic of Canadian society, thus affect the manner in which the system responds to religious cleavages in two ways: conflicts have not reached the intensity observed in countries like Ireland, Belgium, Austria, or Holland, for instance, and it has been easier than elsewhere for politicians to handle such religiously-based crises as did develop without structuring the party system in response to them.

THE MEANING OF "RELIGIOUS VOTING"

The foregoing notwithstanding, religious voting is very much in evidence in Canada. Before examining its character we must clarify what is meant by the term. Unless in what follows it is specifically stated otherwise, "religious voting" refers simply to a statistical relationship between members of two religious groups and the support they give a specified party. It does not here refer to the degree of religious awareness or commitment on the part of the voters. It would be wrong to assume that even when members of a particular denomination show a strong preference for a given party this necessarily reflects a judgement related to a religious matter. The religious factor may be unperceived, completely social or communal in origin, and it may also be part of a spurious relationship, strongly reflecting some other causal characteristic—economic well-being, for instance, or years of schooling.

258

Most of our data are derived from interviews with a 1968 national sample (N = 2767) which contained several questions tapping the religious background and life of the respondents. The questionnaire did not, however, include any direct inquiries into whether the voting decision was consciously related to religious factors.

Under these circumstances the religious vote can be identified in various ways, each attended by many hazards. Table I shows the percentage of Catholics and Protestants voting for the four main parties and also discriminates between French and English-speaking Catholics and between Protestants belonging to the five high status denominations (Anglican, United Church, Presbyterian, Baptist, Unitarian)[8] and the others, whom we call "Low Protestants" without, naturally, passing any judgement on their personal or religious worth. Columns (2) and (5) reveal that 69 percent of the Catholics voted Liberal as compared with 44 percent of the Protestants. We refer to the difference—25 percentage points—as the religious voting for Catholics and Protestants with respect to the Liberal party. The Conservative figure is 22 percentage points (the difference between 17 and 39 percent) and although it should be negative, we shall, for the sake of simplicity, eschew the sign.

TABLE I

Percentage of French and English Catholics, and High and Low Protestants Voting for the Four Parties in 1968

(1)	(2)	(3)	(4)	(5)	(6)	(7)	(8)
		CATHOLIC			PROTESTANT		ALL
	All	French	English	All	High	Low	
Liberal	69	65	71	44	46	37	55
Conservative	17	20	15	39	38	45	29
NDP	8	6	13	14	14	16	11
SC	6	10	1	2	2	3	4
N	949	531	351	1151	904	247	2100

NOTE: The Catholic total is larger than the sum of French and English-speakers because it includes all Catholics, regardless of their language use.

259

Table I records one of the bizarre aspects of the vanishing act celebrated in this paper's title: it documents the fact that despite the absence of the slightest vestige of religious matters in the dialogue of federal parties, they are all influenced by religious voting. In the case of the "third" parties the reasons are largely regional and ethnic. The NDP has never caught hold in Quebec and in French Canada generally,[9] and by the time of our survey the Social Credit party had shrivelled in the west and had emerged strongly in rural Quebec.

But if religious differences are *passé* as causes for a major Canadian cleavage one cannot say that their disappearance is taking place without a trace: they still leave a vivid imprint on the electoral map. It used to be argued that religious voting masked ethnic voting and that the strong support for the Liberals in French Canada accounts for the massive Catholic component of the Liberal vote. Columns (3) and (4) indicate that English Catholics favour the Liberals even more than their francophone coreligionists, thereby confirming the now well-established fact[10] that although ethnicity reinforces religious voting, it is not its cause: while English Catholics exceed French ones in their Liberal zeal only in Quebec (partly because of the virtually exclusive appeal of the Créditistes to francophones and because of the almost solid Liberal support among Quebec anglophones of any faith), they give the Liberal party a greater edge than the Protestants in all regions, particularly Ontario—the most populous province—where the difference is one of 31 percentage points.

Religious voting is broadly similar (although in the opposite direction) with respect to support for the Conservatives—the major beneficiaries of the Protestants' lesser enthusiasm for the Liberals. Members of the smaller sects, the Low Protestants as we have unceremoniously dubbed them, are revealed in column (7) to have preferred the Conservatives over the Liberals, reversing the pattern exhibited by all the other groups we examined. Enthusiasm for the Liberal party is thus greatest among English Catholics, followed by French Catholics, High Protestants, and lastly by Low Protestants, of whom only a shade over a third voted Liberal.

Our quick overview leaves us, to reverse the inspired quip of the Earl of Birkenhead, "much better informed . . . but none the wiser." To obtain a deeper insight into the nature of religious voting I have introduced a wide range of control variables, the effects of most of which are reported in Tables II to VII.[11]

Out of the welter of somewhat disorienting guideposts provided by the relevant literature I have selected three broad areas each of which could be expected to illumine religious voting. In the first place, the religious factor itself has to be considered. Are religious beliefs, practices, attachments, or social ties influential in determining the voters' partisan choices? Secondly, sociological and psychological approaches direct our attention to various socializing experiences and to the related cluster of diverse demographic variables. Finally, political phenomena are obviously pertinent—attitudes to the political process, to issues, and to the physiognomy of the parties.

Religious Factors (Tables II and III, page 275)

The most telling conclusion to be drawn from scrutinizing the association of a number of religious factors, the voters' denomination, and their vote is that religious voting has very little to do with religion in the narrow sense. No data were available, it is true, permitting the control for doctrinal aspects, spirituality, or orthodoxy, but such tests as we were able to introduce yielded exceedingly weak results.

Of the seven dimensions examined, only church attendance, exposure to sectarian schools, and membership in a religious organization have more than a minimal association with religious voting. The Catholic vote varies less than that of the Protestants. Among the latter, it is those who attend church more frequently and those who belong to religious associations who widen the gap between the two religious groups by registering a below-average level of support for the Liberals and a slightly higher one for the Conservatives. Whatever it is that makes Protestants less disposed than Catholics to vote Liberal (and more inclined towards the Conservatives) is a little enhanced by membership in organizations like the Orange Order and by greater church attendance. Such experiences have no appreciable effect on the voting of Catholics.

It may be more noteworthy that the other aspects we examined produced even more negative results. Religious voting was, to all intents and purposes, unaffected by whether one agreed with the proposition that individuals who break the law because of a religious principle should be punished, by the degree of parental religiosity, by membership in church-affiliated organizations, and by what Lenski calls "communality"[12]—the proportion of friends sharing one's religion.

We are justified in concluding that religious voting in Canada is unrelated to narrowly religious factors, like the people's religious views, and that such social influences on voting as emanate from one's membership in a religious group are not related at all, or only very weakly, to experiences like membership in church groups or church attendance, and even to social exposure to friends sharing one's religion.

Demographic Characteristics (Tables IV and V, pages 276, 277)

Among demographic factors, those related to socialization (Items 1–6, Tables IV and V), sex and marital status (Items 7–9), geographical location (10 and 11), and class (12–14), seem likely potential influences on the effect of religious affiliation on voting. It was possible that some of the dimensions under each of these four areas might wipe out religious voting altogether but this was not the case. Sex and, surprisingly, self-defined class, turned out to lead to no appreciable differences in the partisan choices of Catholics and Protestants.

Voters who received their early socialization outside Canada (i.e., immigrants) displayed a higher level of religious voting than natives. When we control for date of immigration we discover that the more recent arrivals are much less disposed to discriminate between the parties in a manner which can be related to their religious affiliation. And while both Catholics and Protestants among post-World War II immigrants strongly favour the Liberals and downgrade the Conservatives, the *rapprochement* between the two groups is largely the work of Protestants.

Canadians who have experienced political socialization

recently and also those who have done so while being exposed to formal schooling are given to religious voting much less than older citizens and those with less education. The younger cohorts and those with post-secondary education have substantially reduced the margin between the partisan preferences of Catholics and Protestants and, again, while both showed increased support for the Liberals, the movement was greater among Protestants. It seems, therefore, that the prospects for the diminution of religious voting are good, since voting differences between Catholics and Protestants are likely to be reduced as what Butler and Stokes[13] call the "replacement of the electorate" occurs and as the present generation of older voters departs. Increased opportunities for better formal education can be expected to have the same effect.

Age is no doubt responsible for single voters, as distinct from married or widowed ones, appearing to be less influenced by their religion when choosing between Liberals and Conservatives. A look at mixed marriages strengthens the impression conveyed by other aspects of our data: Catholics, when submitted to influences likely to reduce their endemic strong preference for the Liberals and their aversion to the Conservatives are less likely to respond than Protestants under corresponding influences. Those among them who enjoy mixed marriages modify their group's voting pattern much less than similarly placed Protestants.

Among the geographical factors I examined are regional variations and size of community. Four main observations are prompted by this exercise. Religious voting is more pronounced in traditional eastern Canada than in the west. The latter is not only the more recently settled area but also contains a lower proportion of Catholics. Secondly, the aberrant case of Quebec, where a larger proportion of Protestants than Catholics votes Liberal (Item 10, Table V), dramatically reveals the key to an understanding of religious voting in Canada: the Liberal party has succeeded not only in retaining the loyalty of a large majority of Catholics but also makes immensely rewarding inroads among Protestants, gaining lavish support from some sub-groups in this category. Thirdly, religious voting is substantially lower in metropolitan areas than in smaller communities but it is not at its highest in rural regions. Finally,

Protestants but not Catholics show a monotonic preference for the Liberal party (and declining Conservative support) as their vote is recorded in communities increasing in size, from rural areas to villages, towns, cities, and metropolises.

Income is strongly associated with religious voting and the now familiar pattern is repeated in our analysis: differences between Catholics and Protestants are considerably smaller among high income groups than among less fortunate citizens and the shortening of the distance between them is largely caused by the greater "volatility" of Protestants than Catholics. Religious voting persists even among the high income groups and we can conclude from this and some of our other data that class factors do not wash out the effects of religion on voting.

Political Factors (Tables VI and VII, pages 278–280)

In exploring the relation between political phenomena and religious voting I examined some aspects of what is usually thought of as political culture (Items 1–15), reactions to election issues (Items 16–26), and various aspects of the parties (Item 27). Among the first, a high sense of efficacy and trust was shown to reduce religious voting. This relationship was weaker but persisted when controls for income and education were introduced. Interest in the election was unrelated as was knowledge of some of the candidates' characteristics.

Although Catholics and Protestants entertained quite different views on public policy areas impinging strongly on private morality, such as divorce, abolition of the death penalty, and the legal status of homosexuals, these differences failed to affect religious voting. Attitudes to some aspects of the political system, on the other hand, were associated significantly with differences between the partisan preferences of Catholics and Protestants. The gap between the two groups was narrower among those who thought that the monarchy should be abolished, that the constitution should be changed, that Canada and the United States should not become one country, that Communists should not be outlawed, and among those who had a more internationalist outlook. Although one might argue about which position on these dimensions is the "progressive" one, I believe it to be substantially correct to suggest that religious voting persisted where traditionalist, old-fashioned, and even illiberal views prevailed and diminished in association with more flexible, innovative, and progressive preferences.[14] The narrowing of the distance between the Catholic and Protestant vote with respect to both a higher sense of efficacy and trust, and the attitudinal dimensions just discussed was associated with the Protestants moving closer to the strong Liberal support exhibited by the Catholics. The same also applies to the lower level of religious voting associated with positions the voters took on various election issues.

One of these dimensions—attitudes to welfare policies—produced a suggestive glimpse of how parties are perceived by members of the two religious groups: for Protestants, the Conservatives were the preferred vehicle of opposition to welfare programs but Catholics favoured the Liberals (Item 18, Table VII). This pattern was very much less evident among those who opposed extensive economic intervention by the government. Although more Catholics than Protestants holding this view still voted Liberal the gap between the two religious groups here narrowed by comparison with the overall national figure, because both moved towards the centre, so to speak: the Catholic vote was 64 (not 69) and that of the Protestants 49 (not 44).

The secret of the Liberal party's success in Canadian politics is epitomized in the way in which it rallied between 60 and 70 percent of both Catholics and Protestants who favoured separate status for Quebec, as well as of the Catholics opposing it, while still receiving its "normal" 43 percent of votes from Protestants to a great many of whom this option was anathema. Special circumstances in Quebec (as well as very small numbers in some cells) are responsible for this curious instance of a higher percentage of Protestants than Catholics voting Liberal, but the case is striking.

In comparing how Catholics and Protestants reward the parties which come closest to their own position on a number of election issues we find that the former, who normally support the Liberals with enthusiasm, cannot, even when they agree with Conservative policies, bring themselves in anything like equal number to give similarly whole-hearted support to that party. Protestants, on the other hand, similarly in accord with a party's position, virtually abandon their usual Conservative preference: about 80 percent of them vote for the party closest to their views on each of the various issues. This is one of several examples we encounter in which Catholics, even when inducements are present to vote Conservative, appear constrained from doing so; Protestants are not similarly inhibited with respect to the Liberal party. The same pattern of Catholic intransigence in the face of encouragement to vote Conservative is encountered among children of Conservative parents: Catholic offspring of Liberals follow the family tradition in very much larger numbers (data not provided in the tables).

Religious voting was below the usual level among those who reported that the party leaders were most important to them in deciding what to do in the election. This may simply reflect the great appeal of Pierre Trudeau in 1968 to both Catholics and Protestants but is relevant to our purpose because it again shows the flexibility of Protestants who, on this dimension, deviated from their "average" Liberal vote more than Catholics.

The salient points to have emerged from this examination of the political aspects are that political factors alone are incapable of eliminating religious voting but that differences between Catholics and Protestants are less evident among those who enjoy a high level of efficacy and trust, among those who take liberal or progressive positions on attitudes to the polity, and among those who report that leaders are particularly important to their voting decision. The narrowing of the gap invariably follows an increasing approximation on the part of Protestants to the Catholics' Liberal enthusiasm (and their aversion to the Conservatives). Catholics are much less flexible in this sense and are revealed as being securely anchored in their Liberal preference even when circumstances lead one to expect that large numbers of them might abandon their group's usual stance. Protestants respond more readily to such temptations.

CONCLUSION: RELIGIOUS VOTING AND THE INTEGRATIVE
ROLE OF PARTIES

Religious voting, we have noted, has not vanished despite the total absence of religion or religious subjects from the federal political dialogue in Canada. It is being attenuated, particularly by sub-populations among whom one would expect this to happen, but not in the anticipated manner. The quintessence of religious voting, insofar as Catholic and Protestant support for the old parties is concerned, resides in two characteristics: the solid, nearly immobile preference of over two-thirds of the Catholics for the Liberal party and the more balanced and flexible evaluation of the two parties by the Protestants.

The norm, as we have seen, is for the Catholics to divide so as to deliver 69 percent of their votes to the Liberals and 17 percent to the Conservatives. The Protestant proportions are the much more even 44 percent and 39 percent respectively. The pattern of the diminution of religious voting is not one in which certain Catholic and Protestant groups split the difference, as it were, and move towards a position of partisan support roughly halfway between the overall position of their groups taken as a whole. When the gap narrows it is almost always because a sub-group of Protestants displaying certain character- istics—say high income—delivers a very much larger percent- age of its vote to the Liberal party than Protestants as a whole, whereas among Catholics in the same category (those in the upper income brackets) the proportion voting Liberal is only slightly higher or the same as that of all Catholics. That is, Protestants (enjoying high income, for example) "travel"

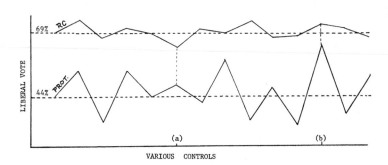

FIGURE I. 'FLUCTUATION' PATTERNS OF CATHOLIC AND PROTESTANT VOTE

267

farther from their group's collective percentage voting Liberal, whereas similarly affluent Catholics "move" only a little from what we may consider their base. Figure I presents the process schematically. At point (a) we ascribe the narrowing of the gap between the two religious groups to the result of what we may term a mutual *rapprochement*.[15] Catholics and Protestants can here take equal credit for reducing religious voting. The usual sequence is illustrated at point (b) where the Protestants come close to the Catholics' "base" of 69 percent and the Catholics' Liberal vote is only a few points above it.

Our search for an explanation of the survival of religious voting was based on the tacit assumption that if we could locate its cause, or causes, the rest would be simple. Not surprisingly, perhaps, no single central explanatory variable emerged and we must conclude that the voting differences betwen Catholics and Protestants are the result of a variety of complex, rather general factors. Historical antecedents are clearly important. The question they pose is why Catholics appear to be more under the spell of historical events and controversies than Protestants, certain groups among whom, as we have seen, are successfully escaping the dead hand of the past. One reason lies in the perpetually simmering ethnic problem in Canada. Despite the fact that, as we have seen, religious and ethnic voting are not the same, it is clear that the two phenomena, and the cleavages which prompt them, are closely related. The Liberal party's success in holding on to its huge following in Quebec has direct consequences for its appeal to non-French Catholics and even to many Protestants.

Since the days of Laurier the Liberal party has nursed its support in Quebec, and in French Canada generally, with consummate skill. It has become the undisputed innovator and champion of policies calculated to bring about compromises between the two major ethnic groups in Canada and it has sought indefatigably to make these arrangements acceptable elsewhere in the country. Unlike the Conservatives, the Liberals have thus not only maintained a very strong presence in French Canada but have also held the intense loyalty of anglophone Quebeckers and of many Canadians everywhere seeking a new accommodation between Canada's two charter groups. And again, unlike the Conservatives, they managed

268

to evolve policies affecting French-English relations without searing internal strife and ceaseless infighting over the matter between regional and ideological factions within their ranks.

Many factors are obviously responsible for giving the Liberal party its wide appeal. The historical legacy of greater acceptability to Catholics and to French Canada, its handling of the conscription crises, recent policies vis-à-vis bilingualism and biculturalism, the recruitment of able francophone militants and candidates, the choice of French-Canadian national leaders, encouragement of immigration from non-Anglo-Saxon countries, establishment of diplomatic ties with the Vatican—all these factors, although they were not explicitly tied to religious issues or controversies, have combined (alongside other Liberal policies and characteristics) to make the Liberal party attractive to Catholics. At the same time, an important segment of the Protestant population also found these and other Liberal initiatives and practices attractive and indeed made it possible for the party to pursue its course in the knowledge that its appeal was more than narrowly sectarian. The Liberals have become the party with by far the broadest appeal and bases of support, not least among most of the country's minorities.[16]

The Conservatives meantime suffered under the historic handicap of being the anti- or at least the non-French party. The leadership has been dominated by anglophones and on the whole, has suffered from weak French-Canadian activists and MP's. The only postwar Conservative administration—that of John Diefenbaker (1957–63)—failed totally to build a viable base for the Conservatives in Quebec. The disappearance of a Quebec provincial Conservative party deprived the federal Conservatives of a vital organizational prop in Quebec. The party's primary electoral base in anglophone and "other-ethnic" areas, particularly rural ones, along with its growing reliance on the west, increased the tendency to be critical of Liberal attempts to cope with French-English tensions. When, under Robert Stanfield (Diefenbaker's successor as party leader), policies more friendly to Quebec were adopted, they lacked credibility, partly because they were widely publicized as causing deep and emotional intraparty conflicts. While these aspects of the party touch primarily on its image in French Canada, the ethnic issue has contaminated the religious one.

The party has not had a Catholic leader since 1940. Even when the top leadership attempts to fashion a party more hospitable to the French and to Catholics, lack of concern and occasionally opposition among many grass roots activists tends to frustrate such overtures. While the Conservative party has, in recent times, shown no signs at all of being hostile to Catholics, and has made some attempts to attract their participation and support, it has continued to present a somewhat uninviting picture to many of them.

The electoral profile presented in this paper indicates that to some extent the pattern imposed on the parties by the past has a tendency to be self-perpetuating. We have seen that the most Liberal sub-groups among Protestants consisted of the young; the better-educated and better off; metropolitan dwellers; people with a high sense of efficacy, with liberal views and who favour change—of individuals, in short, who are more likely than others to influence the world around them, to set patterns for the future, and to have greater access to, or be part of, the elites who dominate political decision-making. Liberal supporters can therefore in one sense be seen as comprising a massive core of Catholics and a group of Protestants among whom progressive, tolerant, better-placed, politically competent people are substantially over-represented. The Liberal constituency is therefore one which could be expected to favour religious (and also ethnic) compromises and generally policies attenuating group conflicts.

There are elements here of a sort of rough-hewn consociationalism within the Liberal party. There is no formal *verzuiling*, to be sure, but the leaders can speak with some assurance of stable support of behalf of impressive majorities of French Canadians and English Catholics, and of important numbers of Protestants who can be counted upon to accept progressive, conciliatory policies affecting intergroup relations. Within the party's top leadership Catholics and Protestants, anglophones and francophones, can work out solutions to vexing problems in the knowledge that their "constituents" will accept their compromises. The Conservative party, on the other hand, lacks this kind of base, and the leaders wishing to shape a party more representative of Canada's kaleidoscopic population are frustrated because they lack an adequate number of appropriate pillars on which to stand. The popular base of the party is thin with respect to francophones and English Catholics, and among Protestants—the party's mainstay—the groups most likely to favour new departures and the adoption of conciliatory ethnic policies are being raided by the Liberals.

This discussion points up the importance, in any examination of party responses to cleavages, of the relation between elites and the mass publics. The former are normally more open, less bigoted, and, naturally, more active in searching for compromises.[17] This is an aspect of our problem which requires treatment in a separate paper. Before abandoning it, we must however note that the reason that the survival of religious voting is rather surprising in Canada is precisely because elites (who provide the audible, visible, and recorded political dialogue) refrain from bringing the religious factor into the open (no doubt for excellent reasons) and that some elements of the mass public are still swayed by it. Our analysis showed, for instance, that in two of the rare instances where religious voting *increased* as the result of Protestants delivering an abnormally low vote to the Liberal party (with the Catholics holding steady), the drop in Liberal support occurred among respondents who reported high church attendance and membership in religious voluntary associations. It is also relevant that although the religious affiliation of candidates is never mentioned from the platform and rarely, if at all, in print, among the Conservative candidates chosen in 1968, 37 percent were Catholics, compared with a Liberal figure of 57 percent.[18]

It is nevertheless highly questionable whether very many Canadians weigh what we might term the religious attractiveness of parties before casting their ballots. Other issues and aspects are obviously more important. It is a well-known fact, however, that partisan choice is not the result of a powerful intellectual and analytical exercise on the part of most voters but rather a loose, often absent-minded response to a wide variety of influences, many of them quite unconscious ones. In situations where no overriding, sharply defined, and deeply penetrating issues dictate a preference for a given party (a very common situation insofar as most voters are concerned) there is undoubtedly a widespread tendency to fall back on traditions and group influences which may, on the face of it, have little to do with current political controversies. Members of minority groups are very likely to resort to a party that has customarily exuded an aura of reassuring hospitality. And there is no doubt that Catholics are a minority in Canada, even if their proportion of the population approaches fifty percent. No French Canadian can escape the feeling of being in some respects a marginal person in the Canadian context and in English Canada Catholics are not only a numerical minority but "Catholic religious affiliation tends to be associated with minority group and lower occupational status."[19] Our data indicate that the group influences which lead to this kind of reaction are extremely subtle and diffused and almost certainly, in many instances, quite unperceived by the individuals affected by them.

The strength of these group influences has never been tested. In recent times, only the twin elections of 1957 and 1958 witnessed a major flight from the Liberals and no survey data are available which would enable us to scrutinize the behaviour and attitudes of Catholics at that time. The results make it obvious that a fairly large number of Catholics abandoned the Liberals and voted for the Conservatives but subsequent events show equally clearly that most of them must have returned to their traditional fold. There has been no cataclysmic event or political crisis resulting in a critical or realigning election. For a diminishing cleavage of low salience to be bleached out of the political fabric altogether it seems that two conditions are required: (1) a widespread and major disenchantment with the parties which had at one time monopolized the favour of the dissenting groups, leading to a loosening of ties not unlike that which has been evident in the relations between Protestants and the Conservative party; (2) the dramatic and sustained transformation of a previously ill-supported party which, in its new guise, can attract the affections of members of groups which had heretofore favoured another party. Had Mr. Diefenbaker, after his triumph over the Liberals in the late fifties, been able to lead a brilliant government and had he reshaped his party so as to make of it a suitable instrument of French-English accommodation, it is quite possible that a great many Catholics who had at that time almost certainly abandoned the Liberals might have freed themselves of the group-inspired link to that party. Diefenbaker did neither of these things and in fact dissipated the immense goodwill which swept him into office.

For reasons we have noted it is most unlikely that the Conservative party will, in the foreseeable future, succeed in broadening its electoral base to include an equitable proportion of Catholics. There are self-perpetuating elements in the relation between the Liberal party and Canada's major ethnic groups which make it almost unavoidable that the Liberals will continue as Canada's governmental party *par excellence*. Regional factors and/or ineptitude will occasionally deprive it of a parliamentary majority or another party—quite possibly the Conservatives—may now and then form a government, but the long-term prospects for the Liberals are excellent. Since their hold on a substantial majority of Catholic voters appears firm and the characteristics of those Protestants who favour the Liberals indicates that the party can expect increased support from this religious group in future, we confront a situation which, if it continues, promises to perpetuate the present one party-dominant system in Canada. More precisely, what will continue is a multi-party system dominated by the Liberals.

There are varying opinions about the general effectiveness of such a system in the Canadian setting at the present time. I shall deftly sidestep this aspect of the problem and focus on its relation to the religious cleavage. As we have seen, the present pattern of partisan support is influenced by factors related to the religious affiliation of the electorate. The political and party systems have effectively defused the once deep cleavage between religious groups. Despite the disappearance of any divisive national religious issues, however, differences with religio-political implications persist, albeit in a low key. The manner in which the parties have responded has, in a sense, neutralized any immediate threat to the system arising from religious cleavages, and has minimized the likelihood of any virulent flare-ups occurring in the future. But at the same time, by the fashion in which it has accommodated itself to the political sentiments which animate the major religious groups, the party system has in its own way contributed to the perpetuation of the religious cleavage at one level. By so doing, the parties help keep in existence a currently mild and benign division that could, however, under certain circumstances turn ugly. This is not likely to happen but the continuation of a religious cleavage with political dimensions, however tenuous, in a country deeply threatened by a closely related ethnic schism, is a possible source of acute future tensions. Religious issues alone are no longer capable of causing crises in Canada; in conjunction with the unresolved French-English split they could provide the darkening landscape against which we might yet see a flash of lightning.

TABLE II

Religious Factors, Religious Affiliation (Roman Catholic/Protestant) and Vote
(In Conditional Yule's Q's)

RELIGIOUS FACTORS			LIBERAL			CONSERVATIVE		
	*	:	*	:	Difference	*	:	Difference
1. Sectarian education	(yes/no)		.22	.46	.24	.38	.46	.08
2. Religious organization	(member/not)		.67	.46	.21	.70	.51	.19
3. Church attendance	(high/low)		.56	.44	.12	.64	.48	.16
4. Punish lawbreakers	(yes/no)		.52	.39	.13	.57	.46	.11
5. Church organization	(member/not)		.54	.45	.09	.57	.50	.07
6. Communality	(high/low)		.45	.53	.08	.53	.58	.05
7. Parents' religious interest	(high/med-low)		.51	.43	.08	.59	.46	.13

TABLE III

Percentage of Catholics and Protestants Voting Liberal and Conservative by Religious Factors

RELIGIOUS FACTORS	* :	LIBERAL *		:		CONSERVATIVE *		:	
		C	P	C	P	C	P	C	P
1. Sectarian education	(yes/no)	71	61	67	43	15	28	20	40
			10		24		13		20
2. Religious organization	(member/not)	73	34	68	45	15	51	17	39
			39		23		36		22
3. Church attendance	(high/low)	69	38	70	48	18	49	16	34
			31		22		31		18

Note: The numbers immediately under the Catholic and Protestant percentages are the percentage differences between them, i.e. the extent of religious voting.

275

TABLE IV

Demographic Factors, Religious Affiliation and Vote
(In Conditional Yule's Q's)

DEMOGRAPHIC FACTORS		LIBERAL						CONSERVATIVE					
		*	:	@	v	^	Diff.	*	:	@	v	^	Diff.
1. Childhood residence	(farm/town/city)	.45	.51	.41			[.10]	.50	.56	.45			[.11]
2. Country of birth	(abroad/Canada)	.63	.45				.18	.73	.50				.23
3. Date of immigration	(pre-1946/post-war)	.82	.35				.47	.87	.48				.39
4. Education	(elem./sec./post-sec.)	.64	.46	.23			[.41]	.61	.51	.47			[.14]
5. Age	(50+/ under 50)	.64	.35				.29	.66	.41				.25
6. Origin	(Germ./Pol./Ukr.-Russ.)	.59	.81	-.05			[.86]	.54	.94	.30			.64
7. Marital Status	(widowed/marr./single)	.65	.47	.30			[.35]	.67	.52	.46			[.21]
8. Homogeneity of marriage	(same rel./diff.rel.)	.49	.16				.33	.56	-.24				.80
9. Sex	(men/women)	.49	.44				.05	.53	.51				.02
10. Region	(Atl./Que./Ont./Prair./B.C.)	.58	-.36	.64	.39	.45	[1.00]	.58	-.07	.78	.41	1.00	[1.07]
11. Size of community	(rural/1-10m/10-100m/100-500m/metro)	.45	.60	.42	.64	.29	[.35]	.49	.70	.35	.74	.35	[.39]
12. Occupation	(manual/non-manual)	.46	.46				.00	.44	.59				.15
13. Self-ascribed class	(working/middle)	.54	.39				.15	.49	.52				.03
14. Income	(less 5m/5-10m/10m)	.59	.46	.28			[.31]	.59	.52	.41			[.18]

TABLE V

Percentage of Catholics and Protestants Voting Liberal and Conservative
by Demographic Factors

DEMOGRAPHIC FACTORS		LIBERAL *	LIBERAL :	LIBERAL @	LIBERAL v	LIBERAL <	CONSERVATIVE *	CONSERVATIVE :	CONSERVATIVE @	CONSERVATIVE v	CONSERVATIVE <
		C P	C P	C P	C P	C P	C P	C P	C P	C P	C P
2. Country of birth	(abroad/Canada)	80 48 / 32	67 44 / 23				8 35 / 27	19 41 / 22			
3. Date of immigration	(pre-1946/post-war)	85 35 / 50	79 64 / 15				5 45 / 40	9 22 / 13			
4. Education	(elem./sec./post-sec.)	66 30 / 36	71 47 / 24	71 61 / 10			19 48 / 29	17 38 / 21	13 30 / 17		
5. Age	(50+/under 50)	72 36 / 36	67 50 / 17				16 48 / 32	18 34 / 16			
6. Origin	(Germ./Pol./Ukr.-Russ.)	81 52 / 29	74 23 / 51	41 43 / -2			15 38 / 23	4 54 / 50	18 29 / 11		
7. Marital status	(widowed/marr./single)	72 36 / 36	69 44 / 25	65 51 / 14			16 49 / 33	17 39 / 22	21 42 / 21		
8. Homogeneity of marriage	(same rel./diff.rel.)	69 43 / 26	64 56 / 8				16 40 / 24	25 17 / -8			
10. Region	(Atl./Que./Ont./Prair./B.C.)	67 34 / 33	66 81 / -15	80 46 / 34	57 37 / 20	76 55 / 21	32 64 / 32	19 17 / -2	7 38 / 31	25 45 / 20	0 15 / 15
11. Size of community	(rural/1-10m/10-100m/100-500m/metro)	59 35 / 24	72 39 / 33	64 42 / 22	77 43 / 34	73 60 / 13	27 52 / 25	12 44 / 32	23 39 / 16	9 40 / 31	12 23 / 11
14. Income	(less 5m/5-10m/10m+)	68 35 / 33	68 44 / 24	73 61 / 12			21 50 / 29	15 35 / 20	15 29 / 14		

Note: The numbers immediately under the Catholic and Protestant percentages are the percentage differences between them, i.e. the extent of religious voting.

277

TABLE VI

Political Factors, Religious Affiliation and Vote
(In Conditional Yule's Q's)

POLITICAL FACTORS	*	LIBERAL *	LIBERAL :	LIBERAL @	LIBERAL Diff.	CONSERVATIVE *	CONSERVATIVE :	CONSERVATIVE @	CONSERVATIVE Diff.
1. Electoral interest	(low/high)	.50	.48		.02	.54	.53		.01
2. Efficacy	(low/high)	.56	.36		.20	.59	.36		.23
3. Trust	(low/high)	.57	.43		.14	.54	.52		.02
4. Efficacy & Trust	(low/high)	.59	.37		.22	.55	.47		.08
5. Candidate information	(low/high)	.53	.39		.14	.56	.47		.09
6. Abolish monarchy	(agree/disagree)	.36	.56		.20	.34	.58		.24
7. Change constitution	(agree/disagree)	.40	.62		.22	.51	.56		.05
8. Canada & USA join	(agree/disagree)	.62	.44		.18	.54	.51		.03
9. Outlaw Communists	(agree/disagree)	.57	.33		.24	.60	.43		.17
10. Abolish death penalty	(agree/disagree)	.41	.49		.08	.51	.46		.05
11. Imprison homosexuals	(agree/disagree)	.45	.46		.01	.56	.47		.09
12. Less severe divorce laws	(agree/disagree)	.45	.48		.03	.51	.59		.08
13. Interest in foreign affairs	(high/low)	.29	.48		.19	.46	.52		.06
14. Maintain peacekeeping	(agree/disagree)	.51	.38		.13	.53	.39		.14
15. Involvement in Latin Am.	(agree/disagree)	.32	.55		.23	.41	.55		.14
16. Treatment of Que.	(sep.status/non ss)	.10	.53		.63	.06	.72		.78
17. Timing of Medicare	(long ago/now)	.56	.45		.11	.56	.37		.19
18. Extent of welfare	(too little/enough/too much)	.47	.32	.80	[.48]	.37	.47	.71	[.34]
19. Govt help economy	(too little/about right/too much)	.56	.22	.30	[.34]	.60	.30	.46	[.30]
20. Party closest-Quebec	(Lib./non-L; Cons./non-C)	.43	.60		.17	.62	.45		.17
21. Party closest-Medicare	(Lib./non-L; Cons./non-C)	.22	.34		.12	.51	.41		.10
22. Party closest-welfare	(Lib./non-L; Cons./non-C)	.44	.40		.04	.57	.29		.28
23. Party closest-economy	(Lib./non-L; Cons./non-C)	.38	.35		.03	.39	.32		.07
24. Party closest-unempl.	(Lib./non-L; Cons./non-C)	.28	.45		.17	.61	.48		.13
25. Party closest-housing	(Lib./non-L; Cons./non-C)	.21	.36		.15	.61	.40		.21
26. Party closest-cost of living	(Lib./non-L; Cons./non-C)	.34	.33		.01	.43	.42		.01
27. Most important factor in voting decision	(leader/candidate/	.47	.54			.52	.53		
	party work/party)	.33	.49		[.21]	.55	.49		[.06]

TABLE VII

Percentage of Catholics and Protestants Voting Liberal and Conservative by Political Factors

POLITICAL FACTORS	category	LIBERAL * (C P / diff)	LIBERAL ∴ (C P / diff)	LIBERAL @ (C P / diff)	CONSERVATIVE * (C P / diff)	CONSERVATIVE ∴ (C P / diff)	CONSERVATIVE @ (C P / diff)
2. Efficacy	(low/high)	63 33 / 30	73 56 / 17		21 50 / 29	16 29 / 13	
4. Efficacy and trust	(low/high)	56 25 / 31	75 58 / 17		24 52 / 28	13 29 / 16	
6. Abolish monarchy	(agree/disagree)	69 51 / 18	71 41 / 30		15 26 / 11	19 46 / 27	
7. Change constitution	(agree/disagree)	68 47 / 21	74 41 / 33		15 35 / 20	18 43 / 25	
8. Canada & USA join	(agree/disagree)	69 34 / 35	69 47 / 22		19 43 / 24	17 38 / 21	
9. Outlaw Communists	(agree/disagree)	69 38 / 31	68 52 / 16		18 47 / 29	15 31 / 16	
13. Interest in foreign affairs	(high/low)	68 54 / 14	65 39 / 26		16 34 / 18	20 44 / 24	
15. Involvement in Latin Am.	(agree/disagree)	69 54 / 15	73 44 / 29		17 33 / 16	15 37 / 22	
16. Treatment of Quebec	(sep. status/non ss)	61 66 / -5	71 43 / 28		24 22 / -2	16 41 / 25	
18. Extent of welfare	(too little/enough/too much)	66 42 / 24	71 56 / 15	75 25 / 50	17 31 / 14	16 34 / 18	17 55 / 38
19. Govt. help economy	(too little/about right/too much)	69 39 / 30	71 61 / 10	64 49 / 15	16 44 / 28	16 27 / 11	14 31 / 17
20. Party closest-Quebec	(Lib./non-L; Cons./non-C)	89 77 / 12	27 8 / 19		57 85 / 28	7 16 / 9	

TABLE VII (Cont'd)

		LIBERAL						CONSERVATIVE					
	*	*		!		@		*		!		@	
	!	C	P	C	P	C	P	C	P	C	P	C	P
21. Party closest-Medicare	(Lib./non-L; Cons./non-C)	87	81	36	22			45	71	9	19		
			6		14				26		10		
22. Party closest-welfare	(Lib./non-L; Cons./non-C)	91	79	33	17			59	84	7	13		
			12		16				25		6		
23. Party closest-economy	(Lib./non-L; Cons./non-C)	90	81	23	12			75	87	7	12		
			9		11				12		5		
24. Party closest-unempl.	(Lib./non-L; Cons./non-C)	89	82	34	16			64	88	6	15		
			7		18				24		9		
25. Party closest-housing	(Lib./non-L; Cons./non-C)	87	81	33	19			58	85	6	14		
			6		14				27		8		
26. Party closest-cost of living	(Lib./non-L; Cons./non-C)	90	81	27	16			71	86	6	14		
			9		11				15		8		
27. Most important factor in voting decision	(leader/candidate	80	59	50	23			13	31	30	57		
			21		27				18		27		
	party work/party)	55	38	67	41			18	43	17	38		
			17		26				25		21		

Note: The numbers immediately under the Catholic and Protestant percentages are the percentage differences between them, i.e., the extent of religious voting.

280

Yule's Q's: Tables II, IV, and VI consist of conditional Yule's Q's for the religious, demographic, and political factors respectively. Under the appropriate heading—the Liberal party, say—Q's are given for the relationship between Liberal/non-Liberal voting and Catholic/Protestant religious affiliation under the specified condition.

Signs: Since Protestants are more Conservative in their voting than Catholics in all cases but three, the Q's should be negatively signed. To avoid confusion, we have instead given negative signs to the three exceptions only. Thus a negative sign in a Conservative column indicates that Catholics are voting more Conservative than Protestants, contrary to our expectations. A negative sign in a Liberal column has its normal meaning, that Protestants are voting more Liberal than Catholics, contrary to our expectations. Similarly, the percentage differences in Tables III, V, and VII are unsigned unless they run contrary to our expectations.

Square brackets: The conditional Q's for each factor were subtracted from one another in the case of dichotomous controls. Where the control variable has three or more values, the lowest was subtracted from the highest; these ranges are indicated by square brackets.

Selection: The criterion for inclusion of variables in Tables III, V, and VII was a difference of at least .16 on either the Liberal or the Conservative side. The exception to this rule is the inclusion of items (20) to (26) in Table VII.

Control Procedures: J. A. Davis in *Elementary Survey Analysis* (Englewood Cliffs: Prentice-Hall, Inc., 1971), pp. 81–106, outlines four general types of results of control procedures:

(1) the control has no effect—the original relationship between the independent and dependent variable is maintained under the control. In this case the conditional Q's are nearly equal. An example is the control for occupation (Table IV, line 12) where the conditional Q's for Liberal voting are both .46.

(2) the control explains away the original relationship—the original relationship disappears under control. In this case the conditional Q's are zero or near-zero. This does not occur in the data.

(3) the control suppresses the original relationship—it either grows in strength or is reversed in sign. The conditional Q's deviate in the same direction and magnitude. There are no examples in the Tables.

281

(4) the control specifies the conditions under which the relationship assumes different values. The conditional Q's are quite different from one another or have different signs. Virtually all the data fall into this category (except those that had no effect).

These simple types are elaborated in O. Benson, *Poltical Science Laboratory* (Columbus: Charles E. Merrill Publishing Company, 1969), pp. 302–17.

Some caveats are necessary. In discovering that most of the controls specified the relationship, we faced the problem of determining the importance of various degrees of specification. A difference (or range) of .16 between the conditional Q's was arbitrarily deemed the cutting point between important and unimportant degrees of specification.

Secondly, at this point in the research, we have assumed, except where common sense indicated otherwise, that all the specification was attached to the control variable. This assumption can be misleading in two ways: (1) other specification may be mixed in, for example, the effect of marital status appears to be caused by age rather than any difference inherent in marital status and (2) the kind of specification that occurs is a function of the collapsing of the categories; in most cases, we have attempted to establish the categories empirically, by examining the effect of the variables before collapsing them.

Third, the size of the control group is unimportant in determining the effect of groups. However, it is important in determining the explanatory power of the variable. For instance, date of immigration specifies the relationship to a great extent (Table IV). However, the explanatory power of this variable is not great since immigrants comprise a relatively small proportion of the society. Similarly, a large difference in conditional Q's between a group that comprises eighty percent of the population and the group that comprises the other twenty percent does not have the same explanatory status as a similar difference of Q's between two groups each of which comprises 50 percent of the population. In addition, one has more confidence in the latter distribution since the differences are less likely to be caused by sampling error.

NOTES

1. A. Campbell, P. E. Converse, W. E. Miller, and D. E. Stokes, *The American Voter* (New York: John Wiley and Sons, 1960), p. 157.

2. P. E. Converse, "Religion and Politics: The 1960 Election," in A. Campbell, P. E. Converse, W. E. Miller and D. E. Stokes, *Elections and the Political Order* (New York, London, Sydney: John Wiley and Sons, 1966), pp. 97, 124, 123.

3. J. Laponce, "Post-dicting Electoral Cleavages in Canadian Federal Elections, 1949–68: Material for a Footnote," *Canadian Journal of Political Science* V: 2 (June 1972), 270–85. The relationship between religious affiliation and voting for the so-called third parties, particularly the NDP and Social Credit, is less unambiguous—see J. Wilson, "Politics and Social Class in Canada: The Case of Waterloo South," *Canadian Journal of Political Science* I: 3 (September, 1968), 288–309. Extensive reviews and bibliographies of the literature on Canadian voting patterns are contained in M. A. Schwartz, "Canadian Voting Behavior," in R. Rose (ed.), *Comparative Electoral Behavior* (New York: The Free Press, 1974), particularly pp. 608–17, and J. C. Terry and R. Schultz, "Canadian Electoral Behaviour: A Propositional Inventory," in O. M. Kruhlak, R. Schultz and S. I. Pobihushchy (ed.), *The Canadian Political Process*, revised edition (Toronto, Montreal: Holt, Rinehart and Winston of Canada, 1973), pp. 248–85. For an excellent "mapping" and discussion of the interaction among ethnic origin, religion, and voting in Canada see J. Laponce, "Ethnicity, Religion and .Politics in Canada: A Comparative Analysis of Survey and Census Data," in M. Dogan and S. Rokkan (eds.), *Quantitative Ecological Analysis in the Social Sciences* (Cambridge, Mass.: MIT Press, 1969), pp. 187–216.

4. J. M. Beck, *Pendulum of Power* (Scarborough: Prentice-Hall of Canada, 1968), pp. 1–86.

5. Catholics comprise a little over 46 percent of the population, only a few percentage points below Protestants. About six percent have no religious affiliation or belong to very small groups like the Jews, Buddhists, and Confucians. See *Census of Canada*, 1971, catalogue 92–724, vol. 1, part 3 (bulletin 1.3–3), Table 9.

6. J. Meisel, "Cleavages, Parties and Values in Canada," Sage Professional Paper in Contemporary Sociology, 1, 06–003. (London and Beverly Hills: Sage Publications, 1974), pp. 20–23.

7. Ibid., pp. 38–40.

8. The incomes of the adherents of these five groups are decidely higher than those of other Protestants and most observers would classify them as enjoying higher status, with the possible exception of Quakers, who are, however, not numerous enough to distort our grouping.

9. The CCF—the NDP's precursor—was for many years proscribed by the Quebec bishops.

10. P. Regenstreif, *The Diefenbaker Interlude* (Don Mills: Longmans Canada, 1965), p. 93; J. Meisel, "Cleavages, Parties and Values in Canada," pp. 15–17; M. A. Schwartz "Canadian Voting Behavior," p. 581; J. Laponce, "Ethnicity, Religion, and Politics in Canada," p. 203; and W. P. Irvine, "Explaining the Religious Basis of Canadian Partisan Identity: Success on the Third Try," *Canadian Journal of Political Science*, VII: 3 (September 1974), 560–63.

11. I have excluded the detailed description and discussion of each of the variables. They are available on request. The present paper is intelligible without reference to the appended tables. An early draft of this paper contained a detailed discussion of the tables. In an effort to reduce the length, and realizing that the international composition of the Round Table for which the paper was written made it undesirable to enter into the minutiae of Canadian voting behaviour, I suppressed the painstaking exploration of the tables.

12. G. Lenski, *The Religious Factor* (New York: Anchor Books, Doubleday, 1963), p. 23.

13. D. Butler and D. Stokes, *Political Change in Britain* (London: Macmillan, 1969), p. 276.

14. The tests on these dimensions provided the only instances in our entire enquiry in which, very occasionally, the combination of taking the "progressive" view, associated with post-secondary education, high income, or post-war immigration washed out religious voting altogether.

15. In all our calculations this splendidly symmetrical rapport occurred only once, with respect to Liberal voting among those who thought that the government was interfering too much with the economy (see above, p. 265).

16. Ninety-one percent of our Jewish respondents voted Liberal, for example (N = 33).

17. One should not, however, overlook the role of ethnic, religious, and other leaders who became professional spokesmen for their groups and sometimes exacerbate and perpetuate intergroup conflicts.

18. Data provided by John Wilson.

19. J. Porter, *The Vertical Mosaic* (Toronto: University of Toronto Press, 1965), p. 389.

APPENDIX
TABLES TO CHAPTER 1

Notes to Tables

Tables I-IX

NOTES TO THE TABLES

The total number of cases is not uniform for all categories because of differences in response rates between questions.

Occupation refers to occupation of main wage-earner in the household in the case of full-time housewives and students. "Professional" includes owners, managers, business executives and professionals; "Skilled labour" includes those working for service and protective industries.

Class. Respondents placed *themselves* in one of the following: Upper, Upper-middle, Middle, Working or Lower Class. "Upper" includes the first two choices and "Lower" the last two.

Language. Respondents were asked what language they usually spoke at home, at work and among friends. If they spoke any language in all three situations, they were defined as "Pure" English- or French-users; if in only two, as "Partial" users and if they spoke English or French in only one or none, they were called "Mixed" users.

TABLE III

See Notes to Tables I and II.

The deviation represents the difference in percentage points between the percentage in each cell (Table II) and the *total* (all cells) percentage for the relevant region and party. See also footnote 7.

TABLE IV

Respondents were asked what they felt were the most important problems the government should take care of as soon as possible and, if they mentioned more than one or two, to specify which was most and next most important. The first row under each listed problem gives the percentage of respondents who mentioned it and the second row gives the mean discriminating between the degree of importance attached to it.

TABLE V

Respondents were asked how important each of the five listed issues was to their voting decision. The first row under each issue shows the percentage of respondents who said that the given problem was extremely or very important to them. The second row gives the mean, calculated as follows: responses of "Extremely" and "Very" important were scored 4 and 3, respectively; "Fairly" important was assigned a value of 2 and "Not too important", "No opinion" or no answer were counted as 1.

N varies very slightly from problem to problem because of miniscule differences in response rates.

TABLE VI

The importance of each of the five economic issues was probed for respondents who indicated that generally issues concerning the economy were "Extremely" or "Very" important to their vote. See also Notes for Table V.

TABLE VII

With two exceptions, noted below, the percentages indicate what proportion of those scoring Low, Medium or High on the various indices voted for each of the parties. Scores were assigned respondentts according to the way in which they answered the questions used in constructing the indices. The division into the Low, Medium and High categories was effected arbitrarily by trichotomizing. There is thus no normative value to be assigned the terms Low, Medium and High.

The categories reporting attitudes towards the separation of Quebec and Internationalism (Interest in International Affairs) are derived from answers to single questions and are therefore not indices.

The questions used covered the following subjects:

Religiosity: church attendance; proportion of friends of same religion as respondent, expenditures on churches

Moral Liberalism: toleration of homosexuality and divorce; opposition to the death penalty

Authoritarianism: intolerance of communists and homosexuals; approval of the death penalty

Law and Order: sanctions for people breaking a law for religious reasons and for non-religious ones; police action during illegal strikes

Tolerance: preference for a Canada in which all people had the same religion and national origin

Centralism: level of government handling the most important problems and problems affecting respondent personally; importance attached to various corresponding federal and provincial offices

Interest: declared interest in 1968 election; record of voting in 1968 and other (federal and provincial) elections; knowledge of candidates' names

Efficacy: a battery of five of the conventional (i.e. Michigan SRC's) efficacy questions (see Robinson, Rusk and Head, *Measures of Political Attitudes,* 460)

Cynicism: the honesty, fairness, efficiency of the Ottawa government

General Optimism: satisfaction with life so far; general and also economic expectations of the future

Economic Expectations: financial satisfaction at present; present economic condition compared to past and future

Internationalism: the question merely sought to elicit the degree of interest in foreign affairs.

N varies slightly from index to index.

TABLE VIII

The asterisk identifies cells containing fewer than 25 cases.

Respondents were not asked to rate the Social Credit parties in provinces where the latter's electoral effort was nonexistent or insignificant.

TABLE IX

Respondents were asked which of the party aspects listed was most important in deciding "What to do in this election", which was next important and which was least important. The percentages in the table represent the proportion of respondents, in each party, identifying the characteristic as "Most important".

TABLE II - PROPORTION OF V...
(Horiz...

	C A N A D A					Atlantic					
	T	Lib	PC	NDP	RC +SC	T	Lib	PC	NDP	T	L...
Religion	2212	56.1	28.6	11.5	3.8	228	44.7	53.5	1.8	581	67
Catholic	949	68.8	17.1	8.1	6.0	69	66.7	31.9	1.4	525	65
Other	1263	46.6	37.2	14.1	2.1	159	35.2	62.9	1.9	56	85
Occupation	2127	56.3	27.6	12.2	3.9	204	45.1	53.4	1.5	543	68
Professional,/etc.	404	63.9	26.2	8.4	1.5	18	44.4	55.6	–	121	76
Sales, clerical	342	64.6	24.3	9.1	2.0	16	50.0	50.0	–	83	78
Skilled labour	743	55.9	23.3	15.9	5.0	79	46.8	50.6	2.5	195	67
Unskilled labour	278	53.6	28.8	12.9	4.7	52	50.0	50.0	–	73	56
Farmer	191	38.2	44.5	9.9	7.3	20	40.0	60.0	–	33	48
Pensioner, retired	169	47.9	36.1	13.0	3.0	19	26.3	68.4	5.3	38	65
Class	2172	56.5	27.5	12.2	3.8	199	46.2	51.8	2.0	577	67
Upper	179	69.8	22.3	6.1	1.7	8	37.5	62.5	–	69	88
Middle	1035	59.9	27.8	8.6	3.7	63	47.8	49.2	3.2	305	72
Lower	958	50.4	28.1	17.1	4.4	128	46.1	52.3	1.6	203	61.
Education	2272	56.4	27.9	12.0	3.7	229	45.4	52.8	1.7	588	68
0 – 8 yrs.	735	52.8	29.1	11.7	6.4	103	43.7	53.4	2.9	264	65
9 – 13 yrs.	1220	56.3	28.6	12.4	2.7	121	47.1	52.1	0.8	228	70
14 yrs. or more	317	65.3	22.1	11.4	1.3	5	40.0	60.0	–	96	72
Residence in Canada	2280	56.4	27.9	12.0	3.7	229	45.4	52.8	1.7	590	68
Born in Canada	1872	55.3	28.9	11.6	4.2	223	44.8	53.4	1.8	547	66
Arrived before 1946	185	48.6	33.5	15.7	2.2	2	100.0	–	–	10	70
Arrived 1946 or after	223	72.2	14.8	11.7	1.3	4	50.0	50.0	–	33	100
Origin	2284	56.4	27.9	12.0	3.7	231	45.5	52.8	1.7	591	68
British	1015	48.4	36.7	13.2	1.8	148	39.9	58.8	1.4	42	83
French	630	67.1	18.1	6.7	8.1	30	73.3	23.3	3.3	496	64
Other	639	58.5	23.6	15.3	2.5	53	45.3	52.8	1.9	53	92
Language	2284	56.4	27.9	12.0	3.7	231	45.5	52.8	1.7	591	68
Pure French	444	64.9	20.5	5.0	9.7	22	77.3	18.2	4.5	407	63
Part French	93	67.7	14.0	9.7	8.6	2	100.0	–	–	73	63
Mixed	105	82.9	12.4	2.9	1.9	1	100.0	–	–	33	90
Part English	115	65.2	15.7	19.1	–	7	57.1	42.9	–	23	95
Pure English	1527	50.8	32.9	14.3	2.1	199	40.7	57.8	1.5	55	83
Community Size	2284	56.4	27.9	12.0	3.7	231	45.5	52.8	1.7	591	68
Metropolitan	682	67.7	15.8	15.0	1.5	–	–	–	–	263	77
100,000 – 500,000	402	56.0	28.4	12.4	3.2	14	42.9	57.1	–	43	74
1,000 – 99,999	615	53.8	29.4	11.5	5.2	68	41.2	57.4	1.5	179	62
Rural	585	46.2	40.0	8.7	5.1	149	47.7	50.3	2.0	106	54
A g e	2284	56.4	27.9	12.0	3.7	231	45.5	52.8	1.7	591	68
21 – 30 yrs.	498	59.2	24.9	11.2	4.6	42	52.4	47.6	–	158	63
31 – 50 yrs.	1010	58.4	24.8	12.8	4.1	97	47.4	51.5	1.0	250	68
51 yrs. or more	776	51.9	33.9	11.5	2.7	92	40.2	56.5	3.3	183	72
S e x	2284	56.4	27.9	12.0	3.7	231	45.5	52.8	1.7	591	68
Male	1163	55.5	26.9	14.1	3.5	115	42.6	54.8	2.6	295	67
Female	1121	57.4	28.9	9.8	3.9	116	48.3	50.9	0.9	296	68

Quebec PC	NDP	RC	Ontario T	Lib	PC	NDP	Prairies T	Lib	PC	NDP	SC	British Columbia T	Lib	PC	NDP	SC
18.4	*5.0*	*8.8*	804	*56.7*	*27.6*	*15.7*	418	*44.3*	*37.8*	*15.3*	*2.6*	181	*57.5*	*12.7*	*17.7*	*12.2*
19.0	*5.3*	*9.7*	239	*79.5*	*7.1*	*13.4*	91	*57.1*	*25.3*	*13.2*	*4.4*	25	*76.0*	*-*	*16.0*	*8.0*
12.5	*1.8*	*-*	565	*47.1*	*36.3*	*16.6*	327	*40.7*	*41.3*	*15.9*	*2.1*	156	*54.5*	*14.7*	*17.9*	*12.8*
17.7	*4.8*	*9.2*	791	*57.1*	*26.8*	*16.1*	402	*44.3*	*37.1*	*16.2*	*2.5*	187	*55.6*	*11.8*	*20.9*	*11.8*
14.0	*7.4*	*2.5*	151	*57.6*	*32.5*	*9.9*	75	*58.7*	*32.0*	*9.3*	*-*	39	*69.2*	*15.4*	*7.7*	*7.7*
9.6	*6.0*	*6.0*	160	*63.1*	*26.3*	*10.6*	58	*51.7*	*34.5*	*12.1*	*1.7*	25	*68.0*	*20.0*	*8.0*	*4.0*
16.9	*4.1*	*11.3*	275	*54.2*	*21.5*	*24.4*	122	*50.0*	*32.0*	*16.4*	*1.6*	72	*50.0*	*2.8*	*29.2*	*18.1*
26.0	*5.6*	*12.3*	96	*58.3*	*22.9*	*18.8*	32	*43.8*	*25.0*	*25.0*	*6.3*	25	*48.0*	*20.0*	*24.0*	*8.0*
27.3	*-*	*24.2*	47	*55.3*	*38.3*	*6.4*	84	*21.4*	*53.6*	*19.0*	*6.0*	7	*71.4*	*14.3*	*-*	*14.3*
26.3	*-*	*7.9*	62	*53.2*	*35.5*	*11.3*	31	*35.5*	*41.9*	*22.6*	*-*	19	*36.8*	*15.8*	*36.8*	*10.5*
18.4	*4.9*	*8.8*	800	*57.1*	*26.8*	*16.1*	402	*44.5*	*37.1*	*16.2*	*2.2*	194	*55.7*	*12.9*	*19.6*	*11.9*
17.4	*11.6*	*2.9*	64	*70.3*	*26.6*	*3.1*	22	*81.8*	*13.6*	*4.5*	*-*	16	*75.0*	*18.8*	*-*	*6.3*
16.1	*3.9*	*7.9*	385	*59.5*	*29.4*	*11.2*	187	*43.9*	*43.9*	*10.2*	*2.1*	95	*62.1*	*13.7*	*13.7*	*10.5*
22.2	*3.9*	*12.3*	351	*52.1*	*23.9*	*23.9*	193	*40.9*	*33.2*	*23.3*	*2.6*	83	*44.6*	*10.8*	*30.1*	*14.5*
18.0	*4.9*	*8.5*	830	*57.1*	*27.0*	*15.9*	425	*44.7*	*36.9*	*15.8*	*2.6*	200	*55.5*	*12.5*	*20.5*	*11.5*
19.7	*2.7*	*12.5*	206	*56.8*	*27.2*	*16.0*	126	*33.3*	*37.3*	*24.6*	*4.8*	36	*33.3*	*11.1*	*33.3*	*22.7*
18.4	*4.4*	*6.6*	496	*55.8*	*26.6*	*17.5*	241	*47.7*	*38.6*	*11.6*	*2.1*	134	*57.5*	*14.2*	*18.7*	*9.7*
12.5	*12.5*	*2.1*	128	*62.5*	*28.1*	*9.4*	58	*56.9*	*29.3*	*13.8*	*-*	30	*73.3*	*6.7*	*13.3*	*6.7*
18.1	*4.7*	*8.6*	834	*57.2*	*26.9*	*15.9*	426	*44.4*	*37.3*	*15.7*	*2.6*	201	*55.7*	*12.4*	*20.4*	*11.4*
19.2	*4.9*	*9.3*	631	*55.5*	*28.7*	*15.8*	331	*44.1*	*36.6*	*16.3*	*3.0*	140	*53.6*	*10.7*	*23.6*	*12.1*
20.0	*10.0*	*-*	72	*51.4*	*31.9*	*16.7*	68	*41.2*	*41.2*	*16.2*	*1.5*	33	*48.5*	*27.3*	*15.2*	*9.1*
-	*-*	*-*	131	*68.7*	*15.3*	*16.0*	27	*55.6*	*37.0*	*7.4*	*-*	28	*75.0*	*3.6*	*10.7*	*10.7*
18.1	*4.9*	*8.6*	834	*57.2*	*26.9*	*15.9*	427	*44.5*	*37.2*	*15.7*	*2.6*	201	*55.7*	*12.4*	*20.4*	*11.4*
14.3	*2.4*	*-*	519	*49.3*	*34.1*	*16.6*	179	*42.5*	*45.3*	*11.2*	*1.1*	127	*51.2*	*16.5*	*19.7*	*12.6*
20.0	*6.4*	*10.1*	71	*83.1*	*7.0*	*9.9*	25	*76.0*	*12.0*	*12.0*	*-*	8	*37.5*	*-*	*50.0*	*12.5*
3.8	*1.9*	*1.9*	244	*66.4*	*17.2*	*16.4*	223	*42.6*	*33.6*	*19.7*	*4.0*	66	*66.7*	*6.1*	*18.2*	*9.1*
18.1	*4.9*	*8.6*	834	*57.2*	*26.9*	*15.9*	427	*44.5*	*37.2*	*15.7*	*2.6*	201	*55.7*	*12.4*	*20.4*	*11.4*
20.4	*5.2*	*10.6*	12	*83.3*	*16.7*	*-*	3	*33.3*	*66.7*	*-*	*-*	-	*-*	*-*	*-*	*-*
17.8	*8.2*	*11.0*	12	*83.3*	*-*	*16.7*	4	*100.0*	*-*	*-*	*-*	2	*50.0*	*-*	*50.0*	*-*
9.1	*-*	*-*	46	*87.0*	*6.5*	*6.5*	20	*60.0*	*35.0*	*-*	*5.0*	5	*80.0*	*-*	*-*	*20.0*
4.3	*-*	*-*	43	*60.5*	*9.3*	*30.2*	36	*52.8*	*27.8*	*19.4*	*-*	6	*66.7*	*-*	*33.3*	*-*
12.7	*3.6*	*-*	721	*54.2*	*29.8*	*16.0*	364	*42.3*	*38.5*	*16.5*	*2.7*	188	*54.8*	*13.3*	*20.2*	*11.7*
18.1	*4.9*	*8.6*	834	*57.2*	*26.9*	*15.9*	427	*44.5*	*37.2*	*15.7*	*2.6*	201	*55.7*	*12.4*	*20.4*	*11.4*
12.2	*8.4*	*2.3*	244	*61.1*	*21.7*	*17.2*	67	*56.7*	*20.9*	*22.4*	*-*	108	*66.7*	*8.3*	*21.3*	*3.7*
14.0	*-*	*11.6*	172	*60.5*	*25.0*	*14.5*	154	*46.1*	*34.4*	*15.6*	*3.9*	19	*63.2*	*21.1*	*5.3*	*10.5*
24.0	*1.1*	*12.8*	257	*56.8*	*25.3*	*17.9*	63	*41.3*	*42.9*	*15.9*	*-*	48	*41.7*	*14.6*	*25.0*	*18.8*
24.5	*4.7*	*16.0*	161	*48.4*	*39.1*	*12.4*	143	*38.5*	*45.5*	*12.6*	*3.5*	26	*30.8*	*19.2*	*19.2*	*30.8*
18.1	*4.9*	*8.6*	834	*57.2*	*26.9*	*15.9*	427	*44.5*	*37.2*	*15.7*	*2.6*	201	*55.7*	*12.4*	*20.4*	*11.4*
19.0	*7.0*	*10.8*	173	*62.4*	*22.0*	*15.6*	88	*45.5*	*38.6*	*13.6*	*2.3*	37	*67.6*	*5.4*	*16.2*	*10.8*
16.0	*4.8*	*10.4*	391	*58.6*	*23.8*	*17.6*	179	*49.2*	*33.0*	*15.6*	*2.2*	93	*59.1*	*8.6*	*20.4*	*11.8*
20.2	*3.3*	*4.4*	270	*51.9*	*34.4*	*13.7*	160	*38.8*	*41.3*	*16.9*	*3.1*	71	*45.1*	*21.1*	*22.5*	*11.3*
18.1	*4.9*	*8.6*	834	*57.2*	*26.9*	*15.9*	427	*44.5*	*37.2*	*15.7*	*2.6*	201	*55.7*	*12.4*	*20.4*	*11.4*
17.8	*6.4*	*8.1*	439	*54.4*	*26.7*	*18.9*	212	*46.2*	*34.9*	*16.0*	*2.8*	102	*57.8*	*6.9*	*24.5*	*10.8*
18.6	*3.4*	*9.1*	395	*60.3*	*27.1*	*12.7*	215	*42.8*	*39.5*	*15.3*	*2.3*	99	*53.5*	*18.2*	*16.2*	*12.1*

TABLE IV - ISSUE PERCEPTION: PRO

	C A N A D A				RC	Atlantic				
	T	Lib	PC	NDP	+SC	T	Lib	PC	NDP	T
Total N	2284	1288	637	274	85	231	105	122	4	591
Inflation										
% Mentioned	33	32	34	35	35	29	24	34	-	29
Mean rating	1.8	1.8	1.9	1.8	1.8	1.7	1.6	1.9	1.0	1.7
Housing										
% Mentioned	27	26	26	34	21	23	18	27	-	11
Mean rating	1.6	1.6	1.5	1.7	1.5	1.4	1.4	1.5	1.0	1.2
Unemployment										
% Mentioned	22	23	21	20	33	33	31	33	75	30
Mean rating	1.5	1.5	1.5	1.4	1.8	1.8	1.8	1.8	2.8	1.7
Welfare										
% Mentioned	18	17	17	19	22	14	13	15	25	16
Mean rating	1.4	1.3	1.4	1.4	1.5	1.3	1.3	1.3	1.5	1.3
Quebec Issue										
% Mentioned	17	19	15	15	7	6	5	7	-	19
Mean rating	1.4	1.4	1.3	1.3	1.1	1.1	1.1	1.2	1.0	1.5
Other Economic Problems										
% Mentioned	14	14	13	15	8	13	13	12	25	10
Mean rating	1.3	1.3	1.3	1.3	1.2	1.3	1.3	1.3	1.8	1.2
Taxes										
% Mentioned	12	12	10	19	14	8	12	5	-	9
Mean rating	1.3	1.2	1.2	1.4	1.3	1.2	1.3	1.1	1.0	1.2
Medicare										
% Mentioned	11	11	9	14	9	10	8	12	-	13
Mean rating	1.2	1.2	1.2	1.3	1.2	1.2	1.2	1.2	1.0	1.3
Education										
% Mentioned	10	10	10	10	17	5	2	8	-	14
Mean rating	1.2	1.2	1.2	1.2	1.4	1.1	1.0	1.2	1.0	1.3
Labour										
% Mentioned	10	10	9	7	9	3	4	2	-	14
Mean rating	1.2	1.2	1.2	1.2	1.2	1.0	1.1	1.0	1.0	1.3
Foreign Affairs										
% Mentioned	7	8	4	7	4	4	4	4	25	6
Mean rating	1.1	1.1	1.1	1.2	1.1	1.1	1.1	1.1	1.5	1.1

	Quebec				Ontario				Prairies					British Columbi			
	ib	PC	NDP	RC	T	Lib	PC	NDP	T	Lib	PC	NDP	SC	T	Lib	PC	NDP
	04	107	29	51	834	477	224	133	427	190	159	67	11	201	112	25	41
	28	31	35	31	37	35	39	40	32	34	31	30	36	34	32	36	32
	.6	1.8	1.9	1.7	1.9	1.9	2.0	2.0	1.8	1.8	1.8	1.7	1.8	1.8	1.8	1.8	1.8
	11	8	14	10	39	38	38	44	21	22	23	15	18	42	44	20	49
	.2	1.2	1.2	1.2	1.9	1.9	1.8	2.0	1.4	1.4	1.5	1.3	1.5	1.9	1.9	1.4	2.0
	28	29	38	41	17	17	17	19	15	21	12	10	-	25	24	24	24
	.7	1.7	1.8	2.0	1.4	1.4	1.4	1.4	1.3	1.4	1.3	1.2	1.0	1.5	1.5	1.5	1.5
	15	16	3	24	17	17	12	23	18	14	24	12	18	29	30	40	27
	.3	1.4	1.0	1.5	1.3	1.3	1.3	1.5	1.4	1.3	1.5	1.3	1.4	1.6	1.6	1.9	1.5
	22	10	31	8	16	17	17	11	19	23	17	13	-	23	25	32	22
	.5	1.3	1.7	1.1	1.4	1.4	1.4	1.2	1.4	1.5	1.4	1.2	1.0	1.5	1.5	1.8	1.5
	10	10	14	6	14	14	15	13	16	20	10	21	9	18	18	32	15
	.2	1.2	1.3	1.1	1.3	1.3	1.3	1.3	1.4	1.4	1.2	1.5	1.2	1.3	1.3	1.7	1.3
	9	7	3	18	18	16	16	29	10	11	7	15	18	7	5	16	7
	.2	1.1	1.1	1.4	1.4	1.3	1.3	1.6	1.2	1.2	1.1	1.3	1.4	1.1	1.1	1.3	1.1
	14	10	7	12	8	8	7	11	14	14	10	24	9	14	16	12	15
	.3	1.2	1.1	1.3	1.2	1.2	1.1	1.2	1.3	1.3	1.2	1.6	1.2	1.2	1.3	1.2	1.3
	13	12	14	22	9	9	10	8	8	8	8	6	-	15	13	16	24
	.3	1.3	1.2	1.5	1.2	1.2	1.2	1.2	1.1	1.2	1.1	1.1	1.0	1.3	1.2	1.2	1.4
	12	19	17	12	8	8	9	7	12	14	10	8	18	9	13	4	2
	.3	1.4	1.4	1.3	1.2	1.2	1.2	1.1	1.3	1.4	1.3	1.2	1.4	1.2	1.3	1.1	1.1
	7	5	3	6	7	8	5	6	6	9	3	6	-	10	13	-	15
	.1	1.1	1.1	1.1	1.1	1.1	1.1	1.1	1.1	1.2	1.1	1.1	1.0	1.2	1.2	1.0	1.3

TABLE VI - ISSUE PERCEPTION: IMPORTAN(

	C A N A D A					Atlantic				T
	T	Lib	PC	NDP	RC +SC	T	Lib	PC	NDP	
Cost of Living	1354	760	355	194	45	106	51	54	1	32(
% Influenced	90	88	93	91	89	93	88	96	100	9(
Mean rating	3.4	3.3	3.5	3.4	3.5	3.6	3.4	3.7	4.0	3.4
Housing	1338					102				322
% Influenced	67	66	65	69	71	67	67	66	100	6(
Mean rating	2.8	2.8	2.8	2.9	2.9	2.8	2.7	2.9	4.0	2.7
Unemployment	1347					106				321
% Influenced	65	65	62	66	76	74	75	72	100	7(
Mean rating	2.8	2.8	2.7	2.8	3.0	3.0	3.0	3.1	4.0	3.(
Wheat Sales	1210					83				26
% Influenced	49	46	52	56	48	48	47	50	-	4.
Mean rating	2.3	2.2	2.4	2.4	2.3	2.0	1.8	2.2	1.0	2.(
Regional Inequality	1262					93				305
% Influenced	48	48	47	48	48	63	60	66	100	5(
Mean rating	2.3	2.3	2.3	2.3	2.4	2.5	2.4	2.6	4.0	2.(

	Quebec					Ontario					Prairies					British Colu		
	Lib	PC	NDP	RC		T	Lib	PC	NDP		T	Lib	PC	NDP	SC		T	Lib	PC	NI
	222	57	18	29		512	293	129	90		282	120	100	56	6		128	74	15	2
	90	*91*	*89*	*90*		*91*	*89*	*93*	*92*		*87*	*83*	*90*	*91*	*83*		*87*	*84*	*100*	*8*
	3.3	*3.4*	*3.2*	*3.6*		*3.4*	*3.4*	*3.4*	*3.6*		*3.4*	*3.2*	*3.4*	*3.4*	*3.5*		*3.3*	*3.2*	*3.6*	*3.*
						508					278						128		
	59	*63*	*50*	*72*		*75*	*74*	*77*	*77*		*57*	*60*	*51*	*59*	*80*		*69*	*68*	*67*	*7*
	2.6	*2.7*	*2.4*	*3.0*		*3.0*	*3.0*	*3.0*	*3.1*		*2.5*	*2.6*	*2.4*	*2.5*	*2.7*		*2.9*	*2.9*	*2.9*	*3.*
						510					282						128		
	75	*73*	*83*	*86*		*61*	*58*	*65*	*63*		*56*	*63*	*47*	*55*	*67*		*66*	*62*	*67*	*7*
	3.0	*3.0*	*3.0*	*3.3*		*2.6*	*2.6*	*2.7*	*2.8*		*2.6*	*2.7*	*2.4*	*2.6*	*2.7*		*2.8*	*2.7*	*2.5*	*3.*
						464					277						124		
	44	*44*	*7*	*33*		*41*	*38*	*42*	*53*		*73*	*71*	*70*	*82*	*100*		*44*	*41*	*47*	*4*
	2.0	*2.1*	*1.5*	*1.9*		*2.1*	*2.1*	*2.1*	*2.3*		*3.0*	*2.9*	*3.0*	*3.0*	*3.8*		*2.2*	*2.1*	*2.3*	*2.*
						479					259						126		
	58	*57*	*50*	*59*		*43*	*42*	*44*	*49*		*45*	*46*	*36*	*59*	*40*		*36*	*38*	*53*	*2*
	2.5	*2.4*	*2.4*	*2.6*		*2.2*	*2.2*	*2.3*	*2.3*		*2.2*	*2.3*	*2.0*	*2.4*	*2.2*		*2.1*	*2.1*	*2.4*	*2.*

TABLE VIII - PARTY PERCEPTIONS: AFFECT OF THE
EACH OF THE PARTIE?

| | C A N A D A | | | RC+ | | Atlantic | | | | Quel | |
	T	Lib	PC	NDP	SC	T	Lib	PC	NDP	T	Lib
Leader											
Lib	69	82	51	54	49	62	80	48	45*	73	82
PC	57	52	71	47	48	72	57	84	58*	52	50
NDP	54	50	53	78	39	58	53	61	84*	42	41
RC	47	41	49	48	82	–	–	–	–	47	41
SC	50	48	51	44	67*	–	–	–	–	–	–
Party Work											
Lib	57	66	44	47	49	53	68	40	50*	64	68
PC	53	49	64	47	50	61	49	71	50*	51	48
NDP	49	46	45	70	38	50	47	51	72*	40	39
RC	45	40	47	43	77	–	–	–	–	45	40
SC	43	40	43	38	61*	–	–	–	–	–	–
Candidate											
Lib	62	70	50	49	53	56	71	44	45*	67	71
PC	58	51	74	47	46	70	55	82	50*	52	47
NDP	48	44	42	74	40	40	39	41	58*	38	34
RC	40	33	41	32*	74	–	–	–	–	40	33
SC	47	43	46	46	71*	–	–	–	–	–	–
Party											
Lib	66	77	51	52	52	61	79	47	40*	71	76
PC	57	51	72	48	48	67	51	80	50*	54	51
NDP	48	44	43	77	38	50	47	51	71*	41	39
RC	43	37	45	43	74	–	–	–	–	43	37
SC	45	42	48	41	65*	–	–	–	–	–	–
Campaign											
Lib	67	77	54	53	50	60	76	47	43*	72	78
PC	55	52	64	47	45	64	53	73	57*	54	52
NDP	49	46	45	70	39	48	45	49	69*	42	41
RC	46	41	46	45*	73	–	–	–	–	46	41
SC	44	41	47	39	58*	–	–	–	–	–	–

ec			Ontario				Prairies					British Col			
C	NDP	RC	T	Lib	PC	NDP	T	Lib	PC	NDP	SC	T	Lib	PC	NDP
3	61	50	70	81	54	54	63	82	47	48	26*	70	82	47	58
7	50	43	56	53	68	47	58	55	66	46	57*	53	50	72*	48
9	70	36	59	55	54	78	58	53	55	80	36*	57	53	50*	80
9	48	82	-	-	-	-	-	-	-	-	-	-	-	-	-
-	-	-	-	-	-	-	46	39*	50*	50*	99*	51	50	51*	43
4	54	50	58	67	46	50	48	60	40	38	34*	56	62	39	51
5	47	48	51	48	60	45	56	52	64	49	45*	50	46	64	47
7	61	35	53	51	48	71	50	47	44	72	31*	52	50	40*	70
7	43	77	-	-	-	-	-	-	-	-	-	-	-	-	-
-	-	-	-	-	-	-	36	35*	35*	33*	65*	45	42	50*	39
5	49*	55	62	71	52	49	56	65	50	43	46*	63	70	49*	57
1	44*	42	57	53	72	47	60	55	72	49	48*	51	48	67*	47
7	71*	39	51	48	42	72	51	45	44	78	38*	56	52	42*	77
1	32*	74	-	-	-	-	-	-	-	-	-	-	-	-	-
-	-	-	-	-	-	-	39	32*	45*	44*	75*	50	46	46*	46
0	60	53	67	77	53	52	59	75	47	47	25*	67	76	45	56
0	49	46	55	51	68	48	60	53	73	51	48*	50	49	68	41
9	68	34	52	48	43	79	48	42	42	77	42*	49	43	35*	76
5	43	74	-	-	-	-	-	-	-	-	-	-	-	-	-
-	-	-	-	-	-	-	40	35*	44*	41*	75*	47	44	51*	41
1	65	50	68	77	56	53	61	75	52	44	27*	66	76	43	58
7	53	45	53	52	59	47	55	51	63	46	45*	50	50	66	44
9	67	35	52	49	45	72	51	47	47	70	31*	50	47	38*	69
6	45*	73	-	-	-	-	-	-	-	-	-	-	-	-	-
-	-	-	-	-	-	-	41	37*	47*	39*	65*	45	43	46*	39